King of the Wood

Oklahoma Series in Classical Culture

King of the Wood

The Sacrificial Victor in Virgil's *Aeneid*

Julia T. Dyson

University of Oklahoma Press : Norman

Library of Congress Cataloging-in-Publication Data

Dyson, Julia T. (Julia Taussig), 1966–
King of the Wood : the sacrificial victor in Virgil's Aeneid / Julia T. Dyson.
p. cm. — (Oklahoma series in classical culture ; v. 27)
Includes bibliographical references (p.) and index.
ISBN 0-8061-3341-4 (alk. paper)
1. Virgil. Aeneid. 2. Epic poetry, Latin—History and criticism. 3. Turnus (Legendary character) in literature. 4. Aeneas (Legendary character) in literature. 5. Mythology, Roman, in literature. 6. Human sacrifice in literature. 7. Diana (Roman deity)—Cult. 8. Rome—In literature. 9. Rome—Religion. I. Title. II. Series.

PA6825 .D96 2001
873'.01—dc21

2001023066

King of the Wood: The Sacrificial Victor in Virgil's Aeneid is Volume 27 in the Oklahoma Series in Classical Culture.

The paper in this book meets the guidelines for permanence and durability of the Committee on Production Guidelines for Book Longevity of the Council on Library Resources, Inc. ∞

1 2 3 4 5 6 7 8 9 10

matri et in memoriam patris

CONTENTS

Acknowledgments ix

Abbreviations xi

Introduction 3

Part 1: Sacrificial Victory

1. The *Piacula* of Aeneas 29
2. Tiber and Numicus 50
3. The Unburied Dead 74
4. Victor and Victim 95
5. Aeneas and Turnus 112
6. Juno's *Honores* 125

Part 2: The Ghastly Priest

7. The Golden Bough 133
8. The Three Faces of Diana 148
9. Dying Kings 168
10. The *Tropaeum* 184

11. Ida and Alba 195

12. The King of the Wood 210

Conclusion 228

Bibliography 237

Index of Passages Cited 251

General Index 259

Acknowledgments

This project has been brewing for over a decade and has incurred substantial debts of gratitude. Some of its arguments have been presented to audiences at Harvard University (1993), Mount Holyoke College (1993), Tulane University (1993), the University of Texas (1994), the University of Oklahoma (1997), the College of St. Thomas More (1997), the University of Colorado (1997), Baylor University (1998), the University of North Carolina (2001), and meetings of the Classical Association of the Middle West and South (1996, 1999, 2000; Southern Section, 1998, 2000) and the American Philological Association (2001). The 1994 NEH Summer Institute "Reading Virgil's *Aeneid* in the Humanities Curriculum," graciously hosted by Christine Perkell at Emory University, gave me the opportunity to immerse myself in Virgil and to meet some of the world's finest Virgilians. My colleagues at the University of Texas at Arlington, Denny Bradshaw, Charlie Chiasson, and Tim Mahoney, have weathered my screeds and continued to speak to me for years now. Our dauntless secretary Billie Hughes and her staff, Stephen Shepherd, David Stalder, Tung Chau, and Jon Olson, have given me innumerable hours of research assistance. I owe much to the cheerful competence of classics librarian Bobbie Johnson and the Interlibrary Loan Department, *sine qua non*.

I cannot thank adequately all the people who have helped to mold this study from its infancy on. Drafts of various portions have been read by many classicists: Ward Briggs, Wendell Clausen, Denis Feeney, Carin Green, Peter Knox, Sara Mack, James O'Hara, Alden Smith, Richard Tarrant, Richard Thomas, Cliff Weber, and Susan Ford Wiltshire. I wince to think what a deformed creature my book would be without their comments. The editors at the University of Oklahoma Press, Jean Hurtado and Alice Stanton, have given me welcome encouragement and indulged my stylistic whims. I am especially grateful to my copyeditor, Marian Stewart, for courteously identifying more infelicities than I care to remember. Finally, my family has combed through the text with scrupulous care. My grandmother, Lucelia Daldy, discovered more than a few typographical errors. My husband, Matthew Hejduk, responds with alacrity to my requests for comments on most everything I write. My greatest debt is to my mother, Elizabeth Dyson, who is among other things one of the finest editors I know. Needless to say (yet invariably said), any remaining flaws are mine alone.

Abbreviations

A&A	*Antike und Abendland*
AJA	*American Journal of Archaeology*
AJP	*American Journal of Philology*
ANRW	*Aufstieg und Niedergang der römischen Welt*
AVM	*Atti e memorie della Accademia Virgiliana di Mantova*
AW	*Antike Welt*
C&M	*Classica et Mediaevalia*
CA	*Classical Antiquity*
CJ	*Classical Journal*
CP	*Classical Philology*
CQ	*Classical Quarterly*
CR	*Classical Review*
CSSH	*Comparative Studies in Society and History*
CW	*Classical World*
EMC	*Échos du monde classique* (Classical Views)
EV	*Enciclopedia Virgiliana* (ed. F. Della Corte, 6 vols., Rome, 1984–91)
G&R	*Greece and Rome*
HSCP	*Harvard Studies in Classical Philology*
JRH	*Journal of Religious History*
JRS	*Journal of Roman Studies*

LIMC	*Lexicon Iconographicum Mythologiae Classicae* (Zürich, 1981–)
MD	*Materiali e discussioni per l'analisi dei testi classici*
MEFRA	*Mélanges d'Archéologie et d'Histoire de l'École Française de Rome, Antiquité*
MH	*Museum Helveticum*
OCD	*Oxford Classical Dictionary* (eds. Simon Hornblower and Antony Spawforth, Oxford, 1996)
OLD	*Oxford Latin Dictionary* (ed. P. G. W. Glare, Oxford, 1982)
PBSR	*Papers of the British School at Rome*
PCPhS	*Proceedings of the Cambridge Philological Society*
PhQ	*Philological Quarterly*
PLLS	*Papers of the Leeds International Latin Seminar*
PVS	*Proceedings of the Virgil Society*
RE	*Realencyclopädie der classischen Altertumswissenschaft* (eds. A. F. von Pauly, G. Wissowa, W. Kroll, Stuttgart, 1893–)
REL	*Revue des études latines*
RhM	*Rheinisches Museum*
SO	*Symbolae Osloenses*
Syll. Class.	*Syllecta Classica*
TAPA	*Transactions of the American Philological Assocation*
TLL	*Thesaurus Linguae Latinae* (Leipzig, 1900–)
YJC	*Yale Journal of Criticism*

KING OF THE WOOD

INTRODUCTION

stetit acer in armis
Aeneas volvens oculos dextramque repressit;
et iam iamque magis cunctantem flectere sermo
coeperat, infelix umero cum apparuit alto
balteus et notis fulserunt cingula bullis
Pallantis pueri, victum quem vulnere Turnus
straverat atque umeris inimicum insigne gerebat.
ille, oculis postquam saevi monimenta doloris
exuviasque hausit, furiis accensus et ira
terribilis: "tune hinc spoliis indute meorum
eripiare mihi? Pallas te hoc vulnere, Pallas
immolat et poenam scelerato ex sanguine sumit."
hoc dicens ferrum adverso sub pectore condit
fervidus; ast illi solvuntur frigore membra
vitaque cum gemitu fugit indignata sub umbras.

(*Aen.* 12.938–52)

Aeneas stood fierce in his armor, rolling his eyes, and held back his right hand; and now more and more Turnus' speech had begun to sway him, he hesitated—and then the unhappy baldric appeared high on Turnus' shoulder, and the sword-belt gleamed with its well-known ornaments: arms of the boy

> Pallas, whom Turnus had conquered with a wound and slain, and he was wearing the emblem of the enemy on his shoulders. Aeneas, after he drank in with his eyes the reminder of savage pain and the booty, enflamed with fury and terrible in his wrath—"Are you to be stolen hence from me, clothed in the spoils of my own people? Pallas, Pallas with this wound sacrifices you and exacts the penalty from your accursed blood." While saying this he buries his sword in the chest facing him, seething; but the other's limbs are loosed in cold, and with a groan his life flees, resentfully, to the Shades below.[1]

Why Virgil chose to end the *Aeneid* this way is one of the great mysteries of Latin literature. The epic, after all, traditionally has been regarded as Virgil's "temple" to Augustus, as the great patriotic myth glorifying the prehistory of Rome: why then does its final tableau show the victim's soul fleeing resentfully to the Underworld, his supplication denied? Since ancient times, readers have attempted to justify Aeneas' action. They correctly point out that Aeneas had every right to kill his enemy and that his hesitation marks him as unique among epic heroes. But this does not account for the effect of those final lines. It is not so much the killing itself that is troubling but the way it is portrayed—as an act of passion, without the *Iliad*'s reconciliation, without the *Odyssey*'s closure.[2]

In a well-constructed mystery novel, the ending is invariably the goal and culmination of all that went before. Paradoxically, it is both unpredictable and inevitable. When the detective "re-reads" the text for us, pointing out clues that were there all along,

---

1. Unless otherwise noted, all quotations of Virgil are from the Oxford Classical Text of Mynors (1969), and all translations are my own. I have tried to make my translations as literal as possible without damaging the English language.

2. Putnam (1995) 87–89 contrasts the "completion" characterizing the endings of the *Iliad* (reconciliation between Priam and Achilles and burial of Hector), the *Odyssey* (peace between Odysseus and the families of slain suitors), and other epics with the "incompletion" of the *Aeneid*. As Hardie (1997b) 144 notes, "the killing of Turnus inverts the expected sequence of violence followed by ritual."

we realize that the solution could not have been otherwise, no matter how impenetrable it seemed before. The *Aeneid* is no mystery novel; the ending, far from relieving our bewilderment, only deepens it. Those final lines leave us with a question. And yet, they leave us with an answer as well, as if Virgil has revealed the final clue and challenged us to seek the solution for ourselves. A strategy of modern mystery readers may prove helpful: to view the ending not as a momentary flash of pessimism or sign of incompletion, but as the *telos* toward which the entire work has been tending.[3]

To approach the *Aeneid* as a mystery to be solved may seem jarring. Virgil's poetry stirs readers alternately to pity or patriotism, sorrow or hope. Each reader responds to it differently, depending on his or her assumptions, biases, training, and experience. This emotional plane, often more intuitive than rational, is the most important part of our relationship with any text. But there is another level to Virgil's poetry, an intellectual plane of erudite allusions, puzzles, and games designed to challenge the highly educated and alert reader. This "Alexandrianism" is often discussed in brief scholarly notes that emphasize Virgil's cleverness, in contrast or counterpoint to the *Aeneid*'s solemnity of tone and seriousness of purpose.[4] The present study strives, rather, to draw out certain continuous threads whose cumulative effect is to convey a vital message about the fate of Aeneas and of Rome. The *Aeneid* is defined by predictions of events beyond its end; it is

3. Winkler (1985) 57–98 explores the possibility of reading Apuleius' *Golden Ass*—which in its surprise ending is not entirely unlike the *Aeneid*—as a mystery novel.

4. As Hutchinson (1988) 328 observes, the *Aeneid*'s "continuous endeavor for extremes of ὕψος, of intensity, elevation, sublimity," creates an impact quite unlike that of other Alexandrian poetry. Briggs (1981) 969: "the one excess not permitted Alexandrian poetry was too much seriousness."

On Greek Alexandrian poetry in general—that is, the learned, allusive, self-conscious poetry that flourished in Alexandria during the third century B.C.—see (e.g.) Briggs (1981) 949–53; Zanker (1987) 1–3; Hopkinson (1988) 7–11; Bing (1988) 50–90. On Roman Alexandrianism, which flourished during the late Republic and early Empire, see (e.g.) Hutchinson (1988) 277–354; Thomas (1986); Clausen (1987).

"Roman history in the future tense."[5] To read it fully, one must discern what the poet's prophecy implies.[6]

One feature sets the *Aeneid* apart from other poems, deepening the mystery that surrounds it and creating a problem for anyone wishing to discover Virgil's intentions: the *Aeneid* was never finished. The biographical tradition informs us that Virgil wrote a prose draft, which he turned into poetry piecemeal, leaving some passages unfinished and bolstering others with *tibicines*, "props," until he could supply the real "columns" (Suetonius *Vita Vergilii* 23–24). He planned to spend three years revising it, but illness prevented him. His deathbed wish to have the poem burned was disregarded by his friends Varius and Tucca, who published it as it was with only a few minor corrections (35–42). Readers since ancient times, therefore, have assumed that Virgil would have finished the *Aeneid*'s fifty-odd incomplete lines and reconciled its many inconsistencies if he had lived, and they excuse his "blemishes" with the thought that "Virgil never meant them for our eyes."[7] But there is a danger here. Because we have no way of knowing what Virgil would have changed, attempts to exonerate the poet may cause us to miss the meaning of things that he *did* mean for our eyes.

"Those oft are stratagems which errors seem, nor is it Homer nods, but we that dream."[8] In recent years, readers have become more willing to consider the possibility that some of the *Aeneid*'s blemishes as well may be beauties in disguise, ingenious devices designed to suggest covertly what Virgil preferred not to proclaim openly.[9] The hope of discovering *tibicines* has made readers of

5. W. H. Auden, "Secondary Epic" line 3, and the title of Mack (1978) chap. 4. As Mack points out, the *Aeneid* is extraordinarily teleological on every level: "No major action is taken in the poem that is not in response to some summons from the future" (55).

6. For the idea of "Vergil as Poet-Prophet of the *Aeneid*," see O'Hara (1990) 176–84.

7. A. E. Housman, quoted in Hardie (1986) 242.

8. Alexander Pope, *Essay on Criticism* 177–78.

9. E.g., O'Hara (1990) 143: "inconsistency is a deliberate narrative device." See also O'Hara (1994). On a significant pattern of discrepancies in Book 6, see Zetzel (1989). On deliberate "errors" in the *Georgics*, an unquestionably "finished"

Virgil over the centuries particularly alert to such "errors,"[10] many of which are in fact stratagems—and our potential clues.[11]

Some working assumptions about Virgil follow, which underlie this reading of the *Aeneid*. First, he knew by heart more poetry than most people read in a lifetime. Partly for that reason, he understood its nuances better than nearly any other person before or since. His allusive style is natural, not artificial; the poetry of his predecessors was in his blood. Second, he wrote meticulously and self-consciously. Whatever the half-unconscious process that initially produced a line, Virgil generally would be aware, once he had finished, of its various associations, and would have avoided allusions and echoes that did not fit into a meaningful pattern.[12] Third, he wrote for at least two distinct audiences. This

---

poem, see Ross (1987) 104–109. Horsfall (1991) 91–102 rightly observes that many of Virgil's inconsistencies derive from contradictions in his sources—but there is more to it than that.

10. It is uncertain whether Virgil intended to leave some or all of his half-lines incomplete. Moskalew (1982) 12–13 (with bibliography) calls trying to defend Virgil's half-lines as intentional a "pretty hopeless undertaking." Baldwin (1993) 144–51, however, reopens the issue, questioning each of the traditional arguments against intentional incompleteness and pointing out that experimentation, metrical and otherwise, characterized the times in which Virgil wrote. The half-line may even have an imitator in that notorious poetaster and would-be dancer of "Virgil's Turnus" (Suet. *Nero* 54), the emperor Nero. Whether or not Virgil intended to revise his hemistichs, it is hard to imagine how a complete line could better convey the frustration of *hic cursus fuit* ("here our course was," 1.535), or the finality of *numina magna deum* ("the great divinities of the gods," 2.623). Not all the half-lines are so perfect, of course—there is nothing particularly remarkable about, say, *Dardanidae* ("the sons of Dardanus," 1.560) or *stant circum* ("they stand around," 2.767)—but it is striking how incompleteness dramatizes even seemingly ordinary lines.

11. Of course not *all* inconsistencies and apparent infelicities are part of Virgil's design. Much work remains to be done on creating a "typology of errors" in the *Aeneid*. As will become evident in the course of this study, certain types (such as geographical or ritual "errors") are especially likely to be deliberate. It may well be, as Williams (1983) 262–78 argues, that Book 3 (for instance) was written originally as a third-person narrative and imperfectly converted; see also Goold (1970) 114–18 on Book 2. However, much of the evidence often adduced to demonstrate a "change of plan" can be better explained in other ways (see, e.g., the discussion of the Palinurus episode in chaps. 2 and 3).

12. Wigodsky (1972) 15: "No doubt all products of the mind reflect both conscious and unconscious intentions; and if the recollection of the context in which a borrowed expression originally stood adds something to our appreciation of what

sort of assumption in the case of other authors has produced ludicrous results, as in Verrall's rationalizing interpretation of Euripides, which posits a naïve audience that would have accepted supernatural elements and a clever audience that would have constructed alternative explanations for them. But in Virgil's case, we know that he was writing both for an elite group of literati, accustomed to reading between the lines, and for Augustus, who would have frowned on *overt* criticism of his regime.[13] The modern controversy over "optimistic" and "pessimistic" readings of Virgil is partly a natural result of this dual audience.[14] This is not to say that Augustus himself would have been blind to or would have censored anything less than complimentary in the *Aeneid*. The *princeps* may have had a sharper eye, thicker skin, and less direct control over "Augustan poetry" than commonly supposed.[15]

Vergil has done with it, then the allusion must be in some sense intentional." See Lyne (1987) 100–44; Thomas (1986); Farrell (1991) 3–25; Conte (1986) 23–31; Gransden (1984) 3–4; Boyle (1993) 94–98.

Lyne (1994) makes the case for adopting "intertextuality" over "allusion," but uneasily, and his appendix on "Objections to the Term 'Intertextuality' " (200–201) is cogent. I confess that after reading his article I felt even more comfortable with "allusion" and less comfortable with "intertextuality" than I had before. Hinds (1998), as his title *Allusion and Intertext* promises, gives a sympathetic hearing to both camps. He notes that there are "areas in which the rhetoric of allusivity, for all its own flaws and occlusions, just does better" (49). On the other hand, there is no convenient substitute for "intertext" ("text to which a poet alludes"). For a characterization of "Virgil's intertextual practice" in general, see Farrell (1997) 228–29.

13. Whether or not such criticism of the monarch posed an actual danger to the poet, it is certainly the case, as Ahl (1984) 184 notes, that ancient poets "sensed the greater power of oblique suggestion." Hinds (1987) 25 observes that "publicly voiced anti-Augustanism must needs be a rhetoric of ambiguity and innuendo": again, this is true from an artistic standpoint, however tolerant of criticism Augustus may have been in reality. It is also useful to bear in mind that visible tolerance of (some) criticism is a sign of strength. Paradoxically, literature that would seem to be "oppositional" may help to consolidate the position of the ruler; see Kennedy (1992) 45–46.

14. Harrison (1990b) 1–20 and Perkell (1999) 14–22 provide useful historical summaries of this ongoing debate. The terms "optimist" and "pessimist" are crude and do justice neither to Virgil nor to his readers, but (with appropriate caveats and "scare quotes" in place) they are occasionally useful.

15. See White (1993) 206–208 (and passim).

Another strategy of this study is to pay close attention to ancient commentators, especially Servius.[16] Although some of his comments reflect intellectual trends of the four hundred years separating him from Virgil, he incorporates much material stemming from Virgil's day and before.[17] Servius' grammarian instinct to make sense of every detail sometimes leads him to devise apparently absurd explanations, to force Virgil's Latin to say what it cannot, and to derive "traditions" based on no evidence but the passage at hand; then as now, a guess repeated often enough easily achieved the status of fact. His is a school commentary, not a scholarly one,[18] and he often oversimplifes or distorts complex issues. But though he may be no more insightful, reliable, or objective than many modern readers, he has two great advantages simply by virtue of the age he lived in and the language he spoke. First, he had easy access to history, myth, traditions, religion, and literature now lost or opaque to us, whether or not he used this access judiciously. Second, while he certainly had his own biases, they are different from ours. His analysis is untouched by the issues that exercise modern scholars (such as the controversy between the "optimists" and "pessimists"). It is partly because of this salutary naïveté that his comments may be considered valuable evidence. If a modern commentator were to claim that the epithet "holy" conjoined with the Numicus river

16. On Servius' continuing usefulness, see Fowler (1997). For convenience, this work will refer to "Servius" and "Servius Auctus" as if they were separate people. Where their comments are intertwined, I shall generally say simply "Servius," designating the comments of "Auctus" by brackets < >. In fact, as Goold (1970) ably demonstrates, in addition to the text of Servius himself, we have a text somewhat clumsily assembled by a seventh-century "Compiler" ("a hack, without taste or learning or brains," 75). The Compiler has grafted onto his text of Servius comments of the more scholarly Donatus (on whom Servius himself drew), along with comments from a few other sources.

17. As the quintessential "classic," the *Aeneid* enjoyed a continuous stream of commentary, almost from before its birth. We remember Propertius' prophetic advertisement, *nescioquid maius nascitur Iliade* ("something greater than the *Iliad* is being born," 2.34.66). See Goold (1970) 121–24.

18. See Kaster (1988) 169–97 on Servius' "insistent and complacent didacticism" (189). Unlike modern scholarly commentators, whose primary aim is exegesis, Servius sought to instruct his students in the correct use of the Latin language.

refers proleptically to the tradition of Aeneas' death and cult there, we might accuse him or her of overinterpretation. When Servius makes the comment (ad 7.797), even if the same accusation could be leveled at his literary criticism, we gain a useful insight into the historical background familiar to Virgil's ancient readers. However far-fetched Servius' solutions may be, he alerts us to the problems that troubled ancient readers, as well as to the external information that they brought to their reading.

An area in which the ancient commentators are particularly biased, and about which their comments are both useful and treacherous, is Roman religion. Servius and his contemporary Macrobius belonged to a pagan revival that revered the religious traditions of ancient Rome, revered Virgil, and consequently elevated Virgil to the status of omniscient high priest of paganism, intimately familiar with its details and exacting in his use of religious vocabulary.[19] Some of the ancients' comments seem overzealous, to say the least. For instance, Servius starts from the assumption that Aeneas is to be seen as a *flamen Dialis*, a priest of Jupiter hedged with many taboos, and Dido as the *flaminica*, or priest's wife.[20] The

19. See Horsfall (1991) 148–49. Macrobius' *Saturnalia* (fifth century A.D.), a fictional dialogue among pagan intellectuals (including the young Servius), devotes two of its six books to discussion of Virgil's poetry. One participant accuses Virgil of various faults while the others vindicate the poet, casting him as a supreme authority in philosophy, religion, and rhetoric. Virgil is called "our Pontifex Maximus" (1.24.16), and it is claimed that he "used no words with more careful propriety than those pertaining to sacred rites and sacrifices" (*nullis tamen magis proprie usus est quam sacris vel sacrificialibus verbis*, 3.2.1). On the dogmatism of Macrobius' assumption that Virgil never "invented" anything but only alluded to previous sources, see Rauk (1995).

20. See Starr (1997). Aeneas could not possibly fit all the requirements for the *flamen Dialis*, which included never seeing an army marshalled for battle outside the city (not to mention always burying his fingernails under a fruitful tree; never touching or mentioning she-goats, raw flesh, ivy, or beans; always sleeping with a box of sacrificial cakes at the foot of his bed; and many other such things, listed in Aulus Gellius *NA* 10.15). The requirements for *flamines* of other cults were less stringent. Servius is persistent, however, in arguing that Virgil "everywhere presents a *flamen* in the character of Aeneas, a *flaminica* in that of Dido" (*ubique Vergilium in persona Aeneae flaminem, in Didonis flaminicam praesentare*, ad 4.103; cf. ad 4.29, 137, 262, 263, 339, 374, 518, 646). See Treggiari (1991) 21–24 for the special

flaminica was not allowed to climb more than three stairs. When Dido ascends her own "tall funeral pyre" (*altos . . . rogos*, 4.645–46), Servius Auctus, reasoning that "tall" must imply more stairs than three, accuses her of religious impropriety (ad 4.646). Similarly, Aeneas is nearly faulted for riding on horseback (ad 8.552), an activity forbidden to the *flamen Dialis*. He is saved by the commentator's realization that other *flamines* (of Mars and Quirinus) were allowed to travel to provinces and hence must have ridden horses.

In his article "Aeneas as the *Flamen Dialis*," Raymond Starr rightly points out the absurdity of some of the grammarians' claims. Yet one of his underlying assumptions, shared by most readers ancient and modern, deserves careful scrutiny. He notes that "Aeneas definitely rides the horse (8.585–86), and the critic cannot fall back on the explanation used for Dido, that he is committing a religious wrong, without raising unsuitable questions about Aeneas."[21] Why, exactly, is it "unsuitable" for Starr or for Servius to entertain the possibility that Aeneas has committed a religious wrong? In the Roman view, *every* misfortune was attributable, at least in part, to a breach of religious propriety. The *pax deorum* or "state of peace with the gods," a precondition of their granting success to Roman endeavors, was maintained by strict adherence to ritual procedure.[22] As his people's religious and political leader—and for the Romans, the two were rarely separate—Aeneas is responsible for maintaining that state of peace:[23] that things sometimes go badly for the Trojans is prima facie evidence that he has

requirements of this solemn ritual marriage or *confarreatio*. Beard and North (1990) 20–21 provide a useful tabulation of the many Roman Republican "priests," a word that cannot do justice to the complexity of the Roman system of Flamines, Pontifices, Augures, and others. See also Beard, North, and Price (1998a) 18–30.

21. Starr (1997) 68.

22. See Rosenstein (1990) 54–59 (with bibliography).

23. As Jocelyn (1966) 92 succinctly observes, "for the average Roman religion concerned primarily the relations between the unseen divine powers and the social groups to which he belonged, i.e. his own family and the Roman community. The maintenance of these relations was the duty of the leader or leaders of the group, not that of the collectivity of members." On the importance of religion in Augustus' political program, see Gottlieb (1998).

done something wrong, however unwittingly. Aeneas must carry from burning Troy the burden of *religio* along with the burden of the past and the future. If the grammarians go too far in claiming that Virgil "presents [Aeneas] as everywhere having held all the priesthoods" (*ubique omnia sacerdotia inducit habuisse,* Servius Auctus ad 1.706), most modern readers go too far in the other direction, ignoring altogether the technical aspects of Aeneas' religious leadership.

This book will raise "unsuitable questions about Aeneas." Its focus will be on sacrifice—and this could mean two very different things. Literary critics tend to treat sacrifice primarily as a metaphor ("Dido must be sacrificed to the Roman cause"), and it is common to see references to "sacrificial themes" or "levels" or "laws" in the *Aeneid.* Human suffering and death are assumed to be somehow redemptive of the larger community. The title of this book's first section, "Sacrificial Victory," has obvious affinity with "Tragic Victory" and "Pyrrhic victory," phrases from two seminal modern literary analyses of the poem.[24] Scholars of ancient religion, on the other hand, use the term "sacrifice" to specify the ritual slaughter that preceded most important acts in the Roman world ("Aeneas sacrifices four black bullocks before entering the Underworld"). When such scholars take an interest in Virgil at all, they tend to be concerned with issues of classification, such as which animals are sacrificed to which deities in what situations, or what formal category describes a given prayer or prodigy. The daunting array of details and jargon that characterized Roman cult, which was analogous in its complexity to Roman law, contributes to a certain disjunction between the two groups of scholars. Literary critics tend to set aside the technical issues as irrelevant to the poem's larger themes, and scholars of religion tend to set aside the larger themes as irrelevant to the technical issues. The metaphorical and the literal uses of "sacrifice" thus have little in common.

24. "Tragic Victory" is the title of the final chapter of Putnam's *Poetry of the "Aeneid"* (1965), and Clausen (1964) 86 refers to Virgil's "perception of Roman history as a long Pyrrhic victory of the human spirit."

One of the aims of this study is to bridge this gap, to incorporate insights from more technical analyses of Roman religion into the interpretation of a literary text. My concern is not to develop or apply a comprehensive theory of sacrifice,[25] but rather to examine it *at work* in a single poem, with particular attention to aspects that are specifically Roman.[26] Far from being an issue of interest only to specialists, Roman cult forms a vital "intertext" of the *Aeneid.* Virgil alludes to religious practices much as he alludes to the *Iliad*: he assumes that his readers will possess a certain body of knowledge and expects them to derive meaning from comparing his poem with the "model." Aeneas' opening words are meant to be interpreted in light of those of Odysseus; Aeneas' first sacrifice, similarly, is meant to be interpreted in light of a well-known ritual prohibition, which he violates. In order for Roman sacrifices to be pleasing to the gods, they had to be performed *correctly,* and Aeneas frequently does not perform them correctly. Unsuccessful offerings were dire omens with potentially dangerous consequences. Many of the poem's metaphorical human sacrifices, in turn, violate essential principles in a manner analogous to faulty offerings of animals. Reading the *Aeneid* against the "text" of Roman religious practice has startling implications for the interpretation of Aeneas' character, his relationship to the gods, and ultimately the poem's broad design.

♦ ♦ ♦

This study consists of two parts, each of which could stand alone but which reinforce one another taken together. The first part

---

25. Much modern sacrificial theory is based on the work of Girard (1977), whose study includes little Roman evidence. See Smith (1999), especially 504–508, for an overview of Girard's ideas and of Virgilian scholarship that draws on them. Smith's analysis of the Sinon-Laocoön episode in *Aeneid* 2 highlights some of the ways in which the Girardian model does *not* fit Virgil's text.

26. Feeney (1998) addresses the common assumption that Roman religion, especially as manifested in Roman literature, is derivative and therefore somehow inauthentic. In particular, he refutes the idea that the "real" meaning of ritual lies in its origin rather than in its use: as he notes, "ritual is not something underpinning or outside or before culture, but something enmeshed in culture's manifold forms" (118).

explores in general terms the theme of "sacrificial victory," the grim logic whereby Aeneas' sacrifice of others implicitly will result in his own sacrificial death after the poem's end. The second part focuses on Virgil's sustained allusion to a specific Roman cult, that of the Rex Nemorensis or "King of the Wood," that is the quintessential example of this logic: the priest who sacrifices his predecessor must inevitably become the victim of his successor. As the thesis of the second part is the more monolithic and the more daring, I have avoided arguments in the first part that would depend upon acceptance of it.

The book opens by arguing that Aeneas repeatedly violates fundamental principles of Roman ritual in his communications with and offerings to the gods. Discerning some of these violations depends upon outside knowledge of Roman cult. For instance, there were strict rules about which animals should be sacrificed to which deities; Aeneas makes the (for the Romans) fatal mistake of sacrificing an uncastrated bull to Jupiter, an act that ancient commentators held to be responsible for the grotesque prodigy of bleeding trees that immediately follows. Some other violations are evident simply from close reading of the text. At several critical junctures, prophet figures (Helenus, Sibyl, and Tiber) instruct Aeneas on how and when to perform propitiatory sacrifices; though Aeneas and the narrator claim that he has performed them correctly, an examination of the text reveals that he has failed to follow the proper order, thus rendering the offerings ineffective. It was a distinguishing feature of Roman religion that sacrifices marred by a ritual error (*piaculum*) had to be atoned for by offering another victim. The gods would remain angry until this expiatory offering was made. Though no explicit statement ever appears in the *Aeneid* about the gods' response to a given sacrifice, their continuing anger (as ancient commentators realized) is evident from the troubles that continue to plague Aeneas and his people. This necessity for expiation by repetition forms an important backdrop to the entire poem.

In fact, Aeneas himself may be the offering required to atone for his ritual violations. A mythico-historical subtext of the *Aeneid* is the tradition that Aeneas disappeared into the Numicus river, near which he was subsequently worshipped as a deity. This tradition can have positive or negative implications, depending on whether one emphasizes apotheosis (the best possible fate) or drowning (the worst possible fate). Jupiter twice foretells Aeneas' eventual deification. The specter of drowning, however, is continually raised more covertly by a series of allusions, inconsistencies, prophecies, and parallels that center on the Tiber river. This river plays a major role in the second half of the poem, both because it represents the Italian landscape that is to become Aeneas' home and because the river-god delivers to him a crucial prophecy of events soon to take place. Yet Tiber's meeting with Aeneas in Book 8 has far more ominous overtones than are usually recognized. Virgil goes to some lengths to link the great Tiber with the relatively minor Numicus, which tradition invariably makes the site of Aeneas' death. Tiber identifies himself as *caeruleus,* a color term that in the *Aeneid* nearly always describes gloomy or dangerous phenomena such as mourning garb, storm clouds, sea monsters, Charon's barge, or snakes (with whom Tiber is also associated in other ways). Finally, Aeneas' journey up the river preternaturally calmed resembles in uncanny ways the death of Palinurus, the helmsman cast overboard as an offering to Neptune. Tiber's prophecy to Aeneas, "as victor, you will pay me my honor in full," may have a deceptive second meaning that predicts Aeneas' sacrificial death by drowning.

The multiplication of characters who combine sacrifice with lack of burial both reminds the reader of Aeneas' death and calls into question whether sacrificial death is of any use. Palinurus is often seen as the paradigm of sacrifice in the *Aeneid,* the "one given for many." Modern assumptions about the redemptive nature of his death, however, overlook an essential principle that causes it to have quite different implications. It was an unvarying requirement of ancient sacrificial ritual that the victim approach the altar willingly. Manifest unwillingness revealed the gods' displeasure and meant that another victim must be offered in expiation. Palinurus' sacrificial death is indeed paradigmatic for the *Aeneid,* but not in the way commonly supposed: his resistance vitiates the offering and may even make it destructive rather than redemptive. The many narrative inconsistencies throughout the Palinurus episode, which are usually seen as Virgil's "errors" and taken as evidence for its late composition, are actually deliberate devices to associate Palinurus with Aeneas' comrades Orontes (whose ship capsizes near rocks called "The Altars") and Misenus (who drowns after a contest with the sea-god Triton). Deliberate inconsistencies also contribute to parallels between Aeneas and other characters said to lie unburied. Priam is killed at an altar in the middle of his house, but his corpse strangely appears on the "shore." Aeneas taunts his enemy Tarquitus with lack of burial and being eaten by birds and fishes, though no body of water has been mentioned. Even the prospect of immortality, which could be the positive side of Aeneas' remaining "unburied," is darkened by the lament of Juturna, a nymph of the Numicus who grieves over spending eternity bereft of her mortal brother. The poem's repetition of unwilling sacrifice and lack of burial provides a chilling comment on the fate of the hero after his death.

That Aeneas will be reciprocally sacrificed is also suggested by the poem's recurring images of priest-become-victim. Literary analyses of the poem frequently discuss "role-reversal," a phenomenon especially evident in Aeneas' assumption of the role of his former enemy, Achilles. An important subset of this phenomenon involves characters who literally or metaphorically perform sacrifices, then die in contexts that allude to ritual slaughter. The link between role-reversal and reciprocal sacrifice is implied when the Trojans put on their enemies' armor—for the Romans, a terrible taboo—in order to pass for Greeks during the Fall of Troy. Coroebus, who devises the scheme, is killed at Minerva's altar. The priest Panthus is killed despite his *infula,* a sacred headband worn by both priests and sacrificial victims; this scene parallels one in Book 10 where Aeneas "sacrifices" (*immolat*) the priest Haemonides, the *Aeneid*'s only other wearer of the ambiguous *infula.* Another priest, Laocoön, is killed while performing a sacrifice and is compared to a bull who runs screaming from the altar, a reversal that emphasizes both the theme of priest-become-victim and the dire omen created by victims' unwillingness. Achilles' son Pyrrhus kills King Priam at an altar and is later killed at an altar himself. Role-reversal and sacrifice are also prominent in the boxing match in Book 5, in which a boxer makes a dramatic comeback and then slaughters the prize bull as a substitute for his opponent. This scene foreshadows events in the Italian War: a human (Aulestes) is killed at an altar as a substitute for an animal, and Turnus and Aeneas are compared to fighting bulls allusively associated with sacrificial bulls. The pattern created by such reversals implies that Aeneas' final sacrifice of Turnus may have deadly consequences for himself.

By associating Turnus with the Italian countryside and with Aeneas himself, Virgil underscores the danger to Aeneas posed by killing the Italian hero. In contrast to Aeneas, Turnus has a harmonious relationship with the Tiber River, which saves his life in a manner reminiscent of the great Roman hero Horatius Cocles. Turnus also is assimilated allusively to the Tiber in various ways, such as being compared to a boiling cauldron in a simile modeled on Homer's description of an enraged river. When Aeneas' spear is caught by the stump of the sacred tree of Faunus, who openly favors Turnus, a reference to "sailors saved from the waves" reminds the reader of Faunus' shrine on the Tiber island and of the tradition of Aeneas' death by drowning. In addition to associating Turnus with natural forces hostile to Aeneas, Virgil also implies that the deaths of Aeneas and Turnus are linked. For instance, Virgil's version of the Homeric scene where Zeus weighs the fates of Hector and Achilles lacks the clear outcome of Homer's: whereas Homer states explicitly that Hector is doomed, Virgil's linguistic ambiguity suggests that both Turnus and Aeneas will die. Associations between Aeneas and the suicide of Ajax also suggest that Aeneas' fight with Turnus may bring about his own death. Finally, the simile of fighting bulls applied to Turnus and Aeneas brings in the shadow of Juno, both through allusions to Juno's torment of Io and through the assimilation of fighting bulls to sacrificial bulls.

It may be that Juno is pacified only by the promise of endless human sacrifices. The final interview between her and Jupiter points in several ways toward a dark future for Aeneas and his people. Parallels with the conversation between Jupiter and Mercury in Book 4, which leads to a new series of adventures for Aeneas, imply that Juno, too, may be at the beginning rather than the end of her intervention in Aeneas' affairs; this possibility is left open by mysterious silence about her destination when she "leaves the cloud." More importantly, Jupiter's closing promise that the Roman people will excel in giving her *honores* answers the indignant question posed by her opening speech: "Will anyone place a sacrifice (*honor*) on my altars?" Aeneas' sacrifice of Turnus brings not closure but continuity.

Human sacrifices endlessly repeated characterized the cult of the Rex Nemorensis, or "King of the Wood," the subject of the study's second half. This famous yet mysterious priest of Diana Nemorensis lived in her sacred grove near Aricia, less than twenty miles from Rome. In commemoration of the cult's mythical foundation by a fugitive (Orestes or Hippolytus), all contenders for the office in historical times had to be runaway slaves. A Challenger was required to break off a bough from the goddess's sacred tree before engaging in mortal combat with the reigning Rex. The winner of this fight would sacrifice the loser. The King of the Wood, then, necessarily gained his office by sacrificing his predecessor, and was destined to be sacrificed himself by his successor. The requirement that the Challenger attack the sacred tree before attacking the Rex also suggests a symbolic equation between priest-king and tree. Reciprocal sacrifice was thus inevitably linked to "tree violation," a religious offense with grave consequences in the ancient world. It is my thesis that a sustained allusion to this cult is a structuring principle of the *Aeneid*.

To explain the strange rites of the Rex Nemorensis is the ostensible purpose of Sir James Frazer's monumental work, *The Golden Bough*; paradoxically, modern scholarly aversion to Frazer has drawn attention away from the cult's implications for the *Aeneid*.

But though Frazer's *equation* of the Golden Bough in *Aeneid* 6 with the sacrificial bough of the Arican cult is marred by faulty logic, it is reasonable to suppose, as Servius did, that the breaking off of Virgil's Golden Bough *alludes* to the breaking off of the branch from Diana's sacred tree. The cult was notorious: its proximity to Rome, its wealth, its role as the focus of the Latin League, its designation as simply "The Grove," and its replication on the Aventine Hill all ensure that it would have been well known to Virgil's audience. References direct and indirect in Latin poetry, and especially in Lucan's portrayal of the combat between Caesar and Pompey, suggest that it captured the imagination of poets. It was also promising because of its association with two Greek tragedies, for tradition makes either Orestes or the resurrected Hippolytus (Virbius) its founder. The *Aeneid*'s depiction of the mysterious Virbius, lonely denizen of the Arician grove near Diana's altar, implies that he was a Rex Nemorensis figure. In addition, the cult was poetically fruitful because of the symbolic and religious significance of trees: they resemble human bodies, provide material for important wooden artifacts (such as spears, ships, and the Trojan Horse), and represent both Nature and the gods.

One of Virgil's primary means of bringing the Arician cult to the reader's mind is through repeated references to Diana. The goddess called "Diana" was by Virgil's time an amalgam of the deities Luna (= Greek Selene, the moon), Trivia (= Greek Hecate, a sorceress), and Diana (= Greek Artemis, a huntress). Myths attaching to this multiform goddess form an important subtext of the Dido episode: Dido herself takes on each of the "three faces of Diana" in turn (huntress, sorceress, and moon), and her "tragic" affair with Aeneas has much in common with that of Phaedra and Diana's protégé Hippolytus. Aeneas' catabasis and his ambiguous fate after death (apotheosis or drowning) resemble the dubious resurrection of Hippolytus and his father Theseus, both of whom are characterized by contradictory traditions depicting their ability or inability to exit from the Underworld. The similarity between Aeneas and Hippolytus extends to their sons, Silvius and Virbius (junior), both posthumous offspring who hide in the Alban woods and are associated with the Rex Nemorensis. Diana Nemorensis implicitly is present in the beginning of the Italian War, especially in the events surrounding the wounding of Silvia's deer: while wounded deer are naturally Diana's charges, this deer also is associated allusively with cypresses (Diana's tree), and the response to Silvia's complaint culminates in a bugle call reaching "Trivia's lake" in the Arician grove. "Transference" between Diana and other goddesses occurs when Aeneas meets Venus dressed as a huntress, when he invokes his parents "in heaven and hell" (the formula used for Hecate), and when Turnus refers to Iris's epiphany in terms more appropriate to Diana. In the episode of Nisus and Euryalus, Diana's influence is more overt: Nisus' prayer to the goddess is given additional point by the friends' incongruous translation to the Alban woods and by echoes of a scene of tree violation by one of the archery contestants during the Funeral Games in Book 5. Nisus is assimilated momentarily to both priest-king and victim in Diana's cult. The complexity and pervasiveness of these references to Diana suggest that the goddess plays a key role in the poem.

Another aspect of the cult, the symbolic equivalence of priest-king and sacred tree, comes to the fore in Virgil's persistent association of kings with violated trees. In the Fall of Troy, tree imagery figures prominently: for instance, King Priam is slain at an altar standing before a sacred laurel (mirrored in that of king Latinus), his headless corpse is called a "trunk" (*truncus*), and the city itself is compared to an uprooted mountain ash. Latinus' scepter is associated allusively with the Golden Bough in a way that implicitly may draw his ancestral monarchy into the realm of the Rex Nemorensis. Latinus' ancestors are also arboreal: his grandfather Picus turned into a "woodpecker," and his father Faunus is a wood spirit whose sacred tree Aeneas attacks near the end of the poem. Tree violation and human sacrifice are united in the minor king Aulestes, who is killed on an altar by a spear "like a tree trunk." If Priam, Latinus, Latinus' ancestors, and Aulestes are associated metaphorically with trees and tree violation, it is King Mezentius whose final assimilation to a tree is overt. Aeneas commemorates his victory over Mezentius by setting up a *tropaeum* (a tree-trunk monument) decked in the king's armor, and declares "this is Mezentius by my hands." Mezentius' transformation from a monster to a sympathetic character is accomplished partly through his changing relationship to trees: he enters like the Cyclops Polyphemus (whom he resembles in other ways), wielding a pine tree, but he ends as a violated tree himself. Both Polydorus and Polyphemus, who frame the narrative of Aeneas' wanderings (Book 3), have important associations with Mezentius as "tree." The Cyclopes are compared to giant trees in the "forest of Jupiter or the grove of Diana," a collocation perhaps pointing to the Alban Mount and the rites of Diana Nemorensis. Aeneas' threefold assault on the tree that bleeds with the blood of Polydorus is echoed in his battle with Mezentius, where he attempts three times to "pluck out a forest of spears" from his shield.

The transformation of Mezentius into a tree, which culminates in Aeneas' dedication of the trophy ("this is Mezentius"), has important implications for the poem's final scene. The death of Turnus results partly from his symbolic transformation into a living *tropaeum*, a theme to which Virgil devotes a range of allusive strategies. All of the other characters whom Aeneas is said to "sacrifice" (*immolare*) are closely associated with *tropaea*: the arms of the priest-become-victim Haemonides are gathered for the poem's first trophy, and the eight youths whom Aeneas will sacrifice to Pallas' shade march in procession alongside tree-trunks. The "arming" of the trophy for Mezentius parodies a conventional epic arming scene, but with a difference (the conspicuous absence of shin-guards) that also appears in the arming scene for Turnus. Mezentius himself introduces the idea of a man becoming a living *tropaeum* in his prayer that his son will become a trophy "clothed in the spoils" of Aeneas. Turnus is killed precisely because he is "clothed in the spoils" he stripped from Pallas. Evander had wished that Turnus would become a "trunk" like that representing

Mezentius, and this wish is fulfilled in the poem's closing lines. Turnus' transformation into a living *tropaeum* emphasizes his impiety (he should have dedicated Pallas' arms to the gods, not hung them on himself): the symbolic equivalence of man and tree also increases the pathos and the moral complexity of his death, for tree violation implies the culpability of the attacker and evinces sympathy for the attacked.

While Turnus at the end comes to resemble a violated tree, he is also portrayed as himself violating "trees" sacred to Cybele, the Great Mother who represents the Trojans' Asiatic origin. In the *Aeneid*'s carefully developed parallels between Cybele and Diana, Virgil interweaves the theme of East versus West with that of the tree violation preceding the combat of Rex and Challenger. Like Diana with her Virbius, Cybele had a sexually inactive priestly consort, Attis, who was closely associated or even identified with a tree (the pine). Turnus' first appearance, in which he insults a goddess disguised as a priestess, recalls the myth of the notorious tree-violator Erysichthon, who insults a goddess disguised as a priestess reprimanding him for attacking Demeter's sacred grove. Turnus also attacks "trees" from Cybele's Mount Ida when he attempts to burn Trojan ships built from her sacred grove; confusion about this grove's composition echoes similar confusion about the composition of the Trojan Horse and suggests a deliberate parallel. He attacks men conspicuously tree-like when he kills Pandarus and Bitias, sons of a wood-nymph who are compared to twin oak trees, and Phegeus, whose name means "oak-man." Yet Turnus is himself associated with a violated tree in several ways, such as being attacked with Allecto's torch, sweating a "pitchy stream" like a pine tree, and unwittingly echoing words describing the bleeding tree of the Polydorus episode. The clash between Cybele and Diana is most prominent when Diana's votary Camilla attempts to gain the armor of Chloreus, a priest of Cybele and the poem's most obvious Attis figure. In particular, Diana's description of Camilla's youth in flashback narrative, which parallels Cybele's flashback about her sacred pines, emphasizes Camilla's many points of contact with the Arician cult: her fugitive father, her transportation inside a "tree," the meaning of her name ("attendant at a sacrifice"), and the retribution that follows the "violation" of her "sacred" body.

The implicit presence of Diana and the many incidents of tree violation throughout the poem reach their climax in the final combat of Turnus and Aeneas, which allusively reenacts the ritual duel between the Rex Nemorensis and his Challenger. Two related similes in *Aeneid* 12 show a bull (Turnus) butting against a tree that stands in for his opponent, then two bulls (Turnus and Aeneas) locked in mortal combat to determine "who is to rule the grove." Several other elements of the final duel recall features of the Arician cult: the setting near a vast encircled lake, the swordfight, the comparison of Turnus to a fleeing deer (fugitive slaves were called "deer"), and allusions to the Scythians (Diana Nemorensis hailed from Scythia). The hunted deer simile resonates with others throughout the poem that recall tree violation and Diana Nemorensis. In particular, the simile comparing Dido to a deer wounded in the Dictaean groves reminds the reader both of dittany, a magic herb that could expel arrows, and of Diana Dictynna, often equated with Diana Nemorensis. Aeneas' arrow wound and then his miraculous healing allude both to this wounded deer simile and to the strange combination of inextricability and pliancy that characterizes the Golden Bough. This combination is also present when Venus retrieves Aeneas' spear stuck in the sacred tree-stump of Faunus, an incident with elements culled from the poem's many violations of trees. That Faunus' tree is a wild olive worshipped by sailors saved from drowning, and that it appears immediately after the comparison of Turnus to a hunted deer, recalls the myth of Hippolytus, whose chariot became entangled in a wild olive near a lake named for a king who drowned while hunting deer. This reminder of the death of the legendary founder of Diana's priesthood fittingly precedes the final sacrifice performed by Aeneas.

It has long been recognized that allusion, the poet's continual invitation to "compare and contrast" with his model, is one of the most powerful tools of the literate poet. Virgil was a master of this technique. As one modern critic puts it, "to try to make sense of the *Aeneid* without continual recourse to Homer is like trying to read a code whose secret is lost."[27] Another essential clue to Virgil's "code" lies in the intricate passageways of Roman cult. For the Romans, religion consisted in executing correctly a complicated set of procedures; to fail to sacrifice correctly was to incur the gods' wrath until an expiatory offering could be made. The *Aeneid*'s many literal and figurative sacrifices ought to be viewed in this light—that is, with the awareness that they are faulty and that such faults can have dangerous consequences. The unwillingness of Turnus, both as sacrificial victim and as representative of the Italian countryside, promises not closure but the necessity for expiation through repetition of sacrifice. The motifs of death by water and of priest-become-victim point to the sacrificial death of the hero himself, which defines the *Aeneid* as surely as the predicted death of Achilles defines the *Iliad*.

The rites of Diana Nemorensis offer a cultic paradigm for this endless cycle of reciprocal sacrifice. Intrusions of Diana, echoes of Greek tragedy, single combat for kingship, and tree violation associated with human death are unquestionably present throughout the poem. The Arician cult binds these apparently disparate elements into a unified whole and endows them with meaning beyond their individual significance. The first part of this book argues that Aeneas is cast as a priest destined to become a victim; the second part argues that his "sacrificial victory" finds a real and specific model in the haunted reign of the King of the Wood. I am suggesting that Virgil's sustained evocation of a cultic "intertext" is as crucial to the poem's design as its references to literary models. It is my hope that this argument may provoke a reappraisal, not only of the *Aeneid*, but also of the role of religion in Roman literature and Roman life.

Mine is a dark reading of the poem. I do not believe, however, that the *Aeneid*'s darkness lies primarily in criticism of Augustus,

27. Gransden (1984) 4.

or in vilification of Aeneas (representing the Roman conqueror) and idealization of Turnus (representing the conquered). If anything, my interpretation emphasizes that both men—all men, perhaps—are victims of the inscrutable and inexorable anger of the gods.

PART ONE

Sacrificial Victory

CHAPTER ONE

THE *PIACULA* OF AENEAS

Readers often remark that Aeneas' salient characteristic is his *pietas,* the quintessential Roman virtue.[1] In Virgil's time, this virtue had a concrete and practical aim: to ensure the health and safety of the Roman state (*salus publica*) by maintaining the *pax deorum.*[2] The key to keeping the gods happy was to honor them by sacrificing the right animals, in the right way, with the right words. An intentional breach of sacral procedure was considered impious and inexpiable; an unintentional breach, called a *piaculum,* could be rectified by means of an expiatory offering, also called a *piaculum.*[3] Until this expiatory offering was made, the gods would remain angry. It is therefore important in interpreting the poem to recognize that *pius Aeneas,* at several critical junctures, performs prayers and sacrifices incorrectly.

The first sacrifice that Aeneas performs has received little attention from modern readers. Described in no great detail, it seems straightforward and innocent enough:

1. This elevation of Aeneas' *pietas* appears to be largely Virgil's invention: see Galinsky (1969) 61.

2. See Linderski (1993) 610–11.

3. Tromp (1921) gives the most detailed and comprehensive account of Roman *piacula.* See also Scheid (1981); Linderski (1984).

> "*sacra* Dioneae matri divisque ferebam
> *auspicibus* coeptorum operum, superoque nitentem
> caelicolum regi mactabam in litore *taurum*." (3.19–21)

> "I was offering *sacrifices* to my mother, daughter of Dione, and the gods, that they might be *auspicious* toward the works begun, and was slaughtering a gleaming white *bull* on the shore to the high king of the gods."

Neither Aeneas, the narrator of Book 3, nor Virgil says anything more about this incident. Yet it raises issues of crucial importance, especially in light of the episode that follows it, in which Aeneas finds human blood and a human voice proceeding from the tree he attempts to uproot. As Ovid's Janus says, *omina principiis . . . inesse solent*, "omens are customarily present in beginnings" (*Fasti* 1.178)—a key principle in Roman religion, as well as a rule of thumb in literary criticism.

In Roman religious practice it was a *piaculum* to sacrifice a *taurus* (a full-grown uncastrated bull) to Jupiter. Of this we can be fairly certain. Macrobius' anti-Virgilian interlocutor Euangelus points to the Thracian *taurus* as an example of Virgil's religious ignorance (*Sat.* 3.10). Euangelus cites the statute recorded by C. Ateius Capito, a famous Augustan jurist and expert on sacral law,[4] *Iovi tauro verre ariete immolari non licet*, "it is not permitted to sacrifice to Jupiter with *taurus, verres,* or *aries* (uncastrated bull, pig, or ram)."[5] Euangelus is rebutted by the wise Praetextatus, who argues that Virgil deliberately introduced this *piaculum* as a prelude to the following scene:[6]

> Ateius enim Capito quem in acie contra Maronem locasti, adiecit haec verba: "siquis forte tauro Iovi fecerit, piaculum

4. On Capito's role as religious consultant for Augustus' *Ludi Saeculari* in 17 B.C., see Fraenkel (1957) 366.

5. Modern scholars disagree about how to interpret this important piece of evidence. See Montanari (1990) 532–33.

6. As Kleinknecht (1944) 72 notes, prodigies often occur during or after sacrificial rites, both in the *Aeneid* and throughout Roman history and literature. The Roman reader would have seen a natural connection between the sacrifice of the *taurus* and the prodigy of the bleeding tree.

> dato." committitur ergo res non quidem impianda, insolita tamen; et committitur non ignorantia, sed ut locum monstro faceret secuturo. (*Sat.* 3.10.7)
>
> That same Ateius Capito whom you lined up against Virgil adds these words: "If someone sacrifices to Jupiter with a *taurus*, let him pay a *piaculum*." Therefore the thing committed is improper, but certainly not inexpiable; and it is committed not through [the poet's] ignorance, but in order to make way for the prodigy that is to follow.

Similarly, Servius informs us that the sacrifice of a *taurus* to Jupiter was a grave error that led to the prodigy of the bleeding trees immediately following (*contra rationem Iovi taurum sacrificat, adeo ut hinc putetur subsecutum esse prodigium,* "against reason he sacrifices a bull to Jupiter, so that it may be supposed that the prodigy followed from this," ad 3.21). Servius remembers the incident, referring to it later in Book 3 in his comment on the sacrifices preceding the Actian Games:

> LUSTRAMUR IOVI aut 'lustramur', id est purgamur, ut Iovi sacra faciamus; aut certe 'lustramur Iovi', id est expiamur. piaculum enim commissum fuerat tauro in Thracia immolato, ut diximus supra, et licet multa fuissent secuta sacrificia, intellegebatur tamen adhuc numen iratum non desinentibus malis. (ad 3.279)
>
> WE LUSTRATE TO JUPITER either "we make a lustration," that is, we purify ourselves, in order to make sacrifices to Jupiter; or, surely, "we make a lustration to Jupiter," that is, we perform an expiation. For a *piaculum* had been committed when the bull was sacrificed in Thrace, as we said above, and even if many sacrifices had followed, it was understood that the divinity was still angry, since troubles did not cease.[7]

7. Servius seems to be reading "lustramur" as (possibly) indicating Aeneas' awareness of his *piaculum*. More probably, however, the verb means "purify" rather than "expiate" a particular sin, since nothing in the text indicates such self-

Do Servius and Macrobius correctly discern a ritual error in Aeneas' first sacrifice?

We must first decide whether Virgil knew that it was a *piaculum* to sacrifice a *taurus* to Jupiter. Despite the importance of sacrificing the appropriate animal to each god—and the animals' age, sex, color, and potency were all factors—Roman words for cattle are confusing and imprecise, with ritual, poetic, and quotidian vocabulary overlapping only partially.[8] Inscriptional evidence indicates that a *bos mas* was the correct animal to be sacrificed to Jupiter, but Virgil never uses this term, and scholars cannot even agree whether it refers to castrated or uncastrated bulls (i.e., the meaning of the term *bos mas* is unclear).[9] Heinrich Lehr insists that Virgil uses the terms *taurus* (full-grown uncastrated bull), *iuvencus* (young bull), and *bos* (generic word for cattle) interchangeably, prompted by metrical considerations and the desire for *variatio* rather than ritual accuracy. In the boxing match episode (5.362–484), the same animal is referred to by each of these three terms.[10] Virgil's apparent indifference to the distinction between *taurus* and *iuvencus*, however, may actually be a mark of poetic acumen rather than sloppiness. Though it is possible that he was simply unaware of the ritual prohibition against sacrificing *tauri* to Jupiter, it is more likely that, like Ovid, he knew it perfectly well and expected his readers to know it too.[11]

---

awareness on the part of Aeneas. Lloyd (1954) 297 observes that Servius' solution here "seems rather subtle" and argues rather that a lustration to Jupiter as the god chiefly in charge of Aeneas' fate "is quite natural and appropriate," despite the fact that the Actian games ostensibly honor Apollo.

8. See Krause (1931) 258–64.

9. Krause (1894) 9 and (1931) 259 identifies a *taurus* as castrated and a *bos mas* as uncastrated. Latte (1960) 381 says that uncastrated animals could not be sacrificed to Jupiter. Dumézil (1961), however, compares the ancient Indic practice of sacrificing to the major divinities only *sterile* cows, which were thought to have mystical powers. Answering the objections of Capdeville (1976), Dumézil (1979) 251–53 maintains that a *bos mas* was indeed castrated and a *taurus* uncastrated; in this he is followed by Turcan (1988) 8.

10. Lehr (1934) 74–75.

11. As Ryberg (1955) 190 notes, the offering of a steer to Capitoline Jupiter was the ritual most frequently represented in Roman art, for "the cult of the Capitolium

A more difficult question involves the extent to which sacrificing a *taurus* might have negative consequences for Aeneas. Virgil's protagonist is a transitional figure, not quite a Roman, not quite a Homeric hero, but with characteristics of both. The reason his identity matters in the present instance is that it was common for *Greek* heroes of the mythical past to sacrifice *tauri* to Jupiter/Zeus. Ovid's *Fasti* provides an interesting comparison. After his victory over Cacus, Hercules sacrifices a *taurus* to Jupiter (1.579). In the episode immediately following, the *flamen Dialis* offers to Jupiter the entrails of a *semimaris ovis*, "a *castrated* ram" (588). Ovid clearly knew that in *Roman* ritual only castrated animals should be sacrificed to Jupiter, but he seems to have no qualms about showing the Greek Hercules sacrificing a *taurus*.

Whether Aeneas is to be held to the standards of a Homeric hero or those of a Roman priest depends largely upon the nature of the *Aeneid*'s gods. Are they Homeric or Roman? This essential question is rarely addressed directly by either ancient or modern readers. Liebeschuetz' characterization of Roman religion points to the problem: "In *Roman religion, as opposed to Greek-influenced literature,* the personalities of even the great gods are of no practical consequence. As a result the Romans could arrange their relationships with the gods without worrying about so personal an attribute as divine jealousy [emphasis added]."[12] This observation may be accurate in reference to Roman cult, but in reference to Roman literature it implies a false dichotomy. Surely it is incorrect to say that because the *Aeneid* belongs to the category of "Greek-influenced literature," it therefore has no affinities with "Roman religion." Juno's intensely personal "divine jealousy," a "Greek" import, motivates the plot, but the *Aeneid*'s etiological connection to Roman religious institutions is equally apparent. It remains an open question whether Juno's manifest (Greek) jealousy is wedded to a

---

could be used, in visual expression as in literature, as an epitome of the whole pantheon of the old Roman gods."

12. Liebeschuetz (1979) 22.

(Roman) passion for ritual correctness.[13] For unlike Homer, who generally specifies whether an offering is favorably received, Virgil does not tell us immediately how the gods react to humans' continual attempts to placate them.

It may be that the language used to describe Aeneas' first sacrifice gives us a clue about how to interpret the scene. In Cicero's dialogue "On the Nature of the Gods" (*De Natura Deorum*), the neo-Academic Cotta refers to the original two-fold division of Roman religion into *sacra* and *auspicia*, to which was added a third category of prophetic warnings:

> Cumque omnis populi Romani religio in sacra et in auspicia divisa sit, tertium adiunctum sit si quid praedictionis causa ex portentis et monstris Sibyllae interpretes haruspicesve monuerunt, harum ego religionum nullam umquam contemnendam putavi, mihique ita persuasi, Romulum auspiciis Numam sacris constitutis fundamenta iecisse nostrae civitatis, quae numquam profecto sine summa placatione deorum immortalium tanta esse potuisset. (*DND* 3.5)

> Since the whole religion of the Roman people has been divided into sacrifice (*sacra*) and auspicy (*auspicia*), and a third thing has been added, i.e., whatever the Sibyls, prophets, or soothsayers have advised for the sake of prediction from portents (*portenta*) and prodigies (*monstra*), I have decided that none of these religious practices ever ought to be despised, and I have thus persuaded myself that Romulus by *auspicia* and Numa by *sacra* laid the foundations of our state, which certainly never would have been able to be so great without the most extreme placation of the immortal gods.

The practice of *auspicium* that Cotta refers to was a highly developed pseudo-science that involved interpreting the behavior of birds, animals, lightning, and other natural phenomena in order

13. For a concise discussion of the differences between Greek and Roman assumptions about the gods, see Jocelyn (1966) 99–103.

to determine whether the gods favored an impending action. However sceptical Roman intellectuals may have been, they never expressed this scepticism publicly: the taking of auspices was a necessary preliminary to the "inauguration" of every public official, every military campaign, every election, and other national events. Aeneas' description of his first sacrifice, "*sacra* Dionaeae matri divisque ferebam / *auspicibus* coeptorum operum" (3.19–20), points directly and indirectly to the two fundamental practices that Cotta names.[14] It is difficult to say whether the word *auspicibus* alone would have recalled to the Roman mind the practice of *auspicia,* for the adjective *auspex* (of which *auspicibus* is the dative plural) often appears to mean little more than "favorable." Yet the addition of *coeptorum operum* emphasizes that Aeneas wants the gods to favor the *beginning* of his enterprise, and for the Romans every important beginning was marked by the taking of auspices. Although it would be anachronistic to insist that Aeneas must "take the auspices" like a Roman official, the language suggests that Aeneas is to be seen as the forerunner of the founders of the Roman state, Romulus (who brought *auspicia*) and Numa (who brought *sacra*). In this context, Aeneas' sacrifice of a *taurus* may well have caused Virgil's readers a *frisson.*

Their uneasiness would have been confirmed by the *monstrum* that immediately follows, a portentous occurrence corresponding to Cotta's third category. Even Euangelus concedes that "the unlawful acts are excused [that is, the poet's knowledge is vindicated] by what follows" (*eventu excusantur inlicita,* 3.11.1). Aeneas' attempts to pluck up some foliage to deck his altar become a scene of horror:

> "forte fuit iuxta tumulus, quo cornea summo
> virgulta et densis hastilibus horrida myrtus.
> accessi viridemque ab humo convellere silvam
> conatus, ramis tegerem ut frondentibus aras,
> horrendum et dictu video mirabile *monstrum.*

14. The fullest modern treatment of *auspicia* is that of Linderski (1986). See especially 2147–48 on the pairing of *sacra* and *auspicia.*

nam quae prima solo ruptis radicibus arbos
vellitur, huic atro liquuntur sanguine guttae
et terram tabo maculant. mihi frigidus horror
membra quatit gelidusque coit formidine sanguis.
rursus et alterius lentum convellere vimen
insequor et causas penitus temptare latentis;
ater et alterius sequitur de cortice sanguis.
multa movens animo Nymphas venerabar agrestis
Gradivumque patrem, Geticis qui praesidet arvis,
rite secundarent visus *omen*que levarent.
tertia sed postquam maiore hastilia nisu
adgredior genibusque adversae obluctor harenae,
(eloquor an sileam?) gemitus lacrimabilis imo
auditur tumulo et vox reddita fertur ad auris:
'quid miserum, Aenea, laceras? iam parce sepulto,
parce pias scelerare manus. non me tibi Troia
externum tulit aut cruor hic de stipite manat.
heu fuge crudelis terras, fuge litus avarum:
nam Polydorus ego. hic confixum ferrea texit
telorum seges et iaculis increvit acutis.' " (3.22–46)

"By chance there was a mound nearby, on whose summit were cornel shrubs and myrtle bristling with dense spear-like stems. I approached, and when I tried to pluck up a green forest from the ground, in order to cover my altar with leafy boughs, I see a horrible *prodigy,* amazing to relate. For the tree that is first plucked from the soil, its roots broken—from this tree drops of black blood trickle down and stain the earth with putrid liquid. Cold horror shakes my limbs and my icy blood congeals with fear. Yet again I attempt to pluck the pliant branch of another, and utterly to test the hidden causes; black blood follows from the bark of yet another. Moving many things in my soul, I venerated the rural Nymphs and father Gradivus [Mars], who presides over the Getic fields, that they might in due ritual fashion favor these visions and

> lighten the *omen*. But after I accost the spear-like stems a third time, with greater effort, and struggle on my knees against the sand, (should I speak or keep quiet?) a pitiable groan is heard from the depth of the mound and a voice comes back and is sent to my ears: 'Why, Aeneas, do you torture this wretch? Spare the one who has been buried, spare polluting your pious hands. Troy did not bear me as foreign to you, nor does this gore pour out from a tree-trunk. Alas, flee these cruel lands, flee the greedy shore: for I am Polydorus. An iron crop of spears pierced and covered me here and grew up with sharp javelins.'"

This scene reveals some important characteristics of the hero and of Virgil's narrative technique. Aeneas' blood runs cold when he attempts to uproot the tree and finds it dripping with gore, *but he still tries a second time.* When his second attempt produces similar results, he prays to the native nymphs and Mars to lighten the omen, *but he still tries a third time.* He stops only when the voice of Polydorus explicitly orders him to do so. In this episode, there can be no doubt that Aeneas violates fundamental religious principles, not to mention ordinary common sense. The Romans observed a crucial distinction between omens "announced" and "unannounced": only those portents that were publicly acknowledged had to be responded to, and there are several (to us) humorous anecdotes about religious officials shutting their eyes and ears.[15]

---

15. So, for instance, the senate decreed that no one should watch the sky while the bill for Cicero's recall from exile was moving through the assembly (Cicero *Sest.* 129). Pliny observes that, according to the augurs, "neither dire omens nor any auspices affect those who, when beginning any undertaking, deny that they notice them; there is no greater gift of divine mercy than this" (*neque diras neque ulla auspicia pertinere ad eos qui quamcumque rem ingredientes observare se ea negaverint, quo munere divinae indulgentiae maius nullum est, NH* 28.17). See Jocelyn (1966) 101–103 and Rosenstein (1990) 71 on the importance of human acknowledgment and interpretation of signs, as opposed to the inherent meaning of the signs themselves. For the Romans, unlike the Greeks and Etruscans, prodigies always indicated the anger of the gods and demanded expiatory rites; see Bloch (1963) 82–86. On the use of prodigy and expiation as a political tool by the Roman senate, see MacBain (1982) 7–8 and passim.

Paradoxically, Aeneas' horror at the *monstrum* and his prayer to lighten the *omen* establish his culpability in continuing to assault the tree.[16] The proper response to a portent was to abort or postpone whatever action was in progress or about to commence. To fail to respond properly to an *acknowledged* omen or ritual fault was to transform imprudence into impiety.[17]

This accusation seems unfair. Aeneas, after all, does not mean to do anything wrong either by sacrificing the bull or by plucking up the tree—indeed, in each case he is trying to perform a pious religious act. He is not acting *dolo malo,* "with wicked intent," and the Romans did scrupulously distinguish between intentional and unintentional faults. Not a Roman magistrate, he can hardly be held responsible for not taking proper account of the omen. Yet such injustices plague Aeneas throughout the poem. In a world of Roman gods with Greek passions, he is forced to play a game for which no one has taught him the rules. Virgil calls attention to the unfairness and the irony of this situation at the beginning of the poem:

> Musa, mihi causas memora, quo numine laeso
> quidve dolens regina deum tot volvere casus
> insignem pietate virum, tot adire labores
> impulerit. tantaene animis caelestibus irae? (1.8–11)

> Muse, tell me the reasons, by what wound to her divinity, grieving over what, the queen of the gods forced a man outstanding in piety to play out so many misfortunes, to undergo so many labors. Is such wrath in celestial hearts?

By the logic of the Roman religious system, Aeneas' *pietas* should be instrumental in restoring the *pax deorum,* provided that he perform the necessary rituals correctly. Juno's continued anger suggests that he does not. As Servius puts it, *intellegebatur tamen adhuc numen*

16. On tree violation in general, see Thomas (1988b). This theme will be treated extensively in the second part of the book.

17. Scheid (1981) 124. On impiety, see also Scheid (1985) 22–36.

iratum non desinentibus malis ("it was understood that the divinity was still angry, since troubles did not cease," ad 3.279). Consequences, not comments, indicate the gods' response.[18]

The errors attending Aeneas' first ritual act in the poem belong to a pattern repeated throughout. As the *piaculum* of the Thracian bull is followed by a bleeding tree, so disobedience to a prophet's instructions is followed by the hesitation of the Golden Bough, which Aeneas must pluck to gain admittance to the Underworld. The Sibyl gives Aeneas tripartite instructions—to procure the Bough, bury a comrade, and sacrifice black sheep—but though she relates the items in this order, she tells him to perform them (it seems) in the reverse order. It is worth looking at her instructions in some detail:

> ergo alte vestiga oculis et rite repertum
> carpe manu; namque ipse volens facilisque sequetur,
> si te fata vocant; aliter non viribus ullis
> vincere nec duro poteris convellere ferro.
> praeterea iacet exanimum tibi corpus amici
> (heu nescis) totamque incestat funere classem,
> dum consulta petis nostroque in limine pendes.
> sedibus hunc refer *ante* suis et conde sepulcro.
> duc nigras pecudes; ea *prima piacula* sunto.
> sic demum lucos Stygis et regna invia vivis
> aspicies. (6.145–55)

> Therefore track it high up with your eyes, and when it is duly found, pluck it with your hand; for it will follow willingly

18. The gods' anger often could be discerned only *ex post facto*. For instance, the Romans' disastrous defeat by the Gauls at the River Allia in 390 B.C. occurred on July 18; after the battle, the Romans remembered that another major defeat (of the Fabii at the Cremera) had taken place on the same day almost a century earlier. July 18 was then declared a *dies religiosus* (a day unsuitable for military and other activities), but there would have been no way of knowing that the day was unlucky before the outcome of the Allia battle "proved" it so. On this and other examples of ritual faults that could not have been discerned until after their negative consequences, see Rosenstein (1990) 67–72.

> and easily of itself if the fates are calling you; otherwise, not with any strength will you be able to conquer it nor tear it off with hard iron. Moreover, the body of your friend is lying dead (alas, you know not!) and polluting the whole fleet with his death, while you seek advice and hang on our threshold. Return him *before* to his proper place and bury him in a tomb. Lead black sheep; *let these be piacula first.* Thus at last you will see the forests of Styx and the kingdoms impenetrable to the living.

The force of *ante* in 152 must be that Aeneas should bury his friend *before* he looks for the Bough.[19] Aeneas in fact plucks the Bough while his comrades are engaged in felling trees and building a funeral pyre. Virgil emphasizes the simultaneity of these actions by framing Aeneas' search for the Bough with "in the midst of these works" (*opera inter talia,* 183) and "meanwhile" (*interea,* 212), referring to the funeral preparations, and only after tearing off the Bough does Aeneas participate in the funeral rites. Similarly, the Sibyl tells Aeneas to lead black sheep as *prima piacula* (153), an anticipatory expiation to be made, presumably, before the burial.[20] Aeneas in fact makes the offering *after* plucking the Bough and burying Misenus, and he offers only a *single* black sheep and a sterile cow (249–51). The narrator tells us twice that Aeneas and his men are following the Sibyl's instructions expeditiously (*iussa Sibyllae, / haud mora, festinant,* "with no delay, they hurriedly follow the commands of the Sibyl," 176–77; *propere exsequitur praecepta Sibyllae,* "he quickly follows the instructions of the Sibyl," 236). Yet

19. Thomas (1988b) 268: "This line suggests yet another lapse in the ceremonial procedure of Aeneas."

20. The Romans often offered a *piaculum* in advance (called a *hostia praecidanea*), in the hope of averting pollution before it happened. See Tromp (1921) 72–81. In addition, the unburied Misenus is already polluting the fleet, and thus must be buried *first,* before anything else happens. Norden (1957) ad 6.153 takes *prima* as refering to the next line, i.e., "make these offerings first, then you will see the Underworld," but it is more natural to take *prima* as refering back to the previous line, i.e., "make these offerings first, *before* burying the comrade" (the interpretation of Servius).

closer examination reveals that Aeneas has carried out these instructions in precisely the wrong order and possibly has sacrificed the wrong animal.[21] No wonder the Bough is unwilling to yield to Aeneas' greedy pull, a detail highly noticeable and not attributable to conflations of different versions:[22]

> corripit Aeneas extemplo avidusque refringit
> *cunctantem*, et vatis portat sub tecta Sibyllae. (210–11)

> Aeneas seizes it suddenly and greedily breaks it off, *though it hesitates*, and carries it to the house of the prophetess Sibyl.

"Hesitate" is the one thing it should not do, for the Sibyl said it would either come off easily, "if the fates are calling you," or be utterly unmoveable (146–48). This pattern of a prophet's instructions half followed, with half-successful results, forms the rule rather than the exception in the *Aeneid*.

---

21. Does the phrase *nigrae pecudes* (153) refer to sheep, as opposed to cattle, or to both sheep and cattle? *Pecudes* can have either meaning (OLD 1.a = livestock, 1.b = specifically sheep). Virgil uses the word in a variety of ways: to contrast animals with humans (*Aen.* 1.743), sheep with cows (*Geo.* 3.368), sheep with cows and pigs (*Aen.* 11.199), or tame animals with wild ones (*Geo.* 3.480). Only once does *pecudes* refer to cows (*Ecl.* 6.49); more often it refers to sheep (*Geo.* 3.471, *Aen.* 3.120, 3.642, 12.171). Norden (1957) ad 153 is probably right in taking *nigrae pecudes* as a reference to sheep only, and thus in seeing a discrepancy between the Sibyl's instructions and Aeneas' actions. He gives the usual explanation: "Dergleichen Diskrepanzen würden, wie wir annehmen dürfen, der Dichter bei endgültiger Redaktion vielleicht beiseitigt haben" ("We may assume that the poet would probably have reconciled such discrepancies in his final redaction"). See Lehr (1934) 75–76.

22. See Thomas (1988b) 267: though Servius and some modern critics try to read *cunctantem* in a neutral or positive way, "the arguments of others, particularly D'Arms [1964] and Segal [1968], are clearly correct, and now probably represent the *communis opinio*: the state of mind of Aeneas (*avidus*), the manner of his actions (*corripit . . . refringit*), and the resistant animism ascribed to the bough (*cunctantem*) create an uneasiness not dissimilar from that generated at the beginning of Book 3." D'Arms (1964) 265 has a useful summary of the positions of readers since Servius who have tried to ignore or mimimize the significance of the bough's hesitation. See Horsfall (1991) 26–27; I agree with Thomas (1993) 77 that Horsfall's "realismo dendrologico" is an unsatisfying explanation. Closer to the truth is the idea of resistance and delay associated with rites of passage discussed in Bremmer and Horsfall (1987) 110–11.

The Bough's reaction is particularly noteworthy in light of its strange designation as "sacred to infernal Juno" (*Iunoni infernae . . . sacer,* 138), a circumlocution for "Proserpina" prompted by more than metrical considerations.[23] Juno is too central to Aeneas' fate for Virgil to have used her name casually in the context of supplication by means of a sacred object. Rather, the Sibyl's instructions and the hesitating Bough tie into the larger theme of winning Juno's favor. As has often been remarked, the wrathful goddess symbolizes the forces opposed to Aeneas and his destiny; it follows that Aeneas must pacify her to fulfill this destiny. Her primary concern is with her own *honores* (sing. *honor* or *honos*), a word often used in sacral contexts as a euphemism for "offerings" or "sacrifices."[24] Thus Juno, at the end of her opening speech, complains that the Trojans' affront to her divinity diminishes the *honor* that will be placed by suppliants on her altars:

> "ast ego, quae divum incedo regina, Iovisque
> et soror et coniunx, una cum gente tot annos
> bella gero. et quisquam numen Iunonis adorat
> praeterea aut supplex aris imponet *honorem*?" (1.48–49)

> "But I, who stride as queen of the gods, and both sister and wife of Jupiter, wage war with one people for so many years. And does anyone adore the divinity of Juno anymore, or will he, suppliant, place a *sacrifice* on her altars?"[25]

What finally wins her over, near the end of the poem, is Jupiter's promise not only that the Trojan name and customs will die out, but that the new race arising from Trojan and Italian blood will celebrate her *honores* like no other:

---

23. Norden (1957) ad 136 ff. notes that Virgil has coined the phrase on the model of Greek *Zeus katachthonios* to stand for the metrically impossible "Proserpinae," adding that other Latin poets got around the problem more simply by using Greek forms such as "Persephones" or "Persephonae."

24. See Lehr (1934) 64.

25. This somewhat awkward translation reflects the strange tense shift between *adorat* (present) and *imponet* (future).

"hinc genus Ausonio mixtum quod sanguine surget,
supra homines, supra ire deos pietate videbis,
nec gens ulla tuos aeque celebrabit *honores*." (12.838–40)

"The race that will arise hence, mixed with Ausonian blood, you will see go beyond men, beyond the gods in piety, nor will any people equally celebrate your *sacrifices*."

The marked position of these lines—the gods' first and last speeches in the poem, with *honorem / es* the last word of both—suggests that giving the proper offerings to Juno is a structuring principle of the poem and an essential component of Aeneas' eventual victory.[26] The problem is that even though Aeneas is twice told that prayer and sacrifice to Juno will gain him "victory" over her, the sacrifices he performs do not seem to accomplish anything.

His first attempt follows his meeting with Helenus at the substitute Troy at Buthrotum. The prophet exhorts Aeneas in highly emphatic language, promising (it seems) that he can achieve victory over the goddess after leaving Sicily:

"'praeterea, si qua est Heleno prudentia vati,
si qua fides, animum si veris implet Apollo,
unum illud tibi, nate dea, proque omnibus unum
praedicam et repetens iterumque iterumque monebo,
Iunonis magnae primum prece numen adora,
Iunoni cane vota libens dominamque potentem
supplicibus supera donis: sic denique victor
Trinacria finis Italos mittere relicta.' " (3.433–40)

"'Moreover, if there is any foresight in Helenus as prophet, if there is any reliability, if Apollo fills my spirit with true things, that one thing, goddess-born, and one thing before all I shall declare to you and, repeating it, warn you again and

26. Feeney (1984) points out the qualified nature of Juno's reconciliation within the *Aeneid*, since she remained an enemy of Rome until the Second Punic War (as is heavily foreshadowed in the *Aeneid*). Juno's *honores* are discussed further in chap. 6.

again: adore the divinity first of great Juno with prayer, to Juno sing vows willingly, and overcome the powerful mistress with suppliant gifts: thus, victor at last, you shall be sent to the Italian borders, with Trinacria left behind.'"

When the Trojans make their first landing in Italy at the Citadel of Minerva, their first action is described by Aeneas as follows:

> "tum numina sancta precamur
> Palladis armisonae, quae prima accepit ovantis,
> et capita ante aras Phrygio velamur amictu,
> praeceptisque Heleni, dederat quae maxima, rite
> Iunoni Argivae iussos adolemus honores." (3.543–47)

"Then we pray to the holy divinity of Pallas loud in arms, who first received us as we cheered, and veil our heads with Phrygian covering before the altars, and, by the instructions of Helenus, which he had given as most important, we in due ritual fashion make the commanded sacrifices to Argive Juno."

Commentators inform us that Aeneas, with characteristic piety, is here carrying out the instructions that Helenus gave him a hundred lines before. Indeed, the last three lines quoted above encourage this reading: Aeneas describes the veiling that Helenus had prescribed (405) and states that he is following the "most important" (*maxima*) instructions, to make sacrifice to Juno. Yet subsequent events—or prior, from the reader's point of view, for the *Aeneid* opens with Juno's tirade—reveal that Juno's wrath has cooled not one degree. What went wrong?

There are two possibilities. One is that the prophet lied, telling Aeneas that he could win victory over Juno with sacrifices when in fact he could not. James O'Hara has argued that many of the *Aeneid*'s "optimistic" prophecies are carefully worded in such a way as to disguise or suppress distressing knowledge, thus shielding their recipients from pain; they are either misleading or "simply not true."[27]

27. O'Hara (1990) 32.

Yet something seems fundamentally wrong about a prophet telling a pure lie, even a white one.[28] The more appealing possibility is that Helenus has delivered a prophecy accurate but deceptive. Helenus' statement is conditionally worded: "Sacrifice to Juno in this way, (then) you will gain victory." If Aeneas fails in the first half, the prophet cannot be held responsible when the second does not come true. Aeneas clearly has no idea that he has done anything wrong—but as the incidents of the Thracian bull and the Sibyl's instructions show, a god's anger can be discerned more readily from subsequent events than from explicit statements by the narrator or his characters. Verbal assurance that orders have been followed is very likely a signal that they have not.

A close examination of Aeneas' actions reveals that he does indeed fail in the task assigned. The prophet gives Aeneas a specific charge:

> '**Iunonis** magnae *primum prece numen* adora.' (3.437)
>
> 'Adore the *divinity first* of great **Juno** with *prayer*.'

Aeneas describes his own actions in words that echo these:

---

28. Artists violate such unwritten "codes" at their peril. Alfred Hitchcock never forgave himself for creating a flashback (in *Stagefright*) that was simply a lie. Dorothy Sayers puts it well: "Any fool can tell a lie, and any fool can believe it; but the right method is to tell the *truth* in such a way that the *intelligent* reader is seduced into telling the lie for himself" (quoted by Winkler [1985] 123). It is legitimate, of course, to play games with the reader's assumptions about codes—as in the Mad Hatter's non-riddle, "Why is a raven like a writing desk?"—but only if the game turns out to vindicate the author's cleverness.

Moreover, ancient prophecies, as a rule, were phrased ambiguously and often were misinterpreted by the hearer. The notorious cases of Croesus and Pyrrhus spring to mind. Croesus was told by an oracle that he would destroy a great empire, only to find after attacking the Persians that the empire he destroyed was his own. Pyrrhus was told, "You the Romans will conquer" (*vincere te Romanos*); thinking that he would destroy the Romans, he discovered the treacherousness of the double-accusative construction when the Romans conquered him. See Fontenrose (1978) 111–14, 302, 343. Though these oracles are probably apocryphal (the Pyrrhus oracle is undoubtedly Ennius' invention, inspired by Herodotus' Croesus oracle), they are nice examples of prophetic ambiguity in the popular and literary tradition, which is most relevant for interpreting Virgil.

"tum *numina* sancta *precamur*
Palladis armisonae, quae *prima* accepit ovantis." (3.543–44)

"Then we *pray* to the holy *divinity* of **Pallas** loud in arms, who *first* received us as we cheered."

The verbal correspondences are quite close—but Aeneas has "prayed first to the divinity" of the *wrong goddess*. Aeneas legitimately can be charged with a breach of procedure. And if we look back to Helenus' speech, that is just what we should have expected. "I tell you one thing, one thing before all, and warn you again and again": in countless narratives, these words precede the crucial instruction that we may be certain the hero will disobey—eating the forbidden fruit, opening the sealed box, falling asleep at the wrong moment. Though positive precepts ("be sure to") are not quite so prone to disobedience as negative ones ("be sure not to"), the very vehemence of Helenus' words should lead us to suspect that they will not be carried out. While Aeneas says that he has obeyed Helenus' greatest orders—and until now readers have taken him at his word—on another level Virgil makes it apparent that he has not.

An analogous scene five books later shows Aeneas making a similar mistake. This time, having reached his destination at last, Aeneas is instructed by the river Tiber in words that echo those of Helenus:

"*surge* age, nate dea, *primisque cadentibus astris*
Iunoni fer *rite* preces, iramque minasque
supplicibus supera votis. mihi victor honorem
persolves." (8.59–62)

"Go on, *get up*, goddess-born, and *as the first stars are setting* bring prayers to **Juno** in *due ritual fashion*, and overcome her wrath and threats with suppliant vows. As victor, you will pay me my honor in full."

Five lines later, Aeneas wakes up and does the following:

surgit et aetherii spectans *orientia solis*
lumina rite cavis undam de flumine palmis

> sustinet ac talis effundit ad aethera voces:
> "**Nymphae,** Laurentes Nymphae, genus amnibus unde est,
> tuque, o **Thybri** tuo genitor cum flumine sancto,
> accipite Aenean et tandem arcete periclis. . . ." (8.68–73)

> He *gets up* and, gazing at the *rising light of the etherial sun, in due ritual fashion* he raises with hollow palms a wave from the river, and pours out such words to the ether: "**Nymphs,** Laurentian Nymphs, whence is the race of rivers, and you, oh father **Tiber,** with your holy stream, receive Aeneas and, at last, keep him away from dangers. . . ."

Once again, the language describing Aeneas' actions clearly and carefully echoes the language of the prophecy. Tiber's imperative *surge* ("get up") is picked up by *surgit* ("he gets up"); *primisque cadentibus astris* ("as the first stars are setting"), that is, "at dawn," is equivalent to *orientia solis / lumina* ("rising light of the sun"); and *rite* ("in due ritual fashion"), a term emphasizing the importance of ritual correctness, is echoed exactly.[29] Tiber's declaration *mihi victor honorem / persolves* ("as victor, you will pay me my honor in full") implies that Juno should come before himself.[30] We expect that Aeneas will pray to Juno first, and Fordyce even tells us that Aeneas does this: "Aeneas has his vision in the small hours and Tiber tells him to make his offering to Juno at dawn, *primis cadentibus astris* (59); he does so, *spectans orientis solis / lumina* (68 f.), and then sets out when he has manned his ships."[31] The text makes clear, however, that this is *not* what Aeneas does. After praying to the Nymphs and Tiber while watching the rising sun, he mans his ships, and only then does he see the white sow that he will sacrifice to Juno:

> sic memorat, geminasque legit de classe biremis
> remigioque aptat, socios simul instruit armis.

29. Lehr (1934) 13 notes that Virgil's use of the term *rite* calls attention to his self-conscious precision about ritual details.

30. Page (1929) ad 8.61: " 'to me thou shalt pay thy offerings when victorious,' i.e. Juno demands instant service, my honours will come later."

31. Fordyce (1977) ad 8.86.

> Ecce autem subitum atque oculis mirabile monstrum,
> candida per silvam cum fetu concolor albo
> procubuit viridique in litore conspicitur sus. (8.79–83)

> So he speaks, and chooses two biremes from his fleet and fits them with oars, and at the same time equips his allies with arms.
>
> But look—a sudden prodigy, marvelous to the eyes, a gleaming sow is sighted through the woods, the same color as her white brood, lying on the green shore.

Even if Aeneas' prayer to the river deities takes little enough time that he can still pray to Juno "at dawn," it is hardly possible that he can also equip his fleet in those few crepuscular minutes. Poetic license cannot obscure the fact that it must be long past sunrise by the time he sees the sow, so gleaming white, on the green bank. Moreover, Aeneas may have committed a *piaculum* not only in delaying the sacrifice to Juno, but also in choosing inappropriate victims: sows with their young were generally offered to Ceres or Tellus, not to Juno.[32]

As in the parallel passage at the Citadel of Minerva, Virgil nevertheless encourages us to believe that Aeneas has done what he was told. When he finally performs the sacrifice to Juno, he does it in style:

> quam pius Aeneas tibi enim, tibi, maxima Iuno,
> mactat sacra ferens et cum grege sistit ad aram. (8.84–85)

> Which [sow] pious Aeneas sacrifices to you, greatest Juno, to you, bearing sacred emblems, and stands her before the altar with her herd.

As elsewhere, the word *pius* calls attention to Aeneas' fulfillment of his religious obligations.[33] Virgil's emphatic, repeated address

32. See Krause (1931) 253–54.

33. Williams (1973) ad 8.84 (pius): "here with particular reference to the fulfilment of religious obligations in appeasing the hostility of Juno (60f., 3.435f.)."

to Juno seems both to highlight the urgency of Aeneas' action and to add the author's own prayer that the sacrifice be favorably received. So moving is this scene that we hardly notice what Aeneas has done wrong.

Virgil repeatedly shows Aeneas committing ritual errors and failing to follow prophets' instructions correctly. Although none of these errors is explicitly mentioned by the poet when it occurs, the rupture in the *pax deorum* can be discerned from subsequent events (bleeding tree, hesitating Bough, unabated wrath of Juno). It remains to ask what Virgil intended by Aeneas' many mistakes. One thing is certain: in Roman practice, an incorrect sacrifice required another to set it right.[34]

---

34. Plutarch (*Coriolanus,* 25), in illustrating the Romans' meticulous attention to ritual detail, informs us that they once repeated a sacrificial rite thirty (!) times. See Scheid (1981) 122–23. On the various causes for repetition of rites (*instauratio*), see Tromp (1921) 66–72.

CHAPTER TWO

TIBER AND NUMICUS

Seas in the ancient world were dangerous places, navigated only out of necessity; rivers were centers of civilization and objects of love. To cross a river or stream of any size was an act of religious significance, for all bodies of "living water" were thought to be inhabited by deities with tremendous powers for good or ill.[1] In the *Aeneid*, Aeneas' wanderings are repeatedly represented as a journey from the dangers of the sea to the safety of the Tiber, his longed-for destination (3.500, 5.82–83, 5.797, 7.302–303). It is the Tiber who welcomes Aeneas to Italy and delivers to him the first prophecy that he hears in the second half of the poem. Yet by association with other characters and episodes, both within and outside the *Aeneid*, Aeneas' encounter with the Tiber in Book 8 (31–96) foreshadows his own death.[2]

---

1. Servius (ad 7.84) notes simply, *nullus enim fons non sacer* ("for no spring is not sacred"). See Holland (1961) 3–20. Perhaps the most notorious Roman *exemplum malum* for how to treat a river was Crassus: "in spite of unfavorable sacrifices both for crossing and landing, he pressed on over the Euphrates to the destruction of himself and his men" (16). On the sanctity and poetic significance of water, see Edlund (1987) 54–62. As she notes, "It is no coincidence that Aeneas, as the founder of civilization in Italy, arrived by sea, entered the underworld near Lake Avernus, received advice from the river god, Tiber, invoked Springs and Rivers in his solemn prayers, and received his final purification and apotheosis through another river, the Numicus" (54).

2. O'Hara (1990) 104–11 discusses many of the important allusions to Aeneas' death. Christmann (1976) discusses the connections between the end of Book 6,

It was well known to Virgil's readers that Aeneas met his end by disappearing into or near the Numicus river, near which he was worshiped as Indiges (*pater Indiges*, *Iuppiter Indiges*, or *Aeneas Indiges*).[3] Servius, in several places, relates the basic elements of the legend.[4] He recognizes part of Dido's curse, for instance, as a true prediction of Aeneas' eventual fate:

> "sed cadat ante diem mediaque inhumatus harena." (4.620)
>
> "But let him fall before his time, and [lie] unburied in the middle of the sand."

On this line, Servius comments,

> Cato dicit iuxta Laurolavinium cum Aeneae socii praedas agerent, proelium commissum, in quo Latinus occisus est, fugit Turnus: et Mezentii auxilio conparato <renovavit proelium, quo> victus quidem est ab Aenea; qui tamen [Aeneas] in ipso proelio non conparuit. Ascanius <vero> postea Mezentium interemit. alii dicunt quod victor Aeneas cum sacrificaret super Numicum fluvium lapsus est, et eius nec cadaver inventum est: unde dicit 'mediaque inhumatus harena'. postea dictus est inter deos receptus. <quidam eum cum adversum Aborigines pugnaret, †extanginem dicunt repertum.>
>
> Cato says that when the allies of Aeneas were driving away booty near Laurolavinium, Turnus fled the battle that ensued, in which Latinus was killed: and when he had enlisted the help of Mezentius, <he renewed the battle, in which> he was conquered by Aeneas; who nevertheless did not appear in

---

where Aeneas leaves the Underworld through the ivory gate of Sleep (not Dreams), and the end of Book 5, where Sleep is instrumental in Palinurus' death (as well as other ways in which the death of Palinurus foreshadows the death of Aeneas). Kepple (1976) points out Virgil's carefully constructed parallel between Arruns, who is fated to die soon after killing Camilla, and Aeneas, fated to die after killing Turnus (see chap. 4, n.1).

3. The meaning of the cult title is somewhat obscure. See Galinsky (1969) 149–50; Ogilvie (1970) ad Livy 1.2.6; Latte (1960) 43–44.

4. See especially ad 4.620, 1.259, 7.150, 7.797, (Auctus) 7.797, 12.794.

> the battle itself. Ascanius <however> later killed Mezentius. Others say that when Aeneas, as victor, was sacrificing on the banks of the Numicus river, he fell in, and not even his corpse was found: whence she says "and unburied in the middle of the sand." Afterward, he was said to have been received among the gods. <Some say that when he fought against the Aborigines, he was found dead.[5]>

This comment includes various traditions that Virgil does not use, but the salient facts about Aeneas' death are that he either fell into the Numicus river or was killed in a battle with the Aborigines. The first of these seems to be the dominant tradition, for in other places Servius states simply that Aeneas fell into the Numicus, either while sacrificing or while fleeing an enemy (e.g., ad 12.794).

Accounts of Aeneas' end written shortly before or after the *Aeneid* show a certain ambivalence about his ultimate fate. Livy says that a victorious battle was the last of Aeneas' mortal labors and that he was subsequently buried and worshipped on the banks of the Numicus:

> Situs est, quemcumque eum dici ius fasque est, super Numicum flumen: Iovem indigitem appellant. (Livy 1.2.6)

> He is buried on the banks of the Numicus river, whoever it is right and proper for him to be said to be: they call him Jupiter Indiges.

Livy's agnosticism about the proper name for Aeneas is phrased with tantalizing ambiguity. It could mean, "whether he ought to be called a man or a god," as several translators take it; it could also mean, "whatever cult title is appropriate for him," as Ogilvie takes it.[6] Dionysius of Halicarnassus, on the other hand, explicitly states that Aeneas' end was a subject of controversy at the time:

---

5. Whatever we read for *extanginem*—conjectures include *exsanguinem, extinctum, exsanguem*, and *exanimem*—the context clearly suggests some word for "dead."

6. Ogilvie (1970) ad Livy 1.2.6.

μάχης δὲ γενομένης καρτερᾶς οὐ πρόσω τοῦ Λαουϊνίου καὶ πολλῶν ἑκατέρωθεν ἀπολομένων τὰ μὲν στρατεύματα νυκτὸς ἐπελθούσης διελύθη, τὸ δὲ Αἰνείου σῶμα φανερὸν οὐδαμῇ γενόμενον οἱ μὲν εἰς θεοὺς μεταστῆναι εἴκαζον, οἱ δ' ἐν τῷ ποταμῷ, παρ' ὃν ἡ μάχη ἐγένετο, διαφθαρῆναι. καὶ αὐτῷ κατασκευάζουσιν οἱ Λατῖνοι ἡρῷον ἐπιγραφῇ τοιᾷδε κοσμούμενον· Πατρὸς θεοῦ χθονίου, ὃς ποταμοῦ Νομικίου ῥεῦμα διέπει.'

(*Roman Antiquities* 1.64.4–5)

The battle becoming fierce not far from Lavinium and many having died on both sides, the armies separated when night came, but the body of Aeneas was nowhere to be found. Some guessed that it had been translated to the gods, while others guessed that it had perished in the river by which the battle took place. And the Latins built him a hero-shrine adorned with an inscription like this: "[This is the shrine] of the father and god of this place, who presides over the stream of the Numicus river."

In this account, the source of uncertainty is made clear: the disappearance of Aeneas' body meant either the greatest honor, instant apotheosis, or the worst horror, drowning and lack of burial. Ovid's rendition of Aeneas' death in the *Metamorphoses* puts a positive spin on his disappearance into the river and focuses on his apotheosis. The Numicus river washes away "whatever had been mortal in Aeneas" (*quidquid in Aenea fuerat mortale, Met.* 14.603), Venus receives him with nectar and ambrosia, and the Romans worship him ever afterward (*Met.* 14.593–608). In the *Fasti*, Aeneas' death is not treated directly, but his eventual apotheosis is implied by close and obvious parallels between his story and that of Dido's sister Anna, who becomes a divinity of the Numicus.[7]

7. Barchiesi (1997) 21 observes that the story of Anna (*Fasti* 3.545–656) "appears to be a continuation, completion, and replica of the *Aeneid*." See Porte (1985) 142–50 for a comprehensive treatment of the parallels between Anna (in the *Fasti*) and Aeneas (in the *Aeneid*).

The variety in the accounts of Livy, Dionysius, and Ovid suggests that Virgil was working with a tradition richly mysterious and conformable to the biases of each author or reader. The *Aeneid* engages both strains of this tradition. Jupiter's great speeches at the beginning and end of the poem emphasize the positive aspect of Aeneas' death, his translation into heaven (1.259–60, 12.794–95). Disappearance into a river, however, happened also to be the fate reserved for Rome's most nefarious criminals: parricides were sewn into leather sacks and thrown into the Tiber, thereby becoming *piacula* to atone for their own crimes.[8] Virgil's treatment of the Tiber and the Numicus points not only to the horror of drowning, but even to the possibility that Aeneas himself will become in this way a sacrificial offering.

Virgil employs various strategies to associate the Tiber with the Numicus. One of these devices is a famous inconsistency between the poem's opening lines and our first glimpse of the Tiber itself. The proem follows tradition in stating that Aeneas came to the "Lavinian shores" (1.2–3), that is, the coastline near the mouth of the Numicus. When Aeneas actually lands in Italy near the beginning of the poem's second half, however, it is at the mouth of the Tiber (7.30–36), not the Numicus. Horsfall sees poetic justification for Virgil's substitution of a Tiber landing for the anticipated Numicus landing:

> Virgil of course transfers the Trojans' arrival from the seashore to the mouth of the Tiber, yet when telling his Muse of his intentions retains the Trojans' traditional goal (1.2–3): *Laviniaque venit litora*. His relocation of the Trojans' landing is perhaps too innovative, too disconcerting, yet symbolically enriching, to be revealed in a prooemium and we may won-

8. Scheid (1981) 154. On the details of this practice, see Le Gall (1953) 92–93. As Kyle (1998) 213–41 ("Rituals, Spectacles, and the Tiber River") discusses, the Tiber appears to have been the primary receptacle for the corpses of criminals executed in the arena and other enemies of the Roman state. The river offered ritual purgation of hostile spirits, punishment (through lack of burial) for the souls of the despised, and a convenient dumping site.

> der whether the site of Lavinium meant much to Virgil; students of the *Aeneid* are perhaps less eager than once they were to convert Virgil into an eager backpacker who had explored the Roman Campagna in minute detail.[9]

This sort of apology, with the amusing contrast implied between divine poet and "eager backpacker," is ubiquitous among lovers of Virgil. But more is to be gained by focusing on the "error" than by dismissing it. Virgil and his Roman readers knew that Lavinium was at the mouth of the Numicus. The proem creates the expectation that, in accordance with the tradition, Aeneas will land there. When he lands instead at the mouth of the Tiber, the reader wonders why.

While the substitution of the "symbolically enriching" Tiber might have the effect of suppressing the Numicus altogether, Virgil takes care to remind us of the smaller river in such a way as to make it seem a fit companion for the great one. The Numicus is named three times in the *Aeneid*, all in Book 7, and always in the same breath with the Tiber. Aeneas and his men in their initial exploration of the Italian countryside discover two named rivers:

> urbem et finis et litora gentis
> diversi explorant: haec fontis stagna Numici,
> hunc Thybrim fluvium, hic fortis habitare Latinos. (149–51)

> They explore in different directions the city and borders and shores of the country: these [were the] pools of the Numicus spring, this the river Tiber, the brave Latins lived here.

In his speech to Latinus, the Trojan envoy Ilioneus explains that the Trojans have found in Italy the land the gods instructed them to find:

> "hinc Dardanus ortus,
> huc repetit iussisque ingentibus urget Apollo

9. Horsfall (1986) 12–13; see also Horsfall (1991) 49–50 for a more extensive discussion of why the Tiber landing is thematically fruitful.

> Tyrrhenum ad Thybrim et fontis vada sacra Numici."
> (240–42)

> "From here Dardanus arose, hither Apollo recalls us and urges us with great commands to [seek] Tyrrhenian Tiber and the holy shallows of the Numicus spring."

It is surprising to hear the Numicus suddenly added to Apollo's orders, since the Tiber has stood alone in prophetic utterances and expressions of Trojan desire up to this point (2.782, 3.500, 5.83, 5.797, 6.87). The third appearance of the two rivers together is in the list of Turnus' followers in the catalogue of Italian warriors:

> qui saltus, Tiberine, tuos sacrumque Numici
> litus arant . . . (797–98)

> those who plow your groves, Tiber, and the holy bank of the Numicus . . .

Such yokings of the two rivers—three times in close proximity—serve not merely to associate the Tiber and the Numicus, but almost to imply that they have some sort of equal status. Despite their disparity in size, Virgil encourages his readers to think of them as a pair.[10]

Another means of yoking the two derives from the pairing of the Xanthus and Simois rivers in the *Iliad*.[11] Virgil makes the association between the Trojan and the Italian rivers explicit, or nearly so, in at least two ways. One is an unmistakable verbal echo between the end of Aeneas' first speech, where he expresses his longing to have died at Troy,

10. Christmann (1976) 272 points out that the Numicus is always mentioned with the Tiber.

11. Cruttwell (1947) 63–64: "Virgil, in fact, postulates two symbolically parallel riverine systems—an eastern, that of Troy, with its Xanthus and its Simois; and a western, that of Rome, with its Tiber and its Numicus." Horsfall (1999) ad 7.797 comments, "Tiber and Numicus are the Simois and Xanthus (6.88–89) of the *ager Laurens* (paired also at [7.]150f., 242), but on detail V. is clearly not to be pressed."

"ubi tot Simois correpta *sub undis*
scuta virum galeasque et fortia corpora volvit!" (1.100–101)

"Where the Simois *rolls* so many *shields of men*, snatched *under the waves, and helmets, and strong bodies*!"

and his grim declaration of the Italian War:

"quam multa *sub undas*
scuta virum galeasque et fortia corpora volves,
Thybri pater!" (8.538–40)

"How many *shields of men and helmets and strong bodies you will roll under your waves*, Father Tiber!"

These lines, both spoken by Aeneas, are highly marked by content and position. It seems that Virgil intended his readers to remember them and to see the Tiber as the Italian counterpart to the Simois. But there is a complication. Aeneas (or Virgil) appears to have made a mistake in naming the Simois as the river clogged with battle equipment and corpses: in the *Iliad*, it is the Xanthus, correctly named by Neptune elsewhere in the *Aeneid* (5.806–808).[12] Metrical considerations cannot be responsible for the substitution, since "Xanthus" would have fit the meter of 1.100 as well as "Simois" does. The end of Aeneas' opening speech, then, not only introduces the theme of corpses in a river, but also creates confusion between the rivers of Troy—as the openings of the *Aeneid*'s first and second halves create confusion between the rivers of Italy. Aeneas later contrasts the imitation *Xanthus* at Buthrotum with the elusive Tiber (3.497–501). Tiber is thus associated at different times with each of the Trojan rivers, as if it were meant to stand for both.

Another passage linking the Trojan and Italian rivers reinforces Tiber's predominance while also calling attention to the strange-

12. See Moskalew (1982) 128: "The image of Simois whirling along in its waters shields and helmets, though influenced by *Iliad* 12.22–23, evokes above all Achilles' battle against the rivers of Troy in *Iliad* 21, where Scamander [another name for Xanthus] at one point complains that his waters are choked with corpses (218–20, cf. 234–39) [emphasis added]."

ness of having one Italian river equated with two Trojan rivers. "Equated" is a strong term, but this is precisely what the Sibyl does when she predicts the Italian War as a replay of the Trojan War:

> "bella, horrida bella,
> et Thybrim multo spumantem sanguine cerno.
> non Simois tibi nec Xanthus nec Dorica castra
> defuerint. . . ." (6.86–89)

> "Wars, horrible wars, and the Tiber foaming with much blood I see. For you neither the Simois nor the Xanthus nor the Doric camps will be absent. . . ."

It is one thing to associate Tiber with each of the Trojan rivers in turn, but quite another to say explicitly that Aeneas will encounter "both the Simois and the Xanthus" in Italy. Having the Sibyl name one Italian river and two Trojan rivers implicitly encourages the reader to seek the missing member of the equation. The "second-reader" who has seen Tiber and Numicus paired repeatedly in Book 7 will probably guess the answer—as Servius does:[13]

> NON SIMOIS TIBI NEC XANTHUS Tiberis et Numicus, in quem cecidit.

> FOR YOU NEITHER THE SIMOIS NOR THE XANTHUS The Tiber and the Numicus, into which he fell.

Servius' comment here exemplifies the rewards of reading Virgil through the lens of a *grammaticus*. Not only does Servius solve the incomplete equation (Simois + Xanthus = Tiber + ?), but also, prompted perhaps by the mention of Tiber "foaming with blood," he identifies the Numicus almost casually as the river into which Aeneas fell. Indeed, so strongly does the Numicus recall this tradition that Servius tells us about "the corpse of Aeneas" two of the three times the river is named. On 7.150, "these pools of Numicus' spring" (*haec fontis stagna Numici*), he calls it the river "in which the

13. See O'Hara (1990) 107.

corpse of Aeneas was found and consecrated" (*in quo repertum est cadaver Aeneae et consecratum*), a comment the more remarkable because nothing else in the context suggests Aeneas' death. On 7.797, "they plow the holy bank of Numicus" (*sacrumque Numici / litus arant*), he notes that the river's epithet "holy" (*sacrum*) may be "proleptic, for the Numicus was consecrated after the corpse of Aeneas was found there" (*aut prolepsis est: nam consecratus est Numicus, postquam inventum est illic cadaver Aeneae*). As O'Hara points out, "Numicus," like "Ford's Theater," seems to have had a funereal association so strong that to mention the name was instantly to recall the hero's death there.[14]

Virgil goes to some trouble to create an association between the Tiber and the Numicus by means of narrative inconsistency, direct pairing, allusions to literary models, verbal reminiscences, and manipulations of tradition. The reason for this lies partly in the Tiber's role in the *Aeneid*'s symbolic landscape and partly in the Numicus' role in the Aeneas legend. As we have seen, Virgil could hardly mention the Numicus without reminding his readers of Aeneas' death. Tiber, on the other hand, free from such typecasting, is capable of taking on the coloring that Virgil chooses.[15] Virgil uses Tiber to link two dark themes: Aeneas' death by drowning and the hostile reaction of the Italian countryside to the foreign invader. The great river can borrow something of its smaller cousin's ominous role in Aeneas' demise—as it borrows the role in Aeneas' landing—and yet retain the ambivalence that so characterizes Virgil's poetry. By avoiding the obvious,[16] Virgil is able to cloak Tiber's character in mystery, to keep us in doubt whether the river (and

14. O'Hara (1990) 106. Horsfall (1986) 9 notes that death at the Numicus is an aspect of the Aeneas legend that never varies.

15. Le Gall (1953) 10 notes that the Numicus, mentioned three times with the Tiber, is given no anthropomorphic qualities or descriptive details.

16. So, for instance, Virgil uses Apollonius' similes for Medea's passion in connection with Aeneas rather than with Dido. As Harrison (1970) 447 observes, "since Dido is Medea's equivalent in Virgil's poem, one would naturally expect him to recall these similes (if at all) in his treatment of the Carthaginian queen; but in fact in both cases he studiedly avoids such an obvious move."

the Italian landscape it represents) is the friend or the enemy of the Trojan hero.

Associating the Tiber with the Numicus does not necessarily entail a dark interpretation of Aeneas' demise; several other associations of the Tiber are more clearly negative, emphasizing death and drowning rather than apotheosis. At the end of his prophecy to Aeneas, Tiber identifies himself in a slightly surprising way:

> "mihi victor honorem
> persolves. ego sum pleno quem flumine cernis
> stringentem ripas et pinguia culta secantem,
> *caeruleus* Thybris, caelo gratissimus amnis." (8.61–64)

> "As victor, you will pay me my honor in full. I am he whom you see grazing the banks with full stream and cutting the fertile fields, *cerulean* Tiber, river most pleasing to heaven."

The word *caeruleus* ("cerulean"), often translated "blue-green," seems at first glance a natural choice for a river god.[17] Yet Tiber's use of this word is remarkable for three reasons. First, the standard color epithet for the Tiber was *flavus* ("tawny"); commenting on the river's first appearance in the *Aeneid* (7.31), Servius rightly calls this his *epitheton proprium* ("appropriate epithet").[18] Second, despite

---

17. See Edgeworth (1992) 107–12.

18. Ancient color terms are notoriously difficult to map into our own. Though our crude translations of "blue-green" and "tawny" exaggerate the difference between *caeruleus* and *flavus*, ancient readers as well argued about whether the two words were mutually exclusive. Aulus Gellius (*NA* 2.26) describes a conversation between the ex-consul Fronto and the philosopher Favorinus about Greek and Latin words for colors, in which this issue (among others) is discussed. Favorinus quotes lines from Ennius (384–85V, 377–78S):

> verrunt extemplo placidum mare: marmore flavo
> caeruleum spumat mare conferta rate pulsum.

> At once they sweep the placid sea: the cerulean sea foams with tawny marble, struck by dense boats.

He comments that *caeruleum mare* ("cerulean sea") did not seem to him compatible with *marmore flavo* ("tawny marble"), until he heard Fronto's statement that *flavus* was actually a color *e viridi et albo mixtus* ("mixed out of green and white").

its etymological connection with *caelum* ("sky"), the word *caeruleus* is commonly used to mean "dusky, dark, associated with death and the Underworld."[19] Servius informs us that "the ancients understood *caeruleus* as 'black'" (*veteres sane caeruleum nigrum accipiebant*, ad 3.64), and elsewhere glosses the word as "green with black, like the sea" (*viride cum nigro, ut est mare*, ad 7.198). Third (and most important), the word *caeruleus* in the *Aeneid* has such an array of funereal associations that it sounds a sour note in any optimistic context.[20]

It is worth examining the uses of *caeruleus* in the *Aeneid*, not only to illustrate its menacing tone, but also because several of the episodes containing it raise the specter of death by water. The word first appears near the beginning of Aeneas' wanderings in a description of the ceremonial fillets at Polydorus' funeral:

> "stant Manibus arae
> *caeruleis* maestae vittis atraque cupresso." (3.63–64)
>
> "The altars stand to the Shades, gloomy with cerulean fillets and black cypress."

The gloominess of *caeruleus* here is obvious; Servius Auctus, citing Cato, comments that it was the color of mourning garb.[21] Polydorus' fate is also connected more specifically with that of Aeneas. According to tradition, after Polydorus was murdered for gold, his

---

The same passage, however, designates Virgil the *poeta verborum diligentissimus* ("poet most careful in his words"). Even if *caeruleus* and *flavus* are not mutually exclusive, the question remains why Tiber uses a word other than his *epitheton proprium*.

19. See *OLD* s.v. *caeruleus* 9.

20. Fordyce's (1977) comment (ad 8.64) that although the Tiber is "notoriously flavus . . . caeruleus is the conventional epithet of a water god" is correct as far as it goes, but unsatisfying. Why should Tiber identify himself with a generic epithet when a personal one is available? More importantly, *caeruleus*, as Virgil uses it, has taken on too menacing a tone to pass as merely "conventional." Austin (1964) ad 2.381 (*caerula colla*), while citing nearly all of the occurrences of *caeruleus* in the *Aeneid*, omits Tiber's anomalous use. (The comment of Williams [1973], "the god is green, though the river is yellow," is less than enlightening.)

21. See Eitrem (1915) on the significance of the color of ceremonial fillets.

body was thrown into the sea and tossed up on the shore. In Euripides' *Hecuba*, his ghost laments,

> "κεῖμαι δ' ἐπ' ἀκταῖς, ἄλλοτ' ἐν πόντου σάλῳ
> πολλοῖς διαύλοις κυμάτων φορούμενος,
> ἄκλαυτος ἄταφος." (28–30)

> "I lie on the shore, carried sometimes in the salt of the sea by much ebb and flow of the waves, unwept, unburied."

These lines have been recognized as one of the sources for the helmsman Palinurus, whose body, as we learn from his ghost, is also tossed by the waves:[22]

> "nunc me fluctus habet versantque in litore venti." (6.362)

> "Now the wave has me and the winds turn me about on the shore."

The man whose corpse Aeneas encounters at the beginning of his journey (Polydorus) has met a fate like that of the man whose death marks its end (Palinurus).

The word *caeruleus* (or *caerulus*) appears many times in the context of threatening seas or sea-monsters. Twice it describes a storm-cloud (*caeruleus imber*) that mystifies Palinurus and forces Aeneas off course, "bringing night and storm, and the wave bristled with shadows" (*noctem hiememque ferens, et inhorruit unda tenebris*, 3.194–95 ≈ 5.10–11). It is the color of the canine nether half of the sea-monster Scylla (3.432)—a former human who, like the king who gave the Tiber its name (discussed below), metamorphosed into a water-creature. Whereas he is *immani corpore Thybris* ("Tiber with enormous body," 8.330), half of Scylla is an *immani corpore pistrix* ("sea-monster with enormous body," 3.427).[23] This echo, like the

22. Ambrose (1980) 449. He also notes the connection of both Palinurus and Polydorus with Homer's Elpenor, the unfortunate helmsman who, like them, lies *aklauton athapton* ("unwept, unburied," *Od.* 11.72).

23. The phrase *immani corpore* ("huge body") occurs only one other time in the *Aeneid*, in a description of Butes, one of the victims of the boxer Dares (5.372); see chap. 4, n. 31.

shared adjective *caeruleus*, quietly undermines the contrast (lamented by Juno in 7.302–304) between the dangers of the sea, represented in part by Scylla (302), and the safety of the Tiber (303). The boat named "Scylla" is cerulean (5.123), like her namesake. Triton is another sea creature with human top and monstrous bottom (10.211 of Triton ≈ 3.426–27 of Scylla) who appears once as a living character (6.171–74) and once as a ship (10.209–12). In ship form, he terrifies the "cerulean straits" with his conch (*caerula freta*, 10.209–10). His one action in living form is to drown Aeneas' comrade Misenus, who made the mistake of challenging the god to a conch-blowing contest. In each of these instances, *caeruleus* points directly or indirectly to the threat of watery death.[24]

Some of the other uses of *caeruleus* are not connected with seas or sea-monsters but are equally morbid. It describes the barge that is about to carry Aeneas over the Styx (6.410), a vessel earlier called *ferruginea* ("rust-colored," 6.303).[25] As in Tiber's change from *flavus* to *caeruleus*, the discrepancy focuses the reader's attention on the word.[26] It refers to a cloud (*caerula nubes*) in the simile describing Aeneas' "bloody, huge" (*sanguineam, ingentem*) Volcanic breastplate (8.619–23). Here, too, it is surprising, forming part of a unique color tetrad.[27] Three times the word refers to snakes: a serpent's neck in a

24. Some instances of the neuter plural form *caerula* are less remarkable. Evander asks what need drove the Trojans through so many "cerulean shallows" (*vada caerula*, 7.198), implying that such journeys are dangerous. Twice the word describes waters not fatal in themselves, but appearing before negative incidents: 3.208 precedes the landing on the Harpies' island, 4.583 precedes Dido's suicide preparations. These usages in themselves would not create an unusual sense of menace—death and danger are ubiquitous in the poem, after all—but neither do they provide any positive associations to counter the many instances in which the word clearly has negative connotations.

25. See McLeod (1970) 145 for a detailed explanation of why *ferrugineus* and *caeruleus* cannot be referring to the same color. McLeod concludes that in Homer's color discrepancies, Virgil "found dispensation" for his own (149). This may well be, but it does not explain the particular colors Virgil has chosen or his motive for imitating Homer in this way in this passage.

26. Moskalew (1982) 123 notes that "the crossing of the Styx seems to correspond roughly to the voyage on the Tiber," citing the "short repetition" in 6.384 ≈ 8.90.

27. Edgeworth (1992) 52: "The tetrad is red-white-gold-blue, the fourth color being the surprise (it is not present in the passage which serves as principal model

simile describing the Greek warrior Androgeos' reaction to treacherous Trojans (*caerula colla*, 2.381); the hair from which the Fury Allecto hurls a serpent at Amata (*caeruleis crinibus*, 7.346); and the markings on the snake that appears at Anchises' tomb (*caeruleae notae*, 5.87).[28]

The last of these is worth examining more closely. The snake appears immediately after Aeneas' lament for his father:

> "non licuit finis Italos fataliaque arva
> nec tecum Ausonium, quicumque est, quaerere Thybrim."[29]
> dixerat haec, adytis cum lubricus anguis ab imis
> septem ingens gyros, septena volumina traxit
> amplexus placide tumulum lapsusque per aras,
> *caeruleae* cui terga notae maculosus et auro
> squamam incendebat fulgor, ceu nubibus arcus
> *mille iacit varios adverso sole colores*. (5.82–89)

> "It was not permitted to seek with you the Italian borders, and the fated fields, nor Ausonian Tiber, whoever he is." He had spoken this, when from the depths of the sanctuary a slippery serpent, huge, dragged his seven coils, seven folds, embracing placidly the burial mound and gliding through

---

for the simile, *Argonautica* Δ 125f). If the addition of the term is significant, then this departure from the usual color pattern would contribute to the ambiguity of the cloud imagery used in the same episode. . . . The familiar colors are present, but so is another the implications of which are unclear to the reader. The effect is slightly unsettling." See also 31, 182, 189–90.

28. In describing an omen at Aulis that predicts nine years of war, Homer's Odysseus tells us that a "blood-red serpent," *drakõn daphoinos*, devoured a mother bird and her eight chicks (*Il.* 2.308–13). Ovid's version of this omen makes the snake *caeruleus* (*Met.* 12.13). As Musgrove (1997) 273 observes, "To the reader who knew the Iliadic model well, the change in color would be read as an ungrammaticality, a sign that perhaps the wrong, or an incomplete, intertext had been activated." She argues that Ovid associates the adjective *caeruleus* with Virgilian snakes and that the purpose of the color change is to remind the reader of the pervasive snake imagery of *Aeneid* 2 (especially 2.381, *caerula colla*).

29. The words Aeneas chooses in the first two members of the tricolon *finis Italos . . . fatalia arva . . . Ausonium Thybrim* are ambiguous: *finis* can mean both "border/land" and "death," while *fatalia* can mean both "fated" and "fatal." For the importance of wordplay on *finis*, see Mitchell-Boyask (1996) 295–98. These dark second-meanings do not bode well for *Ausonium Thybrim*.

> the altars, on whose back were *cerulean* marks, and a gleam spotted with gold set his scales on fire, as when the bow in the clouds *casts a thousand varied colors when the sun strikes.*

Aeneas is not sure what the snake represents, but he takes it as a positive sign of some sort—he is merely "uncertain whether he should consider it the *genius* ["guardian spirit"] of the place or a servant of his father" (*incertus geniumne loci famulumne parentis / esse putet,* 5.95–96). Virgil (as usual) never explicitly contradicts his character's assumption that the omen is good. Snakes did in fact play a positive role in Roman cult.[30] But in classical literature they are almost always malign, and the description of this one is too reminiscent of the snakes devouring Laocoön to be read without suspicion.[31] Moreover, Iris, as she brings death to Dido, is described in nearly identical words less than a hundred lines before the snake omen:

> mille trahens varios adverso sole colores. (4.701)
>
> [she flies down] drawing a thousand varied colors when the sun strikes.

Rainbows in the Greco-Roman tradition were often evil omens signifying the beginning rather than the end of a storm.[32] This reminder

---

30. See Wissowa (1912) 176–77. Snakes frequently were kept as pets (Pliny *NH* 29.72) and were thought to embody the household *genius.*

31. As Putnam (1965) 67 points out, "A benign snake in classical literature is unusual. In Virgil, who constantly associates snakes with hidden, unwonted death, as we have seen from book II, it is all but unique." See 72–73 on similarities to the snakes that attack Laocoön. See Knox (1950) 125 for a discussion of snake imagery as the "dominant, obsessive metaphor" throughout Book 2, and Kenney (1979) 105–109 for the literary background to the snake simile used for the evil Pyrrhus (2.471–75). Lyne (1987) 211 calls snakes "a familiar symbol of, among other things, death and deceit." On snakes as poetic symbols of *furor* and death, see Nethercut (1974).

Edgeworth (1992) 203 notes that in Book 5 "many motifs are given a positive turn which elsewhere in the poem are baleful," and he lists the snake-omen as an example. This raises a crucial question: is it possible for a word or motif to be genuinely positive in one context, when all of its other uses are negative? Tiber's unique, apparently positive usage of *caeruleus* should raise suspicion that all is not so positive as it seems.

32. As Ketterer (1991) 22 observes, "there is a strong poetic tradition of the rainbow or Iris as the harbinger of evil." See also Moskalew (1982) 131.

of Iris in her capacity as killer does not reflect positively on the snake. Though Aeneas and the Trojans may perceive the snake with cerulean spots as favorable, the reader by now should be wary of so facile an assumption.[33]

There is reason, then, to see ominous implications in Tiber's self-identification as *caeruleus*, a word that in the *Aeneid* almost always holds negative connotations. Several other features also link the Tiber with danger and death. First, in addition to the snake omen, Virgil associates Tiber with snakes in other ways. The serpent in Book 5 emerges immediately after Aeneas' speech, which concludes with the word *Thybris* (83–85). Pyrrhus, in Book 2, is compared first to a snake (471–75) and then to a destructive river (496–99).[34] Snakes and the Tiber are both described as "swollen," *tumens* or *tumidus* (8.86 *tumens* of Tiber; 2.381 *tumens* of a snake; 2.472 *tumidus* of a snake).[35] Most suggestively, Servius ad 8.95 (*superant flexus*, "they pass the curves"), in the context of Aeneas' journey up the Tiber, remarks that "the augural books call the Tiber a 'serpent,' because it has many curves" (*Tiberim libri augurum colubrum loquuntur, tamquam flexuosum*). The word *flexus*, which appears only twice elsewhere in Virgil's poetry, is used of the Mincius river (*Geo*. 3.24) and of the constellation *Anguis*, "the Snake"

---

33. Horsfall (1995) takes Putnam's interpretation of the snake omen as an example of "misguided method" (113), the "dogmatic application of rigid schematism" (140), and argues that the snake clearly is meant to represent the benign spirit of Anchises. This argument is unconvincing. That Aeneas and the Trojans respond "happily," *laeti* (100), tells us nothing about what the serpent actually represents, and the narrator does not enlighten us. Linderski (1993) 615 notes that the term *laetus* "regularly appears in various sources to describe the state of mind after a report of a propitious omen." But Aeneas' astoundingly inappropriate reaction to the manifestly anti-Trojan mural on the temple of Juno at Carthage (1.452–93) shows what kind of "reader" he is (as Horsfall implies, 108). On the complexities of this important scene, see Fowler (1991) 31–33. That the narrator calls the snake *innoxius* ("harmless," 92) implies either that it was perceived as harmless (see Fowler [1990] on "focalization") or that it did no harm in the instant circumstances, not that the entire omen must therefore be unambiguously benign.

34. See Kenney (1979) 109–12; Thomas (1986) 183–84.

35. Mancini (1990) 312–13 notes that *tumeo* and its cognates are especially associated with swollen waters and with the "swelling" of human anger.

(*Geo.* 1.244). Virgil exploits a natural similarity between cerulean, rippling, winding rivers and cerulean, rippling, winding snakes.

Second, Virgil reminds us that the Tiber received its name from a king who drowned in its waters. In concluding his narrative of the prehistory of Rome, Evander summarizes his country's regal period in two words (*tum reges*, "then [there were] kings," 8.330). But he devotes three lines to the story of King Thybris:

> "tum reges asperque immani corpore Thybris,
> a quo post Itali fluvium cognomine Thybrim
> diximus; amisit verum vetus Albula nomen." (8.330–32)

> "Then [there were] kings, and harsh Tiber with enormous body, from whom afterward we Italians have called the river Tiber by his name; the ancient Albula lost its true name."

Page explains, "In Livy 1.3 Tiberinus, who, having been drowned in crossing the Albula, gave his name to the river, is a late descendant of Aeneas; but it is useless to examine such legends closely."[36] Gilbert Highet complains that "Evander's history of central Italy devotes a disproportionate amount of time to such trifles as the origin of the name Tiber."[37] Here again the apology for the variant and the objection to the "trifle" should alert us to Virgil's artistry. Virgil commits these peccadilloes in order to draw attention to the drowning, a legend that reminds us of another king who is to drown and be made a god.[38]

Finally, Virgil associates Aeneas' voyage up the Tiber with the death of Palinurus, who drowns (we think) near the coast of Italy.[39]

36. Page (1929) ad 8.331.

37. Highet (1972) 108.

38. Ovid exhibits a similar inconsistency: relating the story of Picus and Circe, he says that the nymphs of the Albula (*inter alias*) loved Picus (*Met.* 14.328), but in the same story Picus' lover Canens wastes away by the Tiber (14.426). When listing Aeneas' descendants, Ovid follows Livy's version, in which King Tiberinus, half a dozen generations after Aeneas, "drowned in the waves of the Tuscan river, gave the water its name" (*in Tusci demersum fluminis undis / nomina fecit aquae*, 14.615–16).

39. Palinurus will be discussed extensively in the next chapter.

Specifically, the scene in which Palinurus is plunged overboard parallels the scene following Tiber's prophecy, in which the river calms his waters to facilitate Aeneas' passage upstream.[40] Virgil's desire to create similarities between these episodes would help to explain several "errors." As Aeneas is on his way from Sicily to Italy, Neptune calms a stormy sea (5.820–21), though the weather seemed fine when Aeneas set out (5.777). This inconsistency is generally taken as evidence for late composition of 5.779–871, with the assumption that Virgil would have corrected it in his final revision.[41] It is signficant, however, that a phrase describing Neptune's action, *sternitur aequor aquis* ("the sea with its waters is laid smooth," 5.821), is echoed by Tiber's action:

> Thybris ea fluvium, quam longa est, nocte tumentem
> leniit, et tacita refluens ita substitit unda,
> mitis ut in morem stagni placidaeque paludis
> *sterneret aequor aquis*, remo ut luctamen abesset. (8.86–89)
>
> Tiber smoothed his swelling river that night, as long as it was, and subsided, flowing backward with silent wave, so that in the manner of a gentle pool and placid swamp *he laid smooth his surface with his waters*, that struggle might be absent from the oar.

Commentators all note the echo without interpreting it, and their disagreement about proper translation points up the slight strangeness of the phrase in each case.[42] In 5.821, *aquis* seems redundant—"the sea is laid smooth" says as much as "the sea *with its waters* is

---

40. Horsfall (1995) 137 notes two correspondences between Book 5 and Book 8: "Venus' plea to Neptune in 5 and arrival with Aeneas' armor in 8, his sea-journey in 5 and his river journey in 8."

41. See Williams (1960) xxvi–xxvii.

42. Williams (1960) ad 5.820–21, Fordyce (1977) ad 8.89, and Gransden (1976) ad 8.89 note the echo of *sternitur / sterneret aequor aquis*. They disagree on the grammatical function of *aquis*, with Williams taking it in 5.821 as "perhaps possessive dative, perhaps local ablative" (with no comment on 8.89), and Fordyce as instrumental ablative in both cases; Gransden takes it in 8.89 as dative or ablative, translating, "(in such a way as to) spread out a smooth surface for (or on) his waters."

laid smooth." In 8.89, *aequor* is an odd choice, for the word elsewhere in Virgil always refers to sea or plain—one could almost translate *sterneret aequor aquis* as "laid smooth a sea-like plain with his waters."[43] Grammatically and narratively, what is natural in one passage seems out of place in the other. While the Tiber's calming of his waters has far-flung symbolic implications,[44] Neptune's calming of the sea, at first glance, appears unnecessary.

In a narrative inconsistency in Book 8, this scenario is reversed: what seems out of place there is natural in Book 5. Virgil implies that Aeneas' journey up the Tiber will occur during the day; he has already equipped his fleet (8.79–80) before sacrificing the white sow to Juno (84–85), which presumably happened during the day even if not "at dawn." It is therefore surprising to hear next that "Tiber smoothed his swelling river *that night, as long as it was*" (*Thybris* ea *fluvium*, quam longa est, nocte *tumentem / leniit*, 8.86–87)—why begin such a journey at night? Highet lists this among the *Aeneid*'s manifestly unfinished sections, postulating that "surely there is a gap in time and action between 8.85 and 8.86."[45] But filling such a gap would resolve only part of the incongruity, for Virgil describes the journey as taking "a night and a day" (*noctemque diemque*, 94). This leads Fordyce to accuse him of either carelessness in the use of words or indifference to geography:

> [Aeneas] arrives at the site of Rome at mid-day (97)—one might suppose after a morning's journey. *ea quam longa est nocte* and *noctemque diemque* (94) are inconsistent with that supposition and Conington and Heinze (following Servius) conclude that he starts his journey on the following night, having spent the intervening day on preparations. Either Virgil used these romantic clichés (cf. v. 766 'noctemque

43. On Virgil's exploitation of the ambiguity of *aequor* during the flight of Turnus in Book 12, see chap. 12, n. 6.

44. See Gransden (1976) ad 8.86–89: "the idea of the river yielding to the hero on a civilising mission is a very Roman one," with mythical and historical resonances from Romulus and Remus to the spread of Augustan *imperium*.

45. Highet (1972) 167.

> diemque', *Geo.* iii. 341 'diem noctemque', *Aen.* vi. 556 'noctesque diesque', ix. 488 'noctes . . . diesque') without thinking of their implications or else, dealing with the immediate neighbourhood of Rome, he was so indifferent to geography as to make Aeneas spend a night and a morning on a miraculously assisted passage of some twelve miles.[46]

Observations such as these, dismissing discrepancies on the grounds of Virgil's indifference to detail or intention to revise, should spur us to seek a deeper motivation. The nighttime seems strange in Book 8, but it is essential in Book 5: Palinurus, beguiled by Sleep, must be the only one awake at the time. Similarly, the calming of waters seems strange in Book 5, but it is the salient element in Book 8. The two passages are thus associated by means of verbal and thematic echoes—night journeys, calmed waters, the phrase *sternitur* or *sterneret aequor aquis*—and the elements puzzling or inconsistent in each passage make sense in the other.

Why does Virgil go to such lengths to associate the two passages? This is an example of a foreshadowing technique employed frequently in the *Aeneid*: the poet sets up parallel situations, tells us the outcome of one, and leaves us to infer the outcome of the other. That is, Palinurus on the calm sea at night is followed by the death of Palinurus. Aeneas on the calm river at night is followed by—we can only guess. In Book 8, Tiber's uncanny calm seems a sign of favor toward Aeneas, a gesture of welcome on behalf of the Italian countryside. Yet in Book 5, Palinurus calls attention to the danger posed by the calm sea:

> "mene salis placidi vultum fluctusque quietos
> ignorare iubes? mene huic confidere monstro?
> Aenean credam (quid enim?) fallacibus auris
> et caeli totiens deceptus fraude sereni?" (5.848–51)

46. Fordyce (1977) ad 8.86. It is interesting that the phrase *noctemque diemque*, though there are several similar ones, occurs in Virgil only in 8.94 and 5.766, ten lines before the Palinurus episode.

> "Are you ordering me to forget what I know of the face of the placid salt sea and the quiet waves? Am I to trust this monster? Should I entrust Aeneas (for what then?) to the false breezes, and I so often deceived by the treachery of a serene sky?"

Palinurus refers to the calm sea here as a *monstrum*, in the sense of a "monster" or dangerous creature. A far greater *monstrum*, in the sense of an unnatural or prodigious occurrence, is Tiber's uncannily placid *aequor*. When Aeneas wakes up and discovers that his helmsman is gone, he pronounces a mournful epitaph:

> "o nimium caelo et pelago confise sereno,
> nudus in ignota, Palinure, iacebis harena." (5.870–71)

> "Oh you who trusted too much in heaven and sea serene,
> you will lie naked, Palinurus, on an unknown sand."

This bears an eerie resemblance to the curse pronounced by Dido on Aeneas, "let him fall before his time, and [lie] unburied in the middle of the sand" (*sed cadat ante diem mediaque inhumatus harena,* 4.620).[47] We should remember Palinurus' distrust of the calm water, and his subsequent fate, as Aeneas rows confidently up the Tiber preternaturally smooth.

While the calming of the Tiber looks backward to Book 5, it also looks forward to the triumphs of Augustus depicted on the shield of Aeneas at the end of Book 8. The word "caerul[e]us" (8.672, 713) frames the description of the battle of Actium, describing first the sea surrounding the naval battle and then the mourning Nile that receives "the conquered [Cleopatra and Antony] into its cerulean bosom and shadowy streams" (*caeruleum in gremium latebrosaque flumina victos,* 713).[48] This absorption into foreign waters, with its

47. Zarker (1966–67) 220; O'Hara (1990) 109; Christmann (1976) 279. See Brenk (1984) 796–801 for a discussion of Virgil's use of funerary epitaphs. As Brenk points out, "The literary precedent and typology for much of the Palinurus incident is not epic at all, but the *Anthology* tradition of the shipwrecked sailor" (800).

48. The final instance of *caerul[e]us* in the *Aeneid* is in Aeneas' prayer to various divinities in the elaborate treaty near the beginning of Book 12 (175–94).

consequent loss of identity, represents both the greatest horror and the greatest temptation facing the epic hero.[49] The ignominious defeat of Cleopatra and Antony is immediately contrasted with the triple triumph of Augustus, who is carried gloriously within solid Roman walls (*at Caesar, triplici invectus Romana triumpho / moenia,* 714–15). A similar polarity characterizes the closing image on the shield, the parade of conquered rivers (and peoples) led captive in Augustus' triumph:

> Euphrates ibat iam mollior undis,
> extremique hominum Morini, Rhenusque bicornis,
> indomitique Dahae, et pontem indignatus Araxes. (726–28)

> The Euphrates flowed now more gently with its waves, and the Morini, furthest of men, and the two-horned Rhine, the unconquered Dahae, and Araxes chafing at its bridge.

The Euphrates flowing "more gently" represents the pacification of Eastern peoples under Augustus' civilizing sway and has rightly been associated with the calmed Tiber, with which the book began.[50] But the final image is that of the Araxes chafing at its bridge, suggesting the lurking resentment of the conquered.[51] Both rivers, not just the Euphrates, are emblems of cerulean Tiber. Aeneas is caught in the middle—between the glory of Augustus and the ignominy

---

49. Quint (1993) 29 observes, "Aeneas in his opening speech . . . seems to desire just such an anonymous immersion into the waves of his native Simois (1.94–101), and the *Aeneid* must wage a campaign against this deathwish, drawing its hero away from the womblike waters of death."

50. Gransden (1976) ad 8.726; Hardie (1994) ad 9.815–18. Both commentators also point out (without explanation) the parallel in Tiber's welcoming of Turnus "with gentle waves" (*mollibus undis,* 9.816); this important episode will be discussed in chap. 5.

51. Quint (1993) 31: "The river's resentment echoes [in the word *indignatus*] that of the pent-up winds of Aeolus (1.55), of the furious, dying soul of Camilla (11.831), and similarly of the soul of the wrathful Turnus in the final line of the *Aeneid.*" See Thomas (1988a) ad *Geo.* 2.161–62, on another body of water resentful (*indignatus*) at being bridged: "The imposing of barriers (*claustra*) on a natural force, particularly on water, was at best a hazardous undertaking in antiquity." The destructive potential of rivers was proverbial: see Lucretius 1.280–87, Horace *Odes* 3.29.33–41.

of those absorbed into the Nile's "cerulean bosom," between the Euphrates now gentle and the Araxes yearning for revenge.

Virgil associates the Tiber with Aeneas' death by linking that great river with the Numicus, with ominous uses of the word *caeruleus,* with snakes, King Thybris, and Palinurus. Re-reading Tiber's prophecy in light of these associations proves the deceptiveness of this prophecy. The river assures Aeneas at the beginning, "do not be frightened by threats of war; all the swelling and wrath of the gods have subsided" (*neu belli terrere minis; tumor omnis et irae / concessere deum,* 8.40–41), then instructs him at the end to "overcome Juno's wrath and threats with suppliant vows" (*iramque minasque / supplicibus supera votis,* 8.60–61).[52] The previous chapter suggested that Aeneas' failure to pray to Juno *first,* as Tiber admonishes, increases her wrath rather than diminishing it. Tiber next instructs Aeneas, "as victor, you will pay me my honor in full" (*mihi victor honorem / persolves,* 8.61–62). There is no meaningful sense in which the sacrifice of the sow gains him victory over Juno. But the "victory" Tiber refers to may be pointing to something else entirely. Servius tells us, "Others say that when Aeneas, *as victor,* was sacrificing on the banks of the Numicus river, he fell in, and not even his corpse was found" (*alii dicunt quod* victor *Aeneas cum sacrificaret super Numicum fluvium lapsus est, et eius nec cadaver inventum est,* ad 4.620). The *honor* that Tiber mentions could hint at the sacrifice of Aeneas himself.

52. See Lyne (1987) 83.

CHAPTER THREE

The Unburied Dead

Death without burial, especially in the oblivion of the waves, was one of the worst things that could befall an ancient Roman.[1] It was also the epic hero's nightmare.[2] Achilles expresses his fear of it when fighting the river in *Iliad* 21.281, Odysseus when fighting the sea in *Odyssey* 5.312 (identical lines); Aeneas recalls both of these Homeric models in his opening speech (1.94–101). Palinurus, who bemoans treacherous waters and lack of burial, has also been regarded as the paradigm of the victim offered that the community may survive. Yet he is merely the most prominent of several characters combining lack of burial with a death in some way marked as sacrificial. Virgil's multiplication of such characters not only reminds the reader continually of the death of the hero, but also calls into question whether sacrificial death is of any use.

1. See Holland (1961) 11–12 on the necessity of burial to allow the souls of the dead to cross the river Styx and find rest in the Underworld. To see a corpse and leave it unburied was the gravest impiety. As Servius tells us, *cum pontificibus nefas esset cadaver videre, magis tamen nefas fuerat, si visum insepultum reliquerent* ("while it was a great wrong for priests to see a corpse, nevertheless it would have been a greater wrong if they left it unburied once seen," ad 6.176). On *piacula* pertaining to burial, see Tromp (1921) 40–43. On the horror of punishment by drowning and lack of burial, see Le Gall (1953) 89–90.

2. See Nisbet and Hubbard (1970) ad Horace *Odes* 1.28.23.

The reading of Palinurus' death as "sacrificial" is rooted in Neptune's prophecy to Venus during Aeneas' voyage from Sicily to Italy. At the end of his long *consolatio* assuring her of her son's safety (5.800–15),[3] the god declares that this safety comes at a (small) price:

> "unus erit tantum amissum quem gurgite quaeres;
> unum pro multis dabitur caput." (5.814–15)

> "There will be only one whom you will seek, lost in the flood;
> one head will be given for many."

The half-line *unum pro multis dabitur caput* has been called the classic expression of the "general sacrificial law," the principle of one given for many.[4] This symbolic sacrifice of a human complements the ritual slaughter of animals performed by Aeneas throughout the poem. As argued in chapter 1, however, several of Aeneas' actual sacrifices contain faults (*piacula*) that in Roman practice would require expiation. An examination of Palinurus' death and reappearance in the Underworld (5.779–871, 6.333–83) suggests that Virgil's literary metaphor of human "sacrifice" may have darker implications than commonly supposed—that such symbolic offerings may even be destructive rather than redemptive.[5]

---

3. Neptune's speech is rich in odd twists that cannot be explained by differing layers of composition and that seem intended to recall the death of Aeneas: see O'Hara (1990) 107–11. Neptune reminds Venus of how he rescued Aeneas when Achilles was clogging the Trojan rivers with corpses (804–10)—though the incidents occur in reverse order and separate books in the *Iliad* (21.218–20, 20.321–39). Virgil appears to be revising the story in order to bring in rivers full of corpses. Neptune then reassures Venus that her son will reach the harbor of Avernus, gateway to the Underworld, safely (813)—though she had requested safe passage to the Tiber (797). An association between Tiber and Land of the Dead flickers for a moment. Then Neptune states that he will exact "only one" life as his price and proceeds to calm the stormy sea (814–21)—though the weather looked fine when Aeneas set out (5.777).

4. Bandera (1981) 223, followed by Hardie (1993) 32.

5. Most readers take Neptune at his word and regard the death of Palinurus as making possible the Trojans' safe transition to Italy. An allusion to a famous passage from Ennius (65V, 54S) on the apotheosis of Romulus is undoubtedly relevant in this regard but is difficult to interpret. Jupiter declares, *unus erit quem tu tolles in caerula caeli / templa*, "There will be one whom you will raise into the *cerulean* regions of the sky." It is likely that the lines about Romulus were balanced by lines about his brother Remus, so that the passage said something like "*one* you will

The many narrative inconsistencies surrounding the Palinurus episode associate him with other characters who drown and lie unburied. The most glaring discrepancies are those between the end of Book 5 and the appearance of Palinurus' ghost in Book 6. R. D. Williams lists the problems:[6]

1. In Book V the god Sleep throws Palinurus overboard, but in Book VI there is no mention by Palinurus of divine intervention; in fact he explicitly says *nec me deus aequore mersit* ["nor did a god drown me in the sea"].
2. Conversely, in Book V Aeneas thinks Palinurus' death was an accident, but in Book VI asks what god was responsible.
3. In Book V the sea is calm, in Book VI stormy.
4. In Book V Palinurus was on the journey from Sicily to Italy, but in Book VI we read *qui Libyco nuper cursu . . .* ["who recently on his Libyan voyage (fell overboard)"].
5. In Book VI Palinurus says that he was on the sea for three days and nights, but in fact only one day has yet passed since the events at the end of Book V.[7]

The first two entries in this list concern human perceptions of causality and are thus not true narrative inconsistencies. Palinurus does not have the same knowledge as the omniscient narrator. A character can easily shift from thinking "sleep overwhelmed me/him" to thinking "Sleep [the god] overwhelmed me/him," especially a man

---

take into heaven, *one* you will not." This is supported by a passage in Ovid's *Fasti* (2.485–88) in which Mars quotes the Ennian line to Jupiter after conceding that one of the twin sons is a lost cause; see Conte (1986) 57–59. Nicoll (1988) 466–70, followed by Hardie (1993) 33, suggests that Palinurus may be a sort of "Remus" to Aeneas' "Romulus," with the death of the helmsman making possible the apotheosis of Aeneas later on. But the allusion could also serve to contrast the happy fate of Romulus, lifted into the *caerula* above, with that of Palinurus, soon to be lost in the *caerula* below.

6. See also Horsfall (1991) 100–103. After careful scrutiny of inconsistencies of various kinds, most of which reflect discrepancies in Virgil's sources, Horsfall concludes that the Palinurus episode is the one "authentic" inconsistency that Virgil certainly would have revised.

7. Williams (1960) xxv. See also Williams (1983) 281–82 for a discussion of the inconsistencies as evidence of Virgil's "change of plan."

who has just been sprinkled with water from Lethe, the stream of forgetfulness (5.854).[8] The incongruous calming of the sea in Book 5, Williams' #3, is motivated partly by an association with the calmed Tiber in Book 8. The remaining inconsistencies—the "Libyan voyage" (not Sicily to Italy) and the "three stormy nights" (not one calm one)—serve to link Palinurus with other men who meet their death in the waves.[9]

The first death described in the *Aeneid* is that of the Lycian leader Orontes, who drowns during the storm requisitioned by Juno as the epic opens. Before Aeneas' eyes, Orontes' ship is overwhelmed near rocks called The Altars:

> tris Notus abreptas in saxa latentia torquet
> (saxa vocant Itali mediis quae in fluctibus *Aras*,
> dorsum immane mari summo), tris Eurus ab alto
> in brevia et Syrtis urget, miserabile visu,
> inliditque vadis atque aggere cingit harenae.
> unam, quae Lycios fidemque vehebat Oronten,
> ipsius ante oculos ingens a vertice pontus
> in puppim ferit: excutitur pronusque magister
> volvitur in caput, ast illam ter fluctus ibidem
> torquet agens circum et rapidus vorat aequore vertex.
> (1.108–17)

> Three [ships], broken off, the South Wind hurls onto hidden rocks (the Italians call the rocks that are in the middle of the flood *Altars*, a huge ridge at the surface of the sea), three the East Wind forces from the high sea into the shallows and Syrtes, wretched to see, and smashes on the shoals and girds

8. Harrison (1980) 372.

9. Virgil's motivations are always complex, and the argument put forth here does not exclude those of some other scholars who see the inconsistencies in the Palinurus episode as deliberate. For instance, Quint (1993) 87–90 argues that these inconsistencies "can be explained as efforts to bring the episode closer to the Odyssean model that it both imitates and inverts" (87). Mackie (1988) 123–41 sees the inconsistencies as contributing to a larger pattern of contrast between Aeneas' *humanitas* in the Underworld and his *pietas* in the upper world.

with a heap of sand. One, which carried the Lycians and faithful Orontes, before his [i.e., Aeneas'] very eyes the huge sea falling sheer strikes astern: the helmsman is shaken out and rolled face down onto his head, but her [the ship] the flood whirls around three times and the rushing whirlpool devours in the sea.

This death with sacrificial overtones (near "The Altars"),[10] preceded by a helmsman thrown overboard, bears a certain resemblance to the Palinurus episode. In the Underworld, Orontes and Leucaspis, whom Servius identifies as Orontes' helmsman, appear with Palinurus among the crowd of unburied dead who cannot cross the Styx:

cernit ibi maestos et mortis honore carentis
Leucaspim et Lyciae ductorem classis Oronten,
quos simul a Troia ventosa per aequora vectos
obruit Auster, aqua involvens navemque virosque.
  Ecce gubernator sese Palinurus agebat,
qui Libyco nuper cursu, dum sidera servat,
exciderat puppi mediis effusus in undis. (6.333–39)

There he sees men gloomy and lacking the honor due to death, Leucaspis and Orontes, the leader of the Lycian fleet, whom at the same time the South Wind overwhelmed as they were carried through the windy seas, wrapping in water both ship and men.

But look, the helmsman Palinurus was making his way, who recently, on the Libyan voyage, while observing the stars, had fallen from the stern and was poured out in the middle of the waves.

10. See O'Hara (1990) 19–22 and (1996) 78. Bleisch (1998) discusses an additional level of meaning (and virtuosity) in Virgil's play here on the Greek word *Arai*, "Curses," as well as his deliberate geographical conflation: the rocks seem at first to be the "Altars" in midocean between Sicily and Sardinia, but the reference to "Syrtes" (famous North African sandbanks) points to the Altars of the Philaeni, mounds of sand off the coast of North Africa. She observes that "Vergil's sophisticated geographical punning exploits the ambiguity of the place name *Arae* to dislocate his narrative, literally shifting the ground under the reader's feet" (604–605).

Their similarity in manner of death and their juxtaposition in the Underworld point up the parallel between Orontes and Palinurus. The last three inconsistencies in Williams' list reinforce this parallel. Palinurus' ghost claims to have spent "three nights" tossing on the stormy sea before reaching Italy:

> "*tris Notus* hibernas immensa per aequora noctes
> vexit me violentus aqua." (6.355–56)
>
> "The *South Wind*, violent with water, carried me through the immense sea for *three* winter nights."

The phrase *tris Notus* ("three the South Wind") occurs elsewhere in Virgil's corpus only to describe ships swirling during the storm in Book 1, in a line whose rhythm is identical:[11]

> *tris Notus* abreptas in saxa latentia torquet. (1.108)
>
> *Three* [ships], broken off, the *South Wind* hurls onto hidden rocks.

Again, elements out of place in one incident are natural in the other. The "three [ships tossed by the] South wind" blend in with the narrative of Orontes' death, but Palinurus' "three [nights carried by the] South wind" conflict with the supposition that only one night has passed before Aeneas meets him in the Underworld (Williams' #5). Similarly, the storminess of the wind is appropriate in Book 1 but inappropriate in Book 5, since Palinurus plunged into water supernaturally *calmed* (Williams' #3).

The most obvious inconsistency, and the only one related by the poet rather than by a speaking character, is the statement that Palinurus was lost "recently, on the Libyan voyage" (*Libyco nuper cursu*, 6.338, Williams' #4).[12] The reference to Palinurus' Libyan voyage

11. Both lines have the rhythm dactyl-spondee-spondee-dactyl-dactyl-spondee and differ only in the length of the last syllable (which always scans as "long" because of the line break).

12. Brenk (1988) 79 suggests that Virgil may be recalling the shipwreck of 255 B.C. off Camarina during the First Punic War, in which the commanders were blamed for sailing along the outer coast of Sicily, "toward the Libyan sea" (Polybius 1.37.4).

immediately after the reference to Orontes (6.334) is strange, stranger perhaps than has been realized. Virgil explicitly reminds us that Orontes died during a storm at sea (6.335–36). The reader presumably remembers that this occurred at the beginning of the poem, before the Trojan landing in Libya (Dido's land). Williams suggests that Palinurus' "Libyan voyage" may be a remnant of some earlier version of the plot: "the mention of Palinurus comes just after a reference to Orontes and the storm. In many ways (but not all) Palinurus' story in book 6 is consistent with this storm, and it is possible that when composing book 6 Virgil may have thought of the loss of Palinurus as having occurred then."[13] This sounds plausible at first, but falls apart under scrutiny. Palinurus cannot have died at the same time as Orontes, because he is said to have fallen overboard "while he observes the stars" (*dum sidera servat*, 6.338), whereas Orontes is killed during a storm (6.336). He cannot have died after Orontes, because the storm cast the Trojans onto the Libyan shore, and an intervening calm would be absurd. And he can hardly have died before Orontes, because Virgil surely would not have had Palinurus fall overboard on the calm sea right before Orontes dies in a storm. In short, Orontes has already filled the slot for the one who "died on the Libyan voyage"—and Virgil all but declares this just before we meet Palinurus. Far from covering up the inconsistency, the poet seems rather to have gone to some trouble to make it obvious. Williams is right to point out that Palinurus' account in Book 6 is consistent in many ways with the storm in Book 1; but the "Libyan voyage" reference could hardly be a remnant of some hypothetical version in which the men died together.[14] The inconsistency is more likely a deliberate device reinforcing the connection between the two men.[15]

---

13. Williams (1960) xxvii.

14. Virgil's desire to associate the two men also may have played a part in Neptune's incongruous calming of the sea in Book 5, just as he calms the storm during which Orontes is killed in Book 1 (148–53).

15. Taking "Libyan voyage" to mean "the voyage *from* Libya" puts a strain on the language and still requires some unlikely conjectures. Heinze (1993) 137, for instance, reminds us that Virgil (according to Suetonius *Verg.* 32) composed each book to be recited separately, and that when he recited Books 2, 4, and 6 to Augustus

Furthermore, one of the *similarities* in the deaths of Orontes and Palinurus renders it unlikely that Virgil ever conceived of them as dying during the same episode. Virgil places some emphasis on Orontes' ship, with the adjective *unam* ("one") beginning the sentence in which the ship is capsized (1.113–15, quoted above). Later in the book, as Aeneas and Achates watch their comrades at Carthage from a cloud, they remember Venus' description of twelve swans returning safely to land. Not otherwise, she had said, your ships and men will return safely (1.390–400). The only problem is that Aeneas had lost *thirteen* ships.[16] When Achates cheerfully remarks that their comrades have returned safely, he also calls attention to the one who was lost:[17]

---

and his family, the audience would have known about the voyage to Libya, but not the voyage to Sicily. This is an ingenious idea, but it is hard to believe that the poem as it stands reflects Virgil's early efforts to make each book self-explanatory. Even if the story about reciting 2, 4, and 6 is reliable (as much of the material in the *Vita Vergilii* is not), Suetonius tells us that the recitation occurred "after the material was completed" (*perfecta materia*, 32). The appearance of Palinurus in Book 6 would have little point without the events at the end of Book 5.

16. See O'Hara (1990) 10–11: "The numerical precision calls attention to the death of Orontes, and to Venus' failure to mention him."

17. The assertion that "all are safe" immediately qualified by a mention of the one lost resembles the description of Aeneas' ships ignited by the Trojan women, then saved (almost) by Jupiter's thunderstorm: *omnes / quattuor amissis servatae a peste carinae* ("all the keels, with four lost, are saved from the plague," 5.698–99). Nicoll (1988) 460 notes that the sacrifice of Palinurus "can be seen as paralleling the burning of the four ships by the Trojan women using fire from Neptune's four altars."

But why *four* ships? Norden (1957) ad 6.243 ff. and Lehr (1934) 89, commenting on the sacrifice of four black *iuvenci* performed before Aeneas enters the Underworld, note that four was an unlucky number favored by the infernal gods. It is tempting also to connect the ships with human beings "sacrificed," but more difficult to specify which human beings. Quint (1993) 84 suggests that Creusa, Anchises, Dido, and Palinurus, who die at the ends of Books 2, 3, 4, and 5, symbolize "the sacrifice that Aeneas, in his role as leader of the Trojan mission, must make of his own individuality." Bandera (1981) 224–26 observes that Palinurus, Misenus, Orontes, and Creusa are a "fitting sacrificial prelude both to Aeneas' symbolic descent to the realm of the dead, which will reveal to him the future of Rome, and to the terrible violence that awaits him on Italian soil." In a parallel context, Lee (1992) 82–92 connects the Sibyl's order to sacrifice seven bulls and ewes (6.38–39) with the annual sacrifice of seven Athenian youths (6.21–22), the "seven suffering heroines" that Aeneas encounters in the Underworld (6.445–49), and the "seven surrogate sons" that are killed in the course of the narrative (Misenus, Palinurus, Nisus, Euryalus, Pallas, Lausus, and Marcellus, or perhaps Camilla).

"nate dea, quae nunc animo sententia surgit?
omnia tuta vides, classem sociosque receptos.
unus abest, medio in fluctu quem vidimus ipsi
submersum; dictis respondent cetera matris." (1.582–85)

"Goddess-born, what thought now rises in your spirit? You see that all things are safe, the fleet and the allies recovered. *One* is missing, whom we ourselves saw submerged in the flood; the rest corresponds to your mother's words."

Again, *unus* (584) holds an emphatic position, like *unam* (113) before; both act as substantives, with "one" standing for "one man" or "one ship" respectively, and both begin sentences. Virgil several times has the neuter *unum* begin a sentence, as in *unum oro* ("One thing I pray"). The grammatical situation described above, however, with the masculine or feminine adjective functioning substantively and beginning a sentence (as in *unus abest*, "one is missing"), occurs in only one other place in Virgil's corpus. That is in Neptune's prophecy of the loss of Palinurus, *unus erit tantum amissum quem gurgite quaeres* (5.814). Palinurus and Orontes, then, are associated by the "one alone is missing" theme, which would be impossible if Virgil had ever conceived of them as dying at the same time.

And yet, despite the emphasis in Neptune's speech on the "one" that will be missing, Palinurus is *not* the only one. As we have seen, the Sibyl tells Aeneas that one of his men is lying unburied, polluting his fleet (6.149), and must be buried before Aeneas can enter the Underworld. The reader, who has just read about Palinurus' plunge overboard, naturally thinks of Palinurus—but in fact the missing comrade is Misenus (6.171–74). Servius, bothered by the apparent lie in Neptune's statement that "only one will be lost," finds a reference to both Palinurus and Misenus in the sea-god's famous lines:[18]

18. Otis (1964) 281 makes an interesting distinction between the types of sacrifice that Palinurus and Misenus represent: "Misenus is the type of the *profane*, of the pollution incurred by ordinary (non-sacrificial) death and thus of the purification by which Aeneas escapes the lot of the *profani* and becomes able to return. He is, in other words, a sacrifice (the parallel and prelude of the proper *piacula*—black

AMISSUM QUEM GURGITE QUAERES Misenum dicit, de quo legimus "inter saxa virum spumosa inmerserat unda [6.174]."

UNUM PRO MULTIS Palinurum significat: nam falsum erit si unum voluerimus accipere: <duos enim constat occisos, Misenum et Palinurum.>

WHOM YOU WILL SEEK, LOST IN THE FLOOD He refers to Misenus, about whom we read "the foamy wave had overwhelmed the man among the rocks."

ONE FOR MANY He means Palinurus: for it will be false if we wish to take this as "one": <for it is clear that two were killed, Misenus and Palinurus.>

If these lines are really referring to two different men, then Neptune has fooled Venus, and Virgil has fooled his reader. If they are not referring to two different men, then Neptune has told a falsehood, as Servius accuses.[19] However we interpret the lines, it would seem that there is some kind of game going on here, that Virgil wants to surprise and confuse us when he writes of Aeneas' three drowned comrades. We are given Misenus when we expect Palinurus, and Palinurus is described in terms that are appropriate for, and remind us of, Orontes.

Why does Virgil do this? Knauer notes that Virgil has split Homer's Elpenor into three different characters, Palinurus, Misenus, and Caieta (Aeneas' nurse, whose burial opens Book 7),[20] and to this list we could also add Polydorus.[21] While Virgil often combines several characters in one (as Achilles and Odysseus both contribute

---

cattle) to Hecate and the underworld deities . . . ; Palinurus is a sacrifice to the *superi* (Neptune in particular) and thus the pledge of their aid."

19. Heinze (1993) 367 accepts the solution proposed by Heyne: "Neptune is speaking only of the crossing to Italy . . . so that the death of Misenus, which happens *after* the landing, has nothing at all to do with it." It is thus possible to see Neptune's words as literally true, in line with the deceptive veracity of many ancient prophecies.

20. Knauer (1964) 395.

21. See chap. 2, n. 22.

to Aeneas), the "distribution" of such a minor character is remarkable.[22] The repetition certainly signals the importance of sacrificial death. But more importantly, it calls into question the efficacy of sacrifice altogether. Neptune says that "there will be *only one* whom you will seek . . . *one* head will be given for many." This statement is either misleading or untrue—as Servius realized, and as the associations among Palinurus, Misenus, Orontes, and others make clear. One is not enough. The idea of sacrificing the "one" breaks down when that sacrifice is repeated, obsessively, with no end in sight.

It remains to ask why the sacrifice of one is not sufficient, a question that goes to the heart of Virgil's religious and philosophical views. As shown in chapter 1, Aeneas' sacrifices fail to please the gods because they contain *piacula*, ritual errors that make the offerings ineffective and demand expiation by means of more offerings. Though human sacrifices such as that of Palinurus are obviously more symbolic, they violate a principle that applies to all sacrifices, regardless of ritual details: the victims are supposed to go willingly. Obvious reluctance of the sacrificial beast was a clear signal that the sacrifice should be called off because the gods would not receive it favorably.[23] In the case of Palinurus, Virgil goes to some length to show the helmsman's resistance, which is so strong that he actually

22. Hardie (1984) well illustrates the "distribution" of the Lucretian sacrifice of Iphigeneia in *Aeneid* 2, a phenomenon analogous to that of the "distribution" of Elpenor.

23. Macrobius, for instance, commenting on a passage from the *Georgics* in which a goat will "stand" (i.e., without resistance) before the altar (2.395), observes that an animal's resistance was sufficient reason to abort the ceremony:

> Observatum est a sacrificantibus ut, si hostia quae ad aras duceretur fuisset vehementius reluctata ostendissetque se invitam altaribus admoveri, amoveretur quia invito deo offerri eam putabant. (*Sat.* 3.5.8)

> It was the practice of those who performed sacrifices that a victim would be removed if, while it was being led to the altar, it had fought back too vehemently and had made clear that it was being brought to the altar unwillingly, because they supposed that it was being offered to an unwilling god.

On the importance of willingness in sacrificial victims, see Tromp (1921) 60; Latte (1960) 386; Versnel (1981) 145–48; Rosenstein (1990) 64.

tears off the rudder in his fall (5.852). F. E. Brenk notes that, like the hesitation of the Golden Bough, the resistance of Palinurus "suggests all is not perfect with the sacrifice," and concludes that "Virgil appears to be hinting at something dark and difficult to expiate in the past."[24] But the victim's resistance carries even deeper implications for the future.

In Roman ritual, an imperfect sacrifice was *worse* than none, for it required yet another sacrifice in compensation. Virgil presents an explicit example of this phenomenon in the abortive human sacrifice of Sinon. The spy claims that he was to be the scapegoat to save the rest of the Greeks, who "transferred to the destruction of one wretch what each feared for himself" (*quae sibi quisque timebat / unius in miseri exitium conversa tulere*, 2.130–31). After his escape from the altar, however, he expresses the fear that his countrymen will "expiate this fault by the death of [his] wretched [family]" (*culpam hanc miserorum morte piabunt*, 2.140). His resistance, that is, transforms him from the scapegoat who can save many into the failed sacrifice who can harm many—unless other victims are offered in expiation. Palinurus may be no different. The many symbolically sacrificial deaths in the *Aeneid*, nearly all of which involve unwilling victims, only lead to more.

The death of Palinurus is also linked to that of Aeneas in two other ways. First, an allusion to Patroclus and Achilles in the *Iliad* supports seeing Palinurus as postponing, but not obviating, the death of his captain. Virgil associates Achilles/Patroclus with Aeneas/Palinurus by recalling the lamentation for Patroclus as a prelude to Palinurus' plunge overboard. Immediately after Neptune's speech and calming of waters (5.800–21), a group of sea divinities curiously observes Aeneas' fleet:

> tum variae comitum facies, immania cete,
> et senior Glauci chorus Inousque Palaemon

24. Brenk (1988) 78. He suggests that Virgil had in mind the suicide of Dido, the massacre of Carthage in the Third Punic War, and Augustus' brutal subjugation of Sicily after the war with Sextus Pompey.

Tritonesque citi Phorcique exercitus omnis;
laeva tenet Thetis et Melite Panopeaque virgo,
Nisaee Spioque Thaliaque Cymodoceque. (5.822–26)

> Then the various faces of his companions, enormous sea-monsters, and the aged chorus of Glaucus and Palaemon son of Ino, and the swift Tritons and the whole army of Phorcus; Thetis holds the left, and Melite and the maiden Panopea, *Nisaee and Spio and Thalia and Cymodoce*.

With the exception of Panopea, who appears during the boat race (5.240), all of the nymphs here named are found nowhere else in the *Aeneid*. All but Thetis appear only once in the *Iliad*: before the lament for Patroclus (*Il.* 18.39–51), led by Thetis (the first nymph in Virgil's list). In particular, Virgil's last line of nymphs (as commentators point out) yokes the beginning and end of the lines with which Homer's list begins:

ἔνθ' ἄρ' ἔην Γλαύκη τε *Θάλειά τε Κυμοδόκη τε*,
Νησαίη Σπειώ τε Θόη θ' Ἁλίη τε βοῶπις.

(*Il.* 18.39–40)

> There was Glauke and *Thaleia and Kymodoke, Nesaie and Speio* and Thoe and ox-eyed Halie.

With the unusual positioning of *-que* imitating the Greek *-te*, and none of these four nymphs appearing anywhere else in either author's work,[25] Virgil's line is probably a specific allusion intended to recall the Homeric context.[26] In mourning for Patroclus, Homer's nymphs implicitly mourn for Achilles, whose death is postponed

25. The line *Nisaee Spioque Thaliaque Cymodoceque* in *Geo.* 4.338 is an interpolation, as Thomas (1988a) points out ad loc.: "The line is not found in the best MSS, and is clearly an importation from *A*.5.826. Damning proof against it (if needed) is the fact that these nymphs, unlike the rest (333–86n.), *are* Homeric—they appear, over two lines which the later Virgil incorporated into one, at *Il.* 18.39–40."

26. For another instance of Virgil's careful and programmatic use of nymph names, see Thomas (1986) 190–93.

but not prevented by that of the "ritual substitute" who enters battle wearing Achilles' armor.[27]

Second, I, like Neptune, have been telling (or implying) a falsehood about Palinurus' demise. One of the surprises awaiting Aeneas in the Underworld is that Palinurus did not in fact drown, despite Neptune's declaration that "one will be lost in the flood"—a statement literally true, since "lost" (*amissus*) need not mean "killed." The helmsman's actual manner of death provides yet another parallel with Aeneas. On meeting Palinurus in Book 6, Aeneas complains that Apollo lied to him in saying that Palinurus would safely reach the *fines Ausonii* ("land/borders of Italy," 6.343–46) safely. Palinurus points out that the god's statement was true, for he did reach the *borders*, but was killed there by a *gens crudelis* ("cruel race") who mistook him for a wild animal. His body was then returned to the sea, to be tossed by the wind and waves (6.359–62). Virgil has offered, in a sense, two "versions" of Palinurus' death: first (we think) drowning, then being killed by natives and falling into the water. It is no coincidence that these correspond to the two strains of the tradition surrounding the death of Aeneas: in some versions he falls into a river, while in others he is killed (or mysteriously disappears) near the river, during or after a battle with the Aborigines. Palinurus embodies both of these traditions—drowning and being killed by natives—in himself. Moreover, Apollo's prophecy that Palinurus will reach the *fines Ausonii* resembles his prophecy in Book 3 (related by Helenus) that Aeneas will reach the *fines Itali:*

---

27. The concept of the "ritual substitute" harks back to the ancient practice of sacrificing an imposter dressed as the king, thereby fooling the gods into thinking that they were being offered the best human victim. See Nagy (1979) 33–34, 292–93 on Patroclus as ritual substitute for Achilles. Even without recourse to comparative linguistic and anthropological arguments, it is evident on literary grounds that the "death of Patroklos inside the *Iliad* foreshadows the death of Achilles outside the *Iliad*" (33). Brenk (1984) 780–81 observes that the plea of Palinurus' shade for Aeneas either to bury him or to carry him over the Styx (6.364–71) echoes the plea of Patroclus' shade for burial (*Il.* 23.70–76). The narrator also addresses Palinurus in the vocative (*te, Palinure, petens,* "seeking you, Palinurus," 5.840), as Homer addresses Patroclus (*Il.* 16.20, 584, 693, 744, 754, 787, 812, and 843), although, as Williams (1960) notes (ad 5.840), such apostrophe is not uncommon in Virgil.

> 'sic denique *victor*
> Trinacria *finis* Italos mittere relicta.' (3.439–40)
>
> 'Thus, *victor* at last, you shall be sent to the Italian *fines*, with Trinacria left behind.'

The literal but deceptive truth of Apollo's prophecy about Palinurus rests on the ambiguity of *fines*, whose meaning shifts from "Ausonian *land*" to "Ausonian *borders*" to "Ausonian *death*."[28] The other parallels between Palinurus and Aeneas suggest that Apollo's prophecy about Aeneas may contain a similar barb. Like Tiber's declaration, *mihi victor honorem / persolves* (8.61–62), Helenus' words may predict obliquely that Aeneas' "victory" will be inseparable from his death.

In addition to his comrades "lost in the waves," other friends and foes of Aeneas prefigure his manner of death. One is King Priam, over whom Aeneas pronounces an epitaph similar to that of Palinurus:

> "iacet ingens litore truncus,
> avulsumque umeris caput et sine nomine corpus."
>
> "The huge trunk lies on the shore, a head torn away from its shoulders and a body without a name." (2.557–58)

As Edgeworth remarks, "The jolt is violent when, after Priam is murdered in his own palace, we are told, without transition, that his headless corpse lies upon the beach. But Priam's palace was nowhere near the shore!"[29] Aeneas has just told us that Priam was slaughtered "before the very altar" (*altaria ad ipsa*, 2.550) of the Trojan citadel. Virgil is conflating two versions of Priam's death, one that he was killed at the altar, the other that he was killed at the tomb of Achilles and dragged to the Sigean promontory.[30] This

---

28. Mitchell-Boyask (1996) 296–97.

29. Edgeworth (1986) 150. After discussing various unsatisfying solutions (ancient and modern) to the problem, Edgeworth proposes emendation of the text from *litore* ("on the shore") to *limine* ("on the threshold").

30. Austin (1964) ad 2.556. It is likely that Virgil also intended an allusion to the fate of Pompey. See Horsfall (1991) 51 for similar examples of details transferred

importation of an inconsistent detail from the other version is no empty display of erudition. The combination of sacrifice (here, dying at the altar) and lying unburied on the shore is what characterizes the deaths of Palinurus and Orontes—and that of Aeneas.

Aeneas' callous treatment of one of his enemies also foreshadows his own fate. In his rampage after the death of Pallas, modeled on that of Achilles after the death of Patroclus, Aeneas shows no compassion to four men whose resemblance to himself he cannot or will not see.[31] Magus entreats him in terms of *pietas* toward father and son (10.524–25); Haemonides is a priest who becomes a sacrificial victim (10.537–42);[32] Anxur mistakenly believes himself destined for long life (10.545–49);[33] and Tarquitus prefigures him still more specifically (10.550-60). Aeneas not only kills Tarquitus in midspeech, but taunts him about being tossed by the waves:

> "istic nunc, metuende, iace. non te optima mater
> condet humi patrioque onerabit membra sepulcro:
> alitibus linquere feris, aut gurgite mersum
> unda feret piscesque impasti vulnera lambent." (10.557–60)

> "Lie there now, oh terrifying one. Your excellent mother will not bury you in the earth nor burden your limbs with ancestral tomb: you will be left for the wild birds [or flying beasts], or the wave will carry you, immersed in the flood, and the hungry fishes will lick your wounds."

---

from one historical or mythological figure to another. On conflicting versions of Priam's death, see Heinze (1993) 59. Seneca (no doubt following Virgil) conflates the sacrificial death and the trunk lying on the shore: *magnoque Iovi victima caesus / Sigea premis litora truncus* ("A victim sacrificed to great Jupiter, you press the Sigean shore, a headless body," *Tro.* 140–41).

31. Powell (1992a) 147–48 compares the young Octavian's infamous lack of compassion toward his fallen enemies, as when (for example) in response to a foe's plea for burial he quipped that the vultures would see to it (Suetonius *Vita Augusti* 13). Powell suggests that in the *Aeneid* passage "one may see Virgil frankly confronting a damaging element in Augustus' image" (148).

32. The death of this priest is discussed in the next chapter.

33. O'Hara (1990) 113 notes that Anxur's self-deception is like the false confidence into which Aeneas has been lured by reassuring prophecies.

Unlike the parallel scene in the *Iliad*, in which Achilles kicks Lycaon's body into the Xanthus/Scamander, the absence of any explicit reference to a body of water nearby makes Aeneas' threat surprising. Highet justly complains, "Vergil follows his model a little too closely when he makes his hero say (559–560) that Tarquitus, unburied, will be eaten by fishes. Achilles has indeed thrown Lycaon's body into the Scamander, but Aeneas is fighting in the middle of a plain with chariots wheeling all around."[34] Aeneas taunts Tarquitus that no grieving mother will bury him; at the beginning of the book Aeneas' mother, rhetorically exaggerating her devotion to Ascanius, declares that she is willing to "let Aeneas be tossed by unknown waves" (*Aeneas sane ignotis iactetur in undis*, 10.47). The immediate context is his journey to gather allies, but his eventual fate gives her words an ominous second meaning.[35]

Virgil also calls attention to the oddity with the phrase *alitibus linquere feris* ("you will be left for the wild birds/winged beasts"), an allusion operating on several levels. In the proem of the *Iliad*, Achilles is said to bring about the ultimate insult in making his foes "spoil for the dogs and birds" (1.4–5). Catullus, alluding to the Homeric lines, has his abandoned Ariadne complain that she will be left as "prey for the beasts and birds," *feris alitibusque praeda* (64.152–53).[36] The *Aeneid*'s only other instance of the dative plural *alitibus* conforms to the Homeric formula,[37] as Euryalus' mother complains that her son will be "left as prey for the dogs and birds,"

34. Highet (1972) 205.

35. The Romans took such ominously ambiguous remarks very seriously. See, e.g., Liebeschuetz (1979) 25–26.

36. The associations among the Homeric, Catullan, and Virgilian lines quoted above are treated in a series of brief articles: Zetzel (1978), Thomas (1979), Renehan (1979), and Dee (1981). The articles mainly discuss whether the Virgilian and Catullan lines throw light on the famous controversy over the reading *oiōnoisi te daita* ("a feast for the birds") versus *oiōnoisi te pāsi* ("for all the birds") in *Iliad* 1.5. Though this particular issue is not essential to the present argument (in which the operative elements are the birds and dogs, not their dinner), it points to the deliberateness with which Virgil probably created this Homeric/Catullan allusion. I am grateful to Richard Thomas for alerting me to the strangeness of Virgil's *alitibus feris*.

37. Thomas (1979) 476.

canibus praeda alitibusque (9.485–86). Thus the epic tradition—especially without mention of water nearby—leads us to expect a reference to dogs and birds, and the phrase *alitibus feris* seems at first glance to fulfill this expectation.[38] But as we read further, it becomes apparent that Virgil is actually alluding to a tradition from which he is departing. The two nouns in Catullus become a noun and an adjective in Virgil, both referring to birds: whether the dative plural *alitibus feris* corresponds to *alites* (adjective) *ferae* (noun), "winged beasts," or *alites* (noun) *feri* (adjective), "wild birds," it is clear that only birds are meant. In place of dogs (or beasts) and birds, Virgil gives us the unusual birds and *fish*—a surprise artfully signalled as one.

The Homeric passage on which the Tarquitus scene is modeled differs from Virgil's in ways that reflect important differences between Aeneas and Achilles. In both passages, the heroes taunt their victims about the horrors of watery oblivion, particularly lack of burial by a grieving mother and being nibbled on by fish (*Il.* 21.122–27, *Aen.* 10.557–60). But only the *Iliad* shows the river's angry reaction to having a corpse kicked into his waters:

> Ὣς ἄρ' ἔφη, ποταμὸς δὲ χολώσατο κηρόθι μᾶλλον,
> ὅρμηνεν δ' ἀνὰ θυμὸν ὅπως παύσειε πόνοιο
> δῖον Ἀχιλλῆα, Τρώεσσι δὲ λοιγὸν ἀλάλκοι. (*Il.* 21.136–38)
>
> So he [Achilles] spoke, and the river was enraged from the bottom of his heart, and plotted in his mind how he might stop Achilles from his labor and ward off destruction from the Trojans.

The river's simmering anger boils up later in the book into a near-fatal confrontation with Achilles—after Xanthus has called upon his brother Simois for aid. Virgil does not even mention a river, much less a river's reaction. But this absence is the more conspicuous in that Aeneas, unlike Achilles, really will fall prey to a river's revenge.

---

38. So, for instance, Anderson (1969) 84 notes, "Aeneas exults that Tarquitius will not go back to his mother for burial, but will be left out as a prey of birds and beasts."

One other element missing from the Tarquitus scene reveals a crucial difference between Aeneas and Achilles in their attitude toward death. Lycaon, in (unsuccessfully) supplicating Achilles, complains of his wretched fate and declares that his mother bore him to be "short-lived," *minunthadios* (*Il.* 21.84–85). Near the beginning of the epic, Achilles also complains that his mother bore him to be *minunthadios* (*Il.* 1.352). The word is rare and significant in the poem, used elsewhere of a person only to describe Hector (15.612) as he gains a brief *aristeia* but is fated to die soon by Achilles' spear.[39] Achilles recognizes the similarity between himself and Lycaon, pointing out his own mortality and predicting—accurately—the manner of his own death:

> "οὐχ ὁράᾳς οἷος καὶ ἐγὼ καλός τε μέγας τε;
> πατρὸς δ' εἴμ' ἀγαθοῖο, θεὰ δέ με γείνατο μήτηρ·
> ἀλλ' ἔπι τοι καὶ ἐμοὶ θάνατος καὶ μοῖρα κραταιή·
> ἔσσεται ἢ ἠὼς ἢ δείλη ἢ μέσον ἦμαρ,
> ὁππότε τις καὶ ἐμεῖο Ἄρῃ ἐκ θυμὸν ἕληται,
> ἢ ὅ γε δουρὶ βαλὼν ἢ ἀπὸ νευρῆφιν ὀϊστῷ." (*Il.* 21.108–13)

> "Do you not see how I, too, am beautiful and great? I am of noble father, and the mother who bore me was a goddess; but upon me, too, is death and strong doom. There will be either a dawn or an evening or a noontime, when someone in war will take away my spirit, hitting me with either a spear or an arrow from the bowstring."

Aeneas shows no such recognition.[40] His insensitivity is the more ironic in that his own fate is to be tossed unburied by the

---

39. The *aristeia*, in which one hero is given the spotlight and said to kill many warriors (usually minor ones) in rapid succession, is a stock feature of Homeric battle narrative. On Virgil's modification of the Homeric *aristeia*, see Clausen (1987) 92–95 and chap. 10 of this book.

40. Clausen (1987) 91 observes, "in his encounter with Tarquitus, in the death of a vain and foolish young warrior, Aeneas shows himself even more ruthless than Achilles; altogether lacking is the awareness of a common humanity which causes Achilles to see, in the death of Lycaon, whom he will not spare, his own inexorable fate."

waves—perhaps the very waves into which he has just thrust his opponent.

The argument that the *Aeneid*'s many images of watery death and lack of burial prefigure the fate of Aeneas leaves aside an essential aspect of the Aeneas legend. Dido's curse called for Aeneas to remain *inhumatus*, "unburied." Will this be fulfilled literally but in a happier sense than she intended?[41] The "epic voice" of Jupiter declares to both Venus and Juno that Aeneas will become a god (1.259–60, 12.794–95). If the death of Aeneas is indeed followed by such a resurrection, are we meant to feel that his sufferings, however great, will receive more than adequate recompense? Virgil provides no explicit answer. Instead, after the final interview between Juno and Jupiter in which Aeneas' eventual divinity is promised, the voice of Turnus' sister Juturna interrupts the battle narrative with a series of questions:[42]

> "alarum verbera nosco
> letalemque sonum, nec fallunt iussa superba
> magnanimi Iovis. haec pro virginitate reponit?
> quo vitam dedit aeternam? cur mortis adempta est
> condicio? possem tantos finire dolores
> nunc certe, et misero fratri comes ire per umbras!
> immortalis ego? at quicquam mihi dulce meorum
> te sine, frater, erit? o quae satis ima dehiscat
> terra mihi, Manisque deam demittat ad imos?"
> tantum effata caput glauco contexit amictu
> multa gemens et se fluvio dea condidit alto.[43] (12.876–86)

"I recognize the beating of the wings and the lethal sound, nor do the proud commands of magnanimous Jupiter deceive me. Is this the recompense for my virginity? For what did he give eternal life? Why is the condition of death taken away? Now

41. Murgia (1987) 54.

42. On Juturna's lament, see Barchiesi (1978); Lyne (1987) 86–87, 139–44; O'Hara (1990) 114–16; Barchiesi (1994); Perkell (1997).

43. For the reading *at* rather than *aut* in 12.882, see O'Hara (1993) 371–74.

> indeed I would be able to put an end to such great pain, and go as companion to my wretched brother through the Shades! Am I to be immortal? Yes, but will there be any pleasure for me in my own people without you, brother? Oh, what earth might yawn deep enough for me, and send me, a goddess, to the deep Shades?" Having spoken this much, she covered her head in a grey veil, groaning much, and, a goddess, buried herself in the deep river.

Virgil makes Juturna a former mortal who became a divinity of the Numicus, as Aeneas is soon to be.[44] It is she, not Jupiter, who provides the final comment on the justice shown by the god who raped her and on the reward of immortality that awaits the poem's hero.[45]

Many characters in the *Aeneid* who experience death by water and/or lack of burial are also marked as symbolic sacrificial victims (Palinurus the "one given for many," Orontes killed near "The Altars," Priam killed at an actual altar). Despite assurances that "only one" will be given, such offerings are repeated frequently; the unwillingness of the victims may contribute to this necessity for repetition, just as *piacula* (ritual errors) in actual sacrifices require expiation. The resemblance of these deaths to that of Aeneas in one way—drowning/lack of burial—suggests that the sacrificial element that characterizes them may be present in his as well. We have seen hints of this already in Tiber's prophecy, *mihi victor honorem / persolves*. The next chapter suggests that Virgil foreshadows this dark theme more forcefully in repeated images of priests who become sacrificial victims.

---

44. O'Hara (1990) 116: "The experience of Juturna parallels what apparently will happen to Aeneas."

45. Barchiesi (1994) 113 notes that though Jupiter promises immortality to Aeneas, "l'ultima voce divina del poema, prima di sparire nelle sue acque, ci fa guardare con meno ottimismo ai doni di Giove. La rappresentazione del dolore dentro una storia di uomini e dei costringe a una visione bifocale." ("The final divine voice in the poem, before disappearing into her waters, causes us to regard the gifts of Jupiter with less optimism. The representation of pain within a story of men and gods forces a bifocal view.")

CHAPTER FOUR

VICTOR AND VICTIM

It is one of the masterstrokes of Homer to close the *Iliad* on the eleventh day of an armistice that the reader knows will end on the twelfth. Patroclus' soul flies down to Hades, mourning its fate, leaving manhood and youth; Hector's soul flies down to Hades, mourning its fate, leaving manhood and youth; after the poem ends, Achilles' soul. . . . One is left to infer what will happen from what has gone before. Virgil, too, makes ample use of this strategy, creating situations within the poem parallel to situations that will occur after its end.[1] The many characters who drown or lie

1. Kepple (1976) 350 demonstrates Virgil's use of such a technique in the case of the parallel between Arruns/Camilla and Aeneas/Turnus, setting up the following "equation":

> Four elements can be isolated in the climax and denouement of the Camilla story:
>
> 1. she takes over the leadership from Turnus;
> 2. she is killed because of booty;
> 3. the line (11.831)
>
>   vitaque cum gemitu fugit indignata sub umbras;
> 4. her killer, Arruns, is himself killed through divine revenge.
>
> Three elements can be isolated in the climax of the Turnus story:
>
> 1. he takes over the leadership from Camilla;
> 2. he is killed because of booty;
> 3. the line (12.952),
>
>   vitaque cum gemitu fugit indignata sub umbras;
> 4. ?
>
> The reader is left to wonder about a possible final element in this second series: what happens to Turnus' killer, Aeneas?

unburied—Orontes, Priam, Polydorus, Misenus, Palinurus, Tarquitus—foreshadow in this way the death of Aeneas. Another complementary phenomenon arises from the recurrent theme of role-reversal, which creates a pattern with important implications for Aeneas' sacrifice of Turnus: many who assume the role of victor or priest, especially those who perform human sacrifice, come to be sacrificed themselves.[2]

Characters in the *Aeneid* frequently assume the role of either priest or victim in a temporary, figurative sense that may or may not overlap with the literal. It is sometimes remarked that representatives of the Trojan past, such as Creusa and Anchises, must be "sacrificed" to Aeneas' mission; the present chapter will focus instead on characters who kill or die in a way that specifically alludes to ritual slaughter.[3] For instance, a character assumes the role of sacrificial victim if he dies at an altar,[4] is otherwise marked by ritual terms such as *immolare* ("sacrifice") or *victima* ("sacrificial victim"), or is compared to a sacrificial animal. His killer assumes the role of priest.

---

2. On the confusion of victor and victim, see Spence (1991) 18.

3. A character poised tantalizingly between literal and symbolic sacrifice is Dido. Tupet (1970) argues that her suicide, which is preceded by ritual utterances and other magical practices, is to be read as a *devotio*, or self-immolation to curse the enemy (on the equally complex issue of Turnus' *devotio*, see chap. 5, n.12). Hardie (1993) 29 notes that "her suicide is a perversion of, or substitute for, the sacrifice to Stygian Jupiter (4.638-9) that she deceives Anna into thinking that she is going to undertake, and some [e.g., Tupet] see in her death a self-sacrifice that will ensure the future potency of her city's revenge on the Romans, whose dead Dido anticipates as sacrificial offerings (*munera*, 4.624) to her own shade." Panoussi (1998), discussing "Dido's Ritual Slaughter" (41–45), observes that "Dido's sacrificial slaughter, instead of ensuring the restoration of the disturbed cultural order, launches a fresh sacrificial crisis to last for centuries" (44). On a more symbolic plane, Spence (1999) 84 notes that "the image of love's poison as a consuming inner fire is strongly suggestive of sacrificial imagery, a connection underscored by Vergil as he juxtaposes the image in lines [4.]60–66 with Dido's performance of just such a sacrifice."

Because the issue of the *devotio* of Dido and Turnus is so controversial, it is not one of the building blocks of the present argument. The reader may judge whether the rest of the argument lends credence to the *devotio* idea—that is, whether it is plausible that Virgil alludes to a ritual whereby the self-immolation of Aeneas' enemies would ensure his death.

4. Turcan (1988) 9 notes that no Roman sacrifice took place without an altar, the center of the scene and a sort of "pivot sacré."

"Role-reversal" refers to two distinct but related phenomena, "reversal of fortune" and "role-playing." The Iliadic trio of Patroclus, Hector, and Achilles embody both of these. Patroclus, wearing Achilles' armor, dies by Hector's hand; Hector, also wearing Achilles' armor (stripped from Patroclus), dies by Achilles' hand. Hector's temporary victory over Patroclus, which leads to his defeat by Achilles, is a classic reversal of fortune. Patroclus, wearing Achilles' armor in order to masquerade as Achilles (*Il.* 16.41), engages in role-playing with fatal results, inheriting the antagonism between Achilles and the gods (particularly Apollo) and becoming a "ritual substitute" for his friend.[5] Homer emphasizes that these three deaths are causally and thematically linked: the dying Patroclus predicts that Achilles will kill Hector (16.852–54), the dying Hector predicts that Paris and Apollo will kill Achilles (22.358–60), and the souls of both Patroclus and Hector fly down to Hades in identical words that occur nowhere else in the poem (16.855–57, 22.361–63). The deaths of Achilles' best friend and worst enemy thus prefigure his own, in a carefully orchestrated parallel essential to the *Iliad*'s themes of retribution and mortality.

Virgil's *imitatio* of Homer adds a new dimension to role-reversal: in addition to creating parallels within the *Aeneid* similar to those within the *Iliad*, Virgil also creates parallels between the two poems. The *Aeneid* continually raises the question of who is to be identified with the Greeks of the *Iliad* and who with the Trojans, and in particular whether Turnus or Aeneas is the "other Achilles" prophesied by the Sibyl. This opens the field for both intratextual and intertextual role-playing, as Aeneas is made to resemble his Greek enemies both inside and outside the *Aeneid*. But his transformation from victim to victor in war, Virgil implies, will culminate in his becoming a victim in sacrifice.

Virgil adumbrates the Trojans' assumption of the role of the Iliadic Greeks—and the consequences of this reversal—when the

5. See chap. 3, n. 27.

Trojans guilefully put on Greek armor during the sack of Troy.[6] Aeneas has already referred to the Trojans as *victi* ("conquered") and the Greeks as victors (2.367–68). The Trojans' one gleam of hope comes when these Greek victors accidentally mistake them for Greeks. The Trojan Coroebus seizes on this success and urges his companions to press it further by disguising themselves in Greek armor stripped from the warriors they have just killed:

> "'o socii, qua prima' inquit 'Fortuna salutis
> monstrat iter, quaque ostendit se dextra, sequamur:
> mutemus clipeos Danaumque insignia nobis
> aptemus. dolus an virtus, quis in hoste requirat?
> arma dabunt ipsi.' sic fatus deinde comantem
> Androgei galeam clipeique insigne decorum
> induitur laterique Argivum accommodat ensem.
> hoc Rhipeus, hoc ipse Dymas omnisque iuventus
> laeta facit: spoliis se quisque recentibus armat.
> vadimus immixti Danais *haud numine nostro*
> multaque per caecam congressi proelia noctem
> conserimus, *multos Danaum demittimus Orco*." (2.387–98)

> "'O allies,' he says, 'where Fortune first shows the path of salvation, and where she shows herself favorable, let us follow: let us exchange shields and fit the insignia of the Greeks to ourselves. Guile or virtue, who would ask in an enemy? They themselves will give the arms.' Having thus spoken, he then puts on the plumed helmet of Androgeos and the beautiful insignia of his shield, and fits the Argive sword to his side. This Rhipeus, this Dymas himself and all the youth do happily: each man arms himself with the fresh spoils. We go mingled with the Greeks, *under a divine power not our own*, and in close combat we sow many battles through the blind night, *we send down many of the Greeks to Orcus*."

6. On this scene as the first of several in which wearing another's armor leads to death (as it *always* does in the *Aeneid*), see Hornsby (1966) 347–49.

In the Roman view, the arms of an enemy remained full of the enemy's power and had to be destroyed (except in very special circumstances). To bring them within the walls of Rome, let alone *wear* them, was taboo.[7] Roman readers would have shuddered at Coroebus' stratagem, and their misgivings soon would have been confirmed. The haunting phrase *haud numine nostro* ("under a divine power not our own") emphasizes the dangerous supernatural consequences of wearing another's armor.[8] A more specific allusion to Achilles reinforces this theme. The line *multos Danaum demittimus Orco* ("we send down many of the Greeks to Orcus," 2.398) echoes the proem of the *Iliad*, which describes the destructive wrath of Achilles:[9]

> πολλὰς δ' ἰφθίμους ψυχὰς Ἄϊδι προΐαψεν
> ἡρώων. (1.3–4)

> He sent forth many mighty souls of heroes to Hades.

Like Patroclus and Hector, the Trojans find that their temporary transformation into "Achilles" brings only a temporary victory. Coroebus, unable to contain himself when he sees his betrothed Cassandra dragged from the temple of Minerva, rushes in to save her. The Trojans are soon massacred by their own countrymen, then by Greeks who recognize the ruse (2.402–30).

Certain details about the deaths of these Trojans suggest that their role-playing leads to compensatory sacrifice. Aeneas expresses his grief and bitterness at these deaths in a crescendo of pathos:

---

7. Versnel (1970) 309–12. The *spolia opima*, or spoils captured from an enemy general and dedicated to Jupiter, could be handled only by the victorious Roman general who had proved himself superior to the enemy's power. The *spolia provocatoria*, or spoils won in single combat preceded by a challenge, could be kept by the victor, but a *piaculum* had to be offered for bringing them within city walls.

8. Hornsby (1966) 348–49: "They have lost the protection of the divine will because they have lost their own will."

9. The phrases *demiserit Orco* ("he sent down to Hades," 9.527) and *miserit Orco* ("he sent to Hades," 9.785) are used of Turnus as he storms the Trojan camp. See Austin (1964) ad 2.398.

"ilicet obruimur numero, primusque Coroebus
Penelei dextra *divae armipotentis ad aram*
procumbit; cadit et Rhipeus, iustissimus unus
qui fuit in Teucris et servantissimus aequi
(dis aliter visum); pereunt Hypanisque Dymasque
confixi a sociis; nec te tua plurima, Panthu,
labentem *pietas nec Apollinis infula texit*." (2.424–30)

"At once we are overwhelmed by their number, and Coroebus first falls forward by the right hand of Peneleus, *before the altar of the goddess strong in arms*; Rhipeus too falls, the one man who was most just among the Trojans and the most observant of right (the gods had another plan); Hypanis and Dymas perish, stabbed by their allies; nor did your very great *piety*, Panthus, *nor the fillet of Apollo protect* you as you collapsed."

The men are killed at an altar (Coroebus), for all their virtue (Rhipeus), by their allies (Hypanis and Dymas), and despite the piety and sacrosanctity of the high priest (Panthus). But Aeneas' claim that the Trojans are innocent victims is undermined by their recourse to treachery, their deliberate confusion of *dolus* ("guile") with *virtus*.[10] The Trojans' first victim, Androgeos, shares this name with the son of Minos who appears on Apollo's temple at Cumae, for whose death the Athenians were required to pay with "seven bodies of youths" each year (6.18–22).[11] Coroebus, the first Trojan victim—a Virgilian departure from earlier tradition, which shows him killed later in the battle—dies at Minerva's altar (*divae armipotentis ad aram*, 425). Virgil apparently wants to depict Coroebus, like the Athenian youths, as a reciprocal offering in exchange for Androgeos.[12] As Servius points out, the name "Coroebus" is tra-

10. Rauk (1991) 294. Hardie (1993) 23 notes that Coroebus' "deliberate 'dissolution of differences' is an ironic image of civil war."

11. See Lee (1992).

12. Rauk (1991) 291–93.

ditionally associated with a proverbial fool.[13] Austin argues that "Virgil's Coroebus shows no trace of contamination from the 'silly' tradition, and Servius' ground for thinking so is absurd";[14] yet one wonders why Virgil would have chosen the name if he had not wished to hint at the foolishness of Coroebus' strategy. To follow Fortune and take a foe's armor—or a foe's role—leads to disaster.[15]

Coroebus' exhortation to the Trojans to follow Fortune and assimilate themselves to the Greeks is echoed in a passage that states explicitly the importance of role-reversal for the second half of the poem. One of Virgil's clearest signals that he will be writing a "second *Iliad*" occurs when the Sibyl prophesies the Italian War in terms of the Trojan War, or the *Aeneid* in terms of the *Iliad*: the Simois and Xanthus, the Greek camps, goddess-born Achilles, hostile Juno, and a wedding to a foreigner will all be found in Italy (6.86–94). It is no coincidence that Coroebus is betrothed to the other raving prophetess in the *Aeneid* (Cassandra).[16] The end of the Sibyl's speech resembles in word and theme the beginning of that of Coroebus:

---

13. Servius ad 2.341:

> hunc autem Coroebum stultum inducit Euphorion, quem et Vergilius sequitur, dans ei "dolus an virtus, quis in hoste requirat?" cum sit turpis dolo quaesita victoria.
>
> But Euphorion makes Coroebus a fool, and Virgil follows him, giving Coroebus the line "guile or virtue, who would ask in an enemy?" when victory sought through guile is foul.

Austin (1964) ad 2.341 gives several other sources for this tradition (e.g., Callimachus fr. inc. Pf. 587; Lucian *Am.* 53; Aelian, *VH* xiii. 14; Suidas, s.v. Κόροιβος· μωρός τις μετρῶν τὰ κύματα ["Coroebus: some fool who measures the waves"]).

14. Austin (1964) ad 2.341.

15. Nicoll (1988) 464 sees the Coroebus incident as one of several in the *Aeneid* making it plain that "following the lead of what is perceived as chance *Fortuna* is an inadequate yardstick to adopt in coming to moral decisions." See also Quint (1993) 92–93 on "following Fortune" as the paradigm for losers in the *Aeneid*, and Horsfall (1995) 175–77 on the negative consequences of a Roman wearing a foe's armor.

16. Literary depictions of Cassandra and the Sibyl are similar. For instance, Virgil's image of the Sibyl as a horse subject to the "reins" and "goads" of Apollo (6.101–102) recalls Aeschylus' description of Cassandra at Agamemnon's palace:

"'o socii, *qua prima'* inquit *'Fortuna salutis*
monstrat iter, quaque ostendit se dextra, sequamur:
mutemus clipeos *Danaumque* insignia nobis
aptemus.'" (2.387–90) [Coreobus]

"'O allies,' he says, *'where Fortune first* shows the path of *salvation*, and where she shows herself favorable, let us follow: let us exchange shields and fit the insignia of the *Greeks* to ourselves.'"

"tu ne cede malis, sed contra audentior ito,
qua tua te *Fortuna* sinet. via *prima salutis*
(quod minime reris) *Graia* pandetur ab urbe." (6.95–97)
[Sibyl]

"Do not yield to evils, but go against them more boldly, *where* your *Fortune* will allow you. The *first* way of *salvation* (something you least expect) will be revealed from a *Greek* city."

Both Coroebus and the Sibyl counsel the Trojans to follow Fortune and seek help from a Greek source. Coroebus' advice is followed by an allusion likening the Trojans to Achilles; the Sibyl's is preceded by the statement that "another Achilles" will be in Italy (89). Her prophecy seems to be referring to Aeneas' new enemy, but the poem in some ways points to Aeneas himself as the "other Achilles."[17] Like Venus' *perge modo* ("just keep going," 1.389, 401) when she meets her

---

χαλινὸν δ' οὐκ ἐπίσταται φέρειν,
πρὶν αἱματηρὸν ἐξαφρίζεσθαι μένος. (*Ag.* 1066–67)

She does not know how to bear the bridle, before foaming out her strength in blood.

17. See Kinsey (1979) 267: "The real counterpart of Achilles in Latium is Aeneas and it is to Aeneas that the Sibyl is referring—another Achilles *for* Latium with *Latio* a dative. The Sibyl is prophesying woe for Aeneas, but it is not woe he will suffer at the hands of an Achilles but the woe he will suffer as he plays the role of Achilles, namely the loss of his Patroclus, Pallas." Clay (1988) 205 and O'Hara (1990) 51 follow this interpretation of the Sibyl's prophecy. Against this view, see Perotti (1991) and Traina (1992), who argue that the "other Achilles" and "Greek camps" in the prophecy must refer to Turnus and the Rutulians. Traina emphasizes Virgil's use of *alius* ("other") rather than *alter* ("a second"): Turnus, that is, will be the *other* Achilles in the sense of a *different* Achilles—one who loses.

son in the Carthaginian wood, the Sibyl's words encourage Aeneas to go boldly where Fortune leads. In the case of Coroebus, however, the danger in seeking help from Greek armor—and the treacherousness of Fortune's "path of salvation"—is made explicit immediately after his speech. When the Trojans under a *numen* ("divine power") not their own send many to the Underworld, as Homer's Achilles did, it soon becomes their undoing. The Trojans' role-playing creates an unsettling parallel to that final moment when Aeneas at his most Achillean sacrifices his enemy in another's name. Turnus wears the armor of Pallas, but Aeneas symbolically assumes the identity of Achilles. Like those of the Trojans in Book 2, these impersonations will have fatal consequences.

The death of Panthus, the last Trojan killed in this episode (2.429–30), also has sacrificial overtones. This priest (*sacerdos*, 319) of Apollo was introduced a hundred lines earlier in terms similar to those describing Aeneas: carrying the *sacra victosque deos* ("sacred objects and conquered gods") and drawing his little grandchild along with him (320–21), he is clearly meant to recall the depiction of *pius* Aeneas with *penates* in hand and Ascanius in tow. There is obvious irony as Aeneas, the paragon of *pietas*, declares that Panthus' *pietas* did not protect him from death.[18] There is also irony in Aeneas' statement that the *infula* of Apollo yielded no protection either, for the *infula* (a woolen fillet) was worn by both priest and sacrificial victim. Since certain Roman priests were said to be "taken" (*capi*) by the gods they served,[19] it would seem that the *infula* rep-

---

It seems unnecessary to choose either Turnus or Aeneas as *the* "other Achilles." There are clearly elements of Achilles, and of Hector, in both Turnus and Aeneas (as Perotti demonstrates). Virgil tells us that the Sibyl's prophecy is obscure (*obscuris vera involvens*, lit., "rolling up true things in dark ones," 6.100); the ambiguity of *alius Achilles* may not be capable of definitive resolution.

18. Austin (1964) ad 2.320 and Gransden (1985) 129 emphasize the more hopeful aspect of the transfer of the *sacra* of Troy from the old high priest (Panthus) to the new one (Aeneas), and Gransden quotes Dryden's *Dedication to the Aeneis*: "That office . . . was made vacant by the death of Panthus for Aeneas to succeed to, and consequently for Augustus to enjoy."

19. Aul. Gell. 1.12.15: *Plerique autem 'capi' virginem solam debere dici putant. Sed flamines quoque Diales, item pontifices et augures 'capi' dicebantur* ("Now many

resented the change to sacred status of both sacrificer and sacrificed. When Panthus is killed, this emblem of his sacerdotal status associates him with the animals formerly his victims.

If the *infula* of Panthus hints at the resemblance of priest and victim, this theme finds its paradigmatic expression in Laocoön, the other *sacerdos* (201) in *Aeneid* 2.[20] Laocoön warns the Trojans that the Horse is a trick and casts his spear at it, but his correct assessment of the danger is interrupted by the lies of Sinon. The Trojans finally decide to take Sinon's word that the Horse will bring them safety when Laocoön, "in the midst of slaughtering a huge bull at the solemn altar" (*sollemnis taurum ingentem mactabat ad aras*, 2.202), is attacked by twin serpents from the sea. They devour his two sons (203–19) and then attack the priest himself:

> ille simul manibus tendit divellere nodos
> perfusus sanie vittas atroque veneno,
> clamores simul horrendos ad sidera tollit:
> qualis mugitus, fugit cum saucius aram
> taurus et incertam excussit cervice securim.
> at gemini lapsu delubra ad summa dracones
> effugiunt saevaeque petunt Tritonidis arcem,
> sub pedibusque deae clipeique sub orbe teguntur.
> (2.220–27)

At the same time he tries to tear apart the knots with his hands, his fillets bathed in gore and black poison, and raises horrible shouts to the stars: like the bellowing when a bull flees the altar wounded and shakes out the ill-aimed axe from his neck. But the twin serpents flee away slithering to the highest temples and seek the citadel of savage Minerva, and are covered under the feet of the goddess and under the circle of her shield.

---

think that only a Vestal Virgin ought to be said to be 'taken.' But in fact the flamens of Jupiter, pontiffs, and augurs were said to be 'taken' ").

20. For bibliography on Laocoön, see Rauk (1991) 288.

Although Virgil (or Aeneas) never explicitly says that Laocoön is killed, Virgil's similes often fill in gaps in the narrative proper.[21] This simile implies that Laocoön at least momentarily frees himself from the snakes. Whether or not he actually escapes, however, the image of the sacrificial bull who is wounded but flees the axe represents one of the worst possible omens. The imperfect sacrifice of Laocoön points to the potentially dire consequences when a priest becomes a victim against his will.[22]

Achilles' son Pyrrhus, the most brutal warrior in the *Aeneid*, also participates in the dynamic of priest-become-victim. Mocking his father's compassionate treatment of Priam, he takes pleasure in slaughtering the aged king as Priam slips in his son Polites' blood "at the very altar" (*altaria ad ipsa*, 2.550). Anchises complains about this atrocity and refers to Pyrrhus as the one who "cuts down the son before the father's face, the father at the altar" (*natum ante ora patris, patrem qui obtruncat ad aras*, 663). The next book reveals that the vengeful Orestes "cuts down [Pyrrhus] at his father's altar" (*patrias obtruncat ad aras*, 3.332).[23] The force of *patrias* ("father's" or "ancestral") is not entirely clear, for Pyrrhus traditionally was killed at Apollo's temple at Delphi. Servius cites a tradition that Pyrrhus had set up an altar of Achilles there, but this seems suspiciously like an invention based on the passage itself. The word *patrius* serves mainly to associate the deaths of Priam and Pyrrhus by means of the echo *patrem qui obtruncat ad aras* (2.663) and *patrias obtruncat ad aras* (3.332). Once again, a killing occuring at an altar, or otherwise signalled by ritual language, is followed by the sacrificial death of the killer.

21. Lyne (1989) 75–76.

22. The flight of a sacrificial animal in the middle of a sacrifice, leaving no doubt about its unwillingness, heralded disaster. See, e.g., Livy 21.63.13–14. When a sacrificial calf escapes and spatters the spectators with blood, the event is "received by many as an omen of great terror" (*a plerisque in omen magni terroris acceptum*). On the implications of unwillingness in victims, see chap. 3.

23. See Williams (1962) ad 3.332: "Thus Pyrrhus in a sense suffers what he had inflicted on Polites and Priam."

The fate of Pyrrhus is especially relevant to that of Aeneas, because one of the *Aeneid*'s clearest role-reversals occurs when Aeneas in Book 10 acts like Pyrrhus in Book 2.[24] Aeneas' gruesome *aristeia* illustrates several types of role-reversal: he has gone from losing (during the fall of Troy) to winning; he has come to play the role of his enemy (Pyrrhus) in the *Aeneid;* and his actions recall the cruelest moments of Achilles in the *Iliad*.[25] Chapter 3 discusses how the fate of Aeneas is mirrored in that of his victims in this scene, especially Tarquitus, whose body Aeneas kicks into the water. Explicit references to sacrifice also render the scene predictive of the end of the poem. The word *immolare* ("sacrifice") appears only three times in the *Aeneid*, twice in this scene (10.529, 541) and once in the sacrifice of Turnus (12.949). Like Achilles, Aeneas sacrifices youths to the shade of his lost friend (10.518-20).[26] Unlike Achilles, he sacrifices a priest in full priestly regalia:

> nec procul Haemonides, Phoebi Triviaeque sacerdos,
> *infula* cui sacra redimibat tempora vitta,
> totus conlucens veste atque insignibus albis.
> quem congressus agit campo, *lapsum*que superstans
> *immolat* ingentique umbra *tegit*, arma Serestus
> lecta refert umeris tibi, rex Gradive, tropaeum. (10.537–42)

> And not far off is Haemonides, the priest of Phoebus Apollo and Trivia [Diana], whose temples a fillet [*infula*] bound with sacred band, all shining in white garments and insignia. Aeneas attacking drives him over the field, and standing above the *collapsed* man *sacrifices* him and *covers* him with a huge shadow; Serestus gathers the arms and brings them back on his shoulders to you, king Gradivus, as a trophy.

---

24. See the useful discussion of Moskalew (1982) 152–53 (with bibliography). Turnus, too, resembles Pyrrhus in his cruelty; see Traina (1994) 30. The (partial) assimilation of both heroes to Pyrrhus parallels their mutual assimilation to Pyrrhus' father.

25. See, e.g., Putnam (1965) 175; Knox (1950) 137; Moskalew (1982) 153–55.

26. Why eight, when Achilles sacrifices twelve (*Il.* 21.27, 23.175)? Is Virgil implying that Achilles is worse? Or do the warriors Aeneas kills in the subsequent narrative stand in for the "missing" four?

This scene contains the only other *infula* in the *Aeneid* besides that of Panthus, and here the resemblance of priest and victim represented by the sacred fillet becomes obvious.[27] Another verbal similarity reinforces the parallel between the deaths of Panthus and Haemonides: there is an ironic echo of Apollo's failure figuratively to "cover" Panthus as he "collapsed" (*labentem . . . texit*, 2.430) when Aeneas literally "covers" the "collapsed" man with his shadow (*lapsum . . . tegit*, 10.540–41). A deeper significance in both scenes emerges when they are taken together, with one saying what the other leaves unsaid. What stands out in Virgil's portrayal of Panthus is his similarity to Aeneas; the idea that his priestly *infula* also marks him as a victim is latent. Haemonides, on the other hand, has no particular affinities to Aeneas aside from his status as priest. Yet in his death the dual function of the *infula* is highlighted, as Aeneas literally "sacrifices" him.[28] A priest very like Aeneas is killed, the sacrificer becomes the sacrificed—these images, and the message they collectively imply, cast their shadows beyond the end of the poem.

Another paradigmatic reversal of fortune occurs in the boxing match (5.362–484), which anticipates the final duel between Aeneas and Turnus.[29] When the young Trojan Dares seems to be winning, the older Sicilian Entellus makes a comeback, routs his opponent, and sacrifices as a substitute victim the bull he wins as a prize.[30] The episode's complex allusions suggest a confusion of roles culminating in the sacrifice of the sometime "victor."

Virgil's main source for the *Aeneid*'s boxing match is the similar contest in *Argonautica* 2.1–97 between the young heroic Polydeuces and the wicked King Amycus.[31] Apollonius characterizes the match

27. Harrison (1991) ad 10.538: "Vergil here exploits the ambiguity of the identical trappings of priest and sacrificial victim: the priest Haemonides, normally the sacrificer, is here ironically presented as the sacrifice."

28. As Moskalew (1982) 155 notes, "not unlike Priam or Laocoon."

29. See Putnam (1965) 215.

30. Heinze (1993) 132 points out that "Virgil's own contribution, in which he differs from all his predecessors, is the introduction of an unexpected *peripeteia*." See also his insightful remarks about Virgilian *peripeteia* in general (254–55).

31. Virgil signals his debt to this scene in introducing the boxer Dares, one of whose victims (Butes) was a subject of Amycus (5.368–74). This Butes is called

by means of a provocative double simile, in which an image of bulls fighting over a heifer turns into an image of first one and then the other boxer sacrificing his opponent:

> ἂψ δ' αὖτις συνόρουσαν ἐναντίοι, ἠύτε ταύρω
> φορβάδος ἀμφὶ βοὸς κεκοτηότε δηριάασθον.
> ἔνθα δ' ἔπειτ' Ἄμυκος μὲν ἐπ' ἀκροτάτοισιν ἀερθείς,
> βουτύπος οἶα, πόδεσσι τανύσσατο, κὰδ δὲ βαρεῖαν
> χεῖρ' ἐπὶ οἷ πελέμιξεν· ὁ δ' ἀίξαντος ὑπέστη,
> κρᾶτα παρακλίνας, ὤμῳ δ' ἀνεδέξατο πῆχυν
> τυτθόν· ὁ δ' ἄγχ' αὐτοῖο παρὲκ γόνυ γουνὸς ἀμείβων
> κόψε μεταΐγδην ὑπὲρ οὔατος, ὀστέα δ' εἴσω
> ῥῆξεν· ὁ δ' ἀμφ' ὀδύνῃ γνὺξ ἤριπεν· οἱ δ' ἰάχησαν
> ἥρωες Μινύαι· τοῦ δ' ἀθρόος ἔκχυτο θυμός. (2.88–97)

> They rushed back together again, as two bulls, enraged, fight over a grazing heifer. And then Amycus stretched himself up on the tips of his toes, like one sacrificing an ox, and flung down his heavy hand upon the other; but he evaded his thrust, bending his head aside, and received his arm on his shoulder only a little; and he, standing close and slipping knee past knee struck him swiftly above the ear, and broke his bones within; and he fell to his knees in pain, and the Minyan heroes shouted; and his spirit was poured out all at once.

Richard Hunter nicely summarizes Apollonius' strategy:

"victor" in the same breath as the description of his defeat (372–74), a detail that resonates with the theme of reversal. See Hardie (1993) 52. For a concise comparison of Virgil's boxing match with that of Apollonius, see Briggs (1981) 976–77.

The boxing match also has many important affinities with and references to the bullfight (i.e., "fight between two bulls") of *Geo.* 3.219–41: see Hunter (1989). Most importantly for our purposes here, the defeated bull goes into "training" for a comeback, and his ultimate victory is implied by a simile comparing him to a destructive wave rolling in from the sea. In describing Turnus' preparation at the beginning of *Aeneid* 12, Virgil quotes almost verbatim from the *Georgics* bullfight (*Aen.* 12.104–106 ≈ *Geo.* 3.232–34). Both the (predicted) reversal of fortune and the assimilation to a vengeful body of water are relevant to the *Aeneid* context (as will be discussed in the next chapter).

> Whereas Vergil presents his bulls warring over a mate as boxers, Apollonius' boxers are like bulls warring over a mate. The simile of lines 88–9 leads in to that of lines 90–2 where Amycus is compared to a man about to sacrifice a bull; the tables are turned, however, and Amycus himself becomes the sacrificial victim. γνὺξ ἤριπεν (line 96) is appropriate both for a beaten boxer and for the bull at a sacrifice, and the heroes' shout suggests not merely the audience of a sporting-contest but also the ritual cry which attended sacrifice . . .[32]

This transition from fighting bulls to sacrificial bulls has important resonances for Virgil. In Virgil's boxing match, the loss of human life is averted by the substitution of the prize bull for the beaten Dares, a departure from Apollonius' fight to the death. Yet the non-fatal outcomes of Virgil's funeral games prefigure fatal events elsewhere in the poem, as when the helmsman thrown from Gyas' ship in the boat race anticipates the death of Palinurus.[33] When Entellus sacrifices the prize bull by smashing its head with his fist, as Polydeuces did to Amycus, he declares, "As victor, I here pay in full this better life in exchange for the death of Dares" (*hanc . . . meliorem animam pro morte Daretis / persolvo hic victor*, 5.483–84). In Book 12, when Messapus violates the peace treaty by slaughtering Aulestes at an altar, he declares, "This is a better victim offered for the great gods" (*haec melior magnis data victima divis*, 12.296). The substitution of animal for human in the games is morbidly reversed by the substitution of human for animal in the war.[34] *Hanc . . . meliorem animam . . . persolvo hic victor,* says *Entellus* (5.483–84); *mihi victor honorem / persolves*, says Tiber to Aeneas (8.61–62).

Apollonius' related images of two bulls (*taurō*) and an ox-slaughterer (*boutupos*) may help to explain an inconsistency concerning Virgil's prize animal, which is called at different times a *taurus* (382, 472, 473), a *iuvencus* (366, 399, 477), and a *bos* (481).[35] *Bos* is the generic

32. Hunter (1989) 559.
33. Putnam (1965) 75.
34. See Hardie (1993) 52; Williams (1960) ad 5.483; Lehr (1934) 94.
35. See chap. 1 on Aeneas' sacrifice of the Thracian *taurus*.

name for "cattle" and thus includes both *tauri* and *iuvenci*, but *taurus* and *iuvencus* (properly used) are mutually exclusive (Varro *RR* 2.5.6). This shifting designation, if noticed at all, is used by scholars to demonstrate that Virgil was indifferent to the distinctions among various types of cattle—and thus to refute Servius' comment that Aeneas' sacrifice of a *taurus* to Jupiter contains a *piaculum*. But like Virgil's other inconsistencies supposedly due to indifference, this one may have thematic motivation. The bull in the boxing match episode has three distinct functions: it is introduced as a prize, but as a "substitute" for Dares it stands for both competitor and sacrificial victim. The three words reflect these three roles. Aeneas introduces it as a *iuvencus* (366), a prize for the victor, just as a *iuvenca* is the prize for the fighting bulls of *Georgics* 3 (219). When Dares seizes its horn with his left hand, it is called a *taurus* (382); elsewhere in the *Aeneid* to seize an enemy's hair or helmet in one's left hand is a prelude to killing him (2.552, 10.535, 12.302). Only *tauri* fight in Virgil's poetry, never *iuvenci* (a fact that belies Virgil's "indifference"). The word *taurus* here reflects the bull's role as a substitute opponent. The striking line-ending *procumbit humi bos* probably has a complex literary ancestry,[36] but it is notable that in Apollonius' boxing match Amycus is compared to a *boutupos*. The prize is a *iuvencus*, the substitute opponent is a *taurus*, and the sacrificial victim is a *bos*.

Virgil's boxing match, though similar to that of Apollonius in some ways, lacks its clear moral demarcation. Amycus is a hubristic tyrant; Polydeuces is the youthful savior of shipwrecked sailors. Virgil's boxers, like his warriors, defy simple categorization. If the reader's sympathies go first to the aged Entellus, roused by shame to one last fight (5.394–400), they are redirected by the final picture of Dares spitting blood and teeth (5.470). In addition to this moral blurring, the boxing match resembles the final duel between Turnus and Aeneas in more specific ways. We might be tempted to

36. The line-ending *bos* is echoed in the description of Io on Turnus' shield (7.790); see chap. 5, n. 19.

cast Entellus—the ultimate victor, the older man, and the one to perform a sacrifice—as an "Aeneas figure." But as in the question of who is the "other Achilles," Virgil steers away from simple identifications, and his clues lead in opposite directions. At least three phrases occur in Virgil's works only in reference to Entellus and Turnus: the knees of both are shaky, *genua labant* (5.432, 12.905); Entellus' former strength and Turnus' pallor are "in youthful body," *iuvenali in corpore* (5.475, 12.221); and both are roused to action amid failing fortunes by their "self-conscious virtue," *conscia virtus* (5.455, 12.668). This last is an especially memorable phrase, crystalizing an important characteristic of Turnus at a pivotal point in the narrative. Entellus and Turnus are both natives fighting against foreigners. When Entellus finally gains the upper hand, he batters Dares like hail (5.458–60), as Aeneas is battered in Book 10.803–10. The only other hail simile in the *Aeneid* occurs in 9.669–71, where it is used for the clamor of battle without reference to one side or the other. In short, there is some reason to see Entellus as a "Turnus figure," and the consequences of the fight should be interpreted in that light. For what marks the boxing match is a reversal of fortune: a temporarily defeated fighter rises up again, not only to gain a victory, but to sacrifice a substitute of his foreign opponent.

This chapter has treated a variety of episodes that at first appear unrelated (the Trojans' assumption of Greek armor; the deaths of Laocoön, Priam, Pyrrhus, and Haemonides; the boxing match). Taken together, however, these scenes form a pattern: role-reversal culminates in the sacrifice of the sometime victor or "priest." The scene for which this pattern provides a chilling prophecy is the confrontation of Aeneas and Turnus.

CHAPTER FIVE

Aeneas and Turnus

Homer sings of warriors seeking personal glory, Virgil of soldiers seeking the good of their community. This generalization is often made by those wishing to distinguish Virgil's particularly Roman aims in his reworking of Greek models, and there is much truth in it. It is somewhat ironic, therefore, that the *Iliad* should end with the response of a dying city to the death of the warrior who sustained it, whereas the *Aeneid* ends focused on the eyes and hands of individuals struggling with private grief.[1] These individuals nevertheless represent a historic struggle for *imperium*: as Aeneas bears on his shoulder the future of Rome, *famamque et fata nepotum*,[2] so Turnus embodies the totality of external forces that Aeneas must overcome. Yet Virgil suggests that these forces will linger even after Turnus' death—that the sacrifice of Turnus both foreshadows and necessitates the sacrifice of Aeneas.

One means of endowing Turnus with power beyond his own strength is to associate him in various ways with the Tiber. Chapter 2 discusses the menacing undertones in the Tiber's relationship

1. Wiltshire (1989) 137–38.

2. This closing phrase of Book 8 (731) is better left untranslated: literally it says "the fame and fates of his grandchildren." The word *imperium* is also difficult to translate; it means both "empire" and "the power to give commands that will be obeyed."

to Aeneas and suggests that Virgil continually reminds his readers of Aeneas' death in a river. Tiber's relationship to Turnus lacks such dark elements. The difference is highlighted by the parallelism in the beginnings and endings—both involving rivers—of Books 8 and 9.[3] Near the beginning of each book, Aeneas (8.69–70) and Turnus (9.22–24) dip their hands in the Tiber and pray. But Aeneas' prayer to the water nymphs and Tiber displaces the prayer that he should have prayed to Juno. Far from pacifying the goddess, his breach of Tiber's instructions merely adds to his list of *piacula*. Book 8 ends with an image of conquered peoples and conquered rivers, the last of which is the "Araxes chafing at his bridge" (*pontem indignatus Araxes*, 8.728). Book 9 ends with a vignette of harmony between the Italian leader and the Italian river, as Turnus, cornered by the Trojans, escapes into Tiber's nurturing waters:

> tum demum praeceps saltu sese omnibus armis
> in fluvium dedit. ille suo cum gurgite *flavo*
> accepit venientem ac mollibus extulit undis
> et *laetum sociis abluta caede remisit*. (9.815–18)

> Then, finally, headlong with a jump he gave himself to the river with all his arms. He [Tiber] received him [Turnus] with his *tawny* flood as he came, and brought him out with soft waves and sent him back *happy* to his allies, *with the gore washed away*.

Here the Tiber is not *caeruleus*, as he (ominously) described himself to Aeneas, but *flavus*, as he ought to be. Turnus is not only saved but purified, *abluta caede* ("with the gore washed away").[4] He returns to his allies happy, while Aeneas always returns to them in grief (4.396, 6.899). There is symmetry and contrast between Tiber's preternatural assistance to Aeneas in Book 8 and his simple welcome of Turnus in Book 9. Ancient readers were troubled by the river's apparent duplicity. Servius (ad 813) reports,

---

3. Hardie (1994) ad 9.22–24, 815-18.

4. See Le Gall (1953) 67–95 on the Romans' use of the Tiber's "sacred waters" in various rites of purification and purgation.

> sane quaerunt multi, cum Tiberis Aeneae faveat, cur liberavit Turnum.
>
> Of course, many ask why, since Tiber favors Aeneas, he freed Turnus.

His answer is less than satisfying:

> ob hoc Turnum esse liberatum, ut maior Aeneae gloria servaretur.
>
> Turnus was freed on this account, that greater glory might be preserved for Aeneas.

The comment of Servius Auctus is similarly unsupported by anything in the text:

> alii tradunt a Thybride, qui Aeneae favet, nunc Turnum in Iunonis gratiam esse servatum.
>
> Others say that Turnus was saved by Tiber, who favors Aeneas, as a favor to Juno.

As so often, the answer reveals less than the question. We are led to wonder whether it is not Turnus that Tiber "favors" after all.[5]

The suggestion that Turnus is Tiber's favorite is supported by a strange but significant allusion to a famous character in Roman history, Horatius Cocles. Horatius saved Rome from the wicked Lars Porsenna by defending the bridge across the Tiber until it could be destroyed. He then plunged prayerfully into the Tiber, in full armor, and swam across to safety. He was (and is) an exemplar of Roman virtue from ancient to modern times. Of Turnus' plunge into the Tiber, Hardie writes, "It is impossible here not to think of the famous leap of the great Roman patriot Horatius Cocles into the Tiber, alluded to at 8.650: T., throughout this book cast in the role of

5. Heinze (1993) 293 has a nice comment about the emotional tone of this episode: "it is as if the god himself could not help admiring the hero, he receives him in such a friendly way, and something which would endanger the lives of others is only a refreshing dip for Turnus."

a would-be sacker of Rome, at the end surprisingly takes on the role of one of the most famous saviors of the city."[6] Such a "surprising" allusion should cause us to reconsider not only the role of Turnus, but also that of the river who responds favorably to his plight.[7]

Turnus himself also is assimilated allusively to vengeful rivers clogged with corpses. After the Fury Allecto hurls her torch into his breast, he is compared to a simmering cauldron that comes to a leaping boil:

> magno veluti cum flamma sonore
> virgea suggeritur costis undantis aëni
> exsultantque aestu latices, furit intus aquai
> fumidus atque alte spumis exuberat amnis,
> nec iam se capit unda, volat vapor ater ad auras. (7.462–66)

> As when a flame of twigs with great sound is placed beneath the ribs of foaming bronze and the liquid leaps out with the heat, the smoking river of water rages within and jumps up high with its foam, nor does the wave now contain itself, the black vapor flies to the breezes.

This simile cleverly reworks an Iliadic scene. The Homeric river Xanthus, furious at Achilles for filling him with bodies, tries to

---

6. Hardie (1994) ad 9.815–18. This surprising confusion of moral boundaries is not unlike that occasioned by a simile describing Aeneas' *aristeia* in Book 10, where the founder of Rome is compared to an enemy of Jupiter's justice and order, the hundred-armed monster Aegaeon (10.565–70). See Hardie (1986) 154–56; O'Hara (1994) 217–24; Horsfall (1995) 114.

7. Aeneas' prayer to Tiber, *tuque o Thybri tuo cum flumine sancto* ("and you, Father Thybris, with your holy stream," 8.72), echoes an Ennian line that some scholars have supposed to be a prayer of Horatius, *teque pater Tiberine tuo cum flumine sancto* ("and you, Father Tiberinus, with your holy stream," *Ann.* 54 V2, 26 S). In Livy 2.10.11 Horatius utters a similar prayer, *Tiberine pater, te sancte precor, haec arma et hunc militem propitio flumine accipias* ("Father Tiberinus, I beg you, holy one, to receive these arms and this soldier with propitious stream"). It is more likely, however, that the Ennian line was spoken by Aeneas or Ilia. See Klingner (1967) 551–52; Knauer (1964) 279–80; Wigodsky (1972) 46, 62–63; Warmington (1956) 18; Skutsch (1985) 184–85; Gransden (1976) ad 8.72; Hardie (1994) ad 9.816. Hickson (1993) 141 observes that, out of all the prayers in the *Aeneid*, only this one is "phrased in such a way as to suggest that Vergil had in mind a traditional Latin prayer as a model."

drown the hero (*Il.* 21.300–27). The fire-god Hephaestus comes to Achilles' rescue by igniting the river, which boils like a cauldron:

> ὡς δὲ λέβης ζεῖ ἔνδον ἐπειγόμενος πυρὶ πολλῷ,
> κνίσην μελδόμενος ἁπαλοτρεφέος σιάλοιο,
> πάντοθεν ἀμβολάδην, ὑπὸ δὲ ξύλα κάγκανα κεῖται,
> ὣς τοῦ καλὰ ῥέεθρα πυρὶ φλέγετο, ζέε δ' ὕδωρ. (*Il.* 21.362–65)

> As a cauldron assailed by much fire boils within, melting the fat of the plump swine, spurting up everywhere, and the dry logs lie beneath it, so his lovely streams burned with fire, and his water boiled.

Fordyce dislikes Virgil's simile. His objections are revealing:

> Virgil elaborates into a simile (suggested, no doubt, by *Il.* xxi. 362 ff.) the common metaphor of *aestuare* ["boil"] or *fervere* ["seethe"], but the comparison of the surging passions in Turnus' breast to the heaving and bubbling of water in a pot over a roaring fire is not a very happy one: as in the description of the eating of the tables (see on 110 ff.), Virgil sets himself to invest commonplace things with epic dignity by enhancement of language—the extravagant *amnis* and *unda*, the poetic *latices*, the archaic *aquai*.[8]

Two of the words to which Fordyce objects, "the extravagant *amnis* ["river"] and *unda* ["wave"]," are precisely those which signal the Homeric model most clearly. Not only does Virgil make the daring leap from a common metaphor ("seething passion") to the unique simile of a river actually boiling, but his language encourages the reader to think of the Homeric context. Turnus is boiling *like the river Xanthus*. Fordyce's intuition that the Virgilian simile is "not a very happy one" is accurate—unless Virgil's aim was to associate the Italian hero with the enraged Homeric river.

A more oblique internal echo unites Turnus with both the Xanthus/Simois and the Tiber/(Numicus?). As discussed in chap-

8. Fordyce (1977) ad 7.462 ff.

ter 2, Virgil develops an association between the rivers of Troy and the rivers of Italy with the memorable and nearly identical lines describing the rolling of shields, helmets, and corpses by the Simois and Tiber, *scuta virum galeasque et fortia corpora volvit/volves* (1.101, 8.539). When in Book 12 Aeneas is treacherously wounded and withdraws from battle, Turnus is granted a brief *aristeia*:

> multa *virum* volitans dat *fortia corpora* leto.
> seminecis *volvit multos*. . . . (12.328–29)

> Flying, he gives many *strong bodies of men* to death. He *sends many rolling half-dead*. . . .

These lines subtly recall Aeneas' lines describing the clogged rivers. The meter and the number of syllables per word in lines 1.101, 8.539, and 12.328 are identical; the sound patterns are similar, especially *scuta virum galeas* and *multa virum volitans*; the phrase *fortia corpora* ("strong bodies"), which we might expect to be common in a war epic, occurs in these three places only; and the phrase *volvit multos* ("sends many rolling") used of Turnus recalls the rolling of many bodies by the bloody Simois and Tiber (*tot Simois . . . volvit*, "the Simois rolls so many," 1.100–101; *quam multa . . . volves / Thybri*, "how many you will roll, Tiber," 8.538–40). Turnus, then, in addition to being favored by the Tiber, momentarily encapsulates its vengeful resentment of the foreign invader Aeneas.[9]

Another passage emphasizing the Italian countryside's preference for Turnus also alludes to Aeneas' manner of death. Just before the final interview between Juno and Jupiter, Aeneas is thwarted in his pursuit of Turnus by Latinus' father Faunus, whose sacred tree the Trojans impiously cut down. This tree is sacred for a strange reason:

> Forte sacer Fauno foliis oleaster amaris
> hic steterat, nautis olim venerabile lignum,

---

9. On the resentment of the conquered, see Lyne (1983). Turnus is explicitly compared to the Nile in a simile (9.30–32) that comes soon after the description on the Shield of the mourning Nile receiving Antony and Cleopatra into its cerulean bosom (8.711–13, discussed in chap. 2).

> *servati ex undis* ubi figere dona solebant
> Laurenti divo et votas suspendere vestis.
> sed stirpem Teucri nullo discrimine sacrum
> sustulerant, puro ut possent concurrere campo. (12.766–71)

> By chance a wild olive with bitter leaves, sacred to Faunus, had stood here, wood once venerable to sailors, where those *saved from the waves* used to fasten their gifts and hang up votive clothing for the Laurentian god. But the Teucrians had destroyed the sacred trunk indiscriminately, that they might do battle on a clear field.

Servius Auctus alerts us to a problem that troubled ancient readers (ad 768):

> et quaeritur, cur terreno deo nautae dona suspenderent?

> And it is asked, why would sailors hang up gifts to a god of dry land?

Why indeed?[10] His answer is unconvincing:

> quia constat omnes in periculis suis deos patrios invocare et ideo illis vota solvere, quorum familiarius numen opitulari sibi credant.

10. On the dedication of clothing upon salvation from shipwreck, see Nisbet and Hubbard (1970) ad Horace *Odes* 1.5.13–16. The poet, after being "shipwrecked" by Pyrrha, hangs up his wet clothes to the god (or goddess?) of the sea:

> me tabula sacer
> votiva paries indicat uvida
> suspendisse potenti
> vestimenta maris deo [or: deae].

> The sacred wall indicates with a votive tablet that I have hung up my wet clothes to the powerful god [or: goddess] of the sea.

Whether we read *deo* (Neptune) or *deae* (Venus, born from the foam—an emendation that Nisbet and Hubbard prefer), either divinity would be appropriate to the situation of the poet, shipwrecked on the sea of love. Nisbet and Hubbard compare Diodorus *anth. P.* 6. 245. 3–5, in which a saved sailor hangs up a robe outside a temple for one of the Cabiri. These divinities, later conflated with the Dioscuri, are (among other things) traditionally protectors of sailors.

> Because it is agreed that all, in their times of danger, invoke the gods of their fathers, and therefore pay vows to those gods whose more familiar divinity they believe will help them.

If such offerings to "familiar" rather than to appropriate gods were a normal occurrence, the question would never have arisen. More importantly, even if it were not odd for sailors to hang votive offerings to a rural land divinity, why would Virgil mention such a detail at this point? Faunus was in no way associated with the sea—but he was associated with the Tiber. The island in the middle of the river housed an ancient shrine of Faunus, and it is probable that river boatmen, sometimes called *nautae*, made thank-offerings to the god upon being saved from the *Tiber*'s waves.[11] Though Aeneas was once "saved from the waves" of the sea (*servatum ex undis*, 3.209), the Trojans' impious treatment of the sacred tree provides another hint that he may not be so lucky with regard to a river. Just as Tiber saves Turnus at a critical moment, so the god residing (the poet reminds us) on Tiber's island responds favorably to Turnus' prayer.

In addition to these suggestions of alliance or association between Turnus and a river hostile to Aeneas, Virgil also hints that the deaths of Aeneas and Turnus are linked.[12] One way is by manipulating a memorable Homeric passage set during the combat of Hector and Achilles. Homer's Zeus reveals unambiguously what the outcome of their final duel will be:

---

11. This highly plausible explanation of the Virgilian puzzle is put forth by Holland (1961) 158.

12. It is tempting to see in Turnus' *animam . . . devovi*, "I have devoted my life" (11.440–42), a reference to the Roman practice of *devotio*, in which a general offered himself as a sacrifice to the gods in exchange for his army's victory over the enemy (see Livy 8.9, 10.28). The objections of Pascal (1990) to seeing Turnus' declaration and subsequent actions as a "real" *devotio* are cogent. Nevertheless, it is reasonable to see, with Leigh (1993), allusive "traces" of *devotio* in Turnus and other characters. Thomas (1998) 285, following Leigh, states that "Turnus qualifies eminently." Fantham (1999) 277, following Hardie (1993) 28, sees in Turnus' declaration an idiosyncratic and ultimately ineffective reference to *devotio* (since Turnus becomes an *unwilling* victim), but a reference nonetheless. On the parallel issue of the *devotio* of Dido, see chap. 4, n. 3.

> καὶ τότε δὴ χρύσεια πατὴρ ἐτίταινε τάλαντα,
> ἐν δὲ τίθει δύο κῆρε τανηλεγέος θανάτοιο,
> τὴν μὲν Ἀχιλλῆος, τὴν δ' Ἕκτορος ἱπποδάμοιο,
> ἕλκε δὲ μέσσα λαβών· ῥέπε δ' Ἕκτορος αἴσιμον ἦμαρ,
> ᾤχετο δ' εἰς Ἀΐδαο, λίπεν δέ ἑ Φοῖβος Ἀπόλλων.
> (*Il.* 22.209–13)

> And then the Father balanced his golden scales, and put in two fates of wretched death, the one of Achilles, the other of Hector tamer of horses, and held and drew them up by the middle: and Hector's day of doom sank, and went down to Hades, and Phoebus Apollo left him.

Virgil's lines clearly echo these, but with Jupiter's final decision left unstated:

> Iuppiter ipse duas aequato examine lances
> sustinet et fata imponit diversa duorum,
> quem damnet labor et quo vergat pondere letum.
> (12.725–27)

> Jupiter himself raises the two dishes in his balanced scale and puts in the different fates of the two men, whom the struggle would condemn [or: free?] and whither death would incline with its weight [or: with which weight death would incline].

It is typical of Virgil to leave implicit what Homer makes explicit. We are encouraged to extrapolate the outcome of Jupiter's action from that of Zeus' action, in which Hector's scale falls. But there is a problem. After reading about the *two* dishes, and the *different* fates of the *two* men—"Virgil goes far beyond Homer in his emphasis on words of duality"[13]—our expectation is strong that the neatly divided line that follows will say something like "who would die and who would live." The Latin, however, does not say this: it says, in effect, "who would die *and who would die*." Servius goes to great

13. Hardie (1993) 26.

lengths to find opposed rather than parallel meanings in *quem damnet labor* and *quo vergat pondere letum*:

> DAMNET LABOR liberet, <id est quem voto liberet labor proeliandi, parta scilicet victoria, quoniam unusquisque ob incolumitatem recuperatam votis exsolvitur, id est liberatur explicitis sacrificiis,> ut <est> "damnabis tu quoque votis". <non nulli sic tradunt: quem labor suus liberet, quem mors urgeat: nam in iure cum dicitur 'damnas esto', hoc est 'damnatus esto ut des', hoc est damno te ut des, neque alias liber eris. quidam 'labor' pro militia intellegunt.>

> LABOR CONDEMNS frees, <i.e., whom the labor of fighting frees from his vow—when victory has been won, of course—because each man, on account of his regained safety, is released from his vows, i.e., is freed, when the sacrifices have been fully performed,> as <is the case with> "you, too, will oblige them to fulfill their vows." <Some explain it thus: whom his labor frees, whom death presses: for in law, when it is said "let it stand that you are obliged," that means, "let it stand that you have been obliged to give," which means, I oblige you to give, and you will not be free otherwise. Some understand "labor" as standing for "fighting.">

The tortuous translation reflects the difficulty in taking *damnet* to mean "frees" rather than "condemns."[14] Even if the Latin can be contorted into the former meaning, no unbiased reader naturally would take it that way. We are compelled either to see the line as referring twice to the fate of the loser, which contradicts the expectation created by the emphasis on duality in the previous lines, or to see a suggestion that the "diverse fates of the two men" may be more similar than they appear. The balanced scales, the balanced line—there is an indication that the fate of *both* men is death.

---

14. Williams (1973) ad 12.727 comments that Servius' interpretation "is followed by some modern commentators and translators, but seems unlikely in the highest degree."

Another link between the deaths of Aeneas and Turnus is implied in Virgil's allusions to the tragic Ajax, the most famous male suicide in Greek mythology. In Aeneas' parting lines to Ascanius,

> disce, puer, virtutem ex me verumque laborem,
> fortunam ex aliis, (435–36)

> Boy, learn virtue and true labor from me, but fortune from others,

there is an echo of the Ajax of Sophocles (550–51) and especially of Accius' translation of the Sophoclean lines:

> virtuti sis par, dispar fortunis patris. (*trag.* 156)

> may you equal your father in virtue, but not in fortunes.

Aeneas' one speech to his son thus recalls the prelude to a suicide. This allusion is buttressed by the surprising epithet *Rhoeteius* applied to Aeneas (12.456), for Rhoeteium was a town in the Troad most famous for containing the tomb of Ajax.[15] Both allusions specifically recall the warrior's death. By meeting Turnus in battle, Aeneas is also, indirectly, bringing about his own demise.[16]

Finally, the similarity of Turnus and Aeneas, both of whom are subject to the gods' wrath, emerges from the simile of the bullfight that precedes the image of Jupiter's scales. The bulls resemble boxers, and themes that pervade Virgil's boxing match (5.362–484)—revenge, confusion of moral boundaries, and human versus animal sacrifices[17]—are replayed in the single combat between Aeneas

15. Lyne (1987) 8-12.

16. Wigodsky (1972) 96–97: "the echo of Accius 156 in XII 435–36 may be intended as another of the reversals of roles that play so important a part in the poem, implying that even in his victory it is Aeneas who is truly a victim of destiny, like Dido and like Ajax." Traina (1994) 24–26 observes that Virgil is alluding not only to the tragic Ajax but to the epic Hector (*Il.* 6.476–81); he sees Aeneas' bitterness in this speech as a point of contact with Turnus. Rowland (1992) 237–43 argues for a more positive reading of the allusion, with *Rhoeteius* emphasizing that Aeneas, like Ajax, will be "enshrined and venerated" (239).

17. On the sexual element that also characterizes the bullfights, see Lyne (1987) 238.

and Turnus. The bullfight simile in Book 12 also introduces the shadow of Juno:

> ac velut ingenti *Sila* summove *Taburno*
> cum duo conversis *inimica in proelia tauri*
> frontibus incurrunt, pavidi cessere magistri,
> stat pecus omne metu mutum, mussantque iuvencae
> quis nemori imperitet, quem tota armenta sequantur;
> illi inter sese multa vi vulnera miscent
> cornuaque obnixi infigunt et sanguine largo
> colla armosque lavant, gemitu nemus omne remugit:
> non aliter Tros Aeneas et Daunius heros
> concurrunt clipeis, ingens fragor aethera complet. (12.715–24)

> And as on huge *Sila* or the top of *Taburnus* when two *bulls* rush together *into enemy battle* with foreheads opposed, the fearful herders have withdrawn, the whole herd stands mute with dread, and the cows mutter about who is to rule the wood, whom the whole flock is to follow; the bulls mix wounds between themselves with much violence, and butting they drive in their horns and wash their necks and flanks with much blood, the whole wood bellows back with groaning: not otherwise do Trojan Aeneas and the Daunian hero clash with their shields, a huge crash fills the ether.

The names of the mountains in the simile (Sila and Taburnus) are reminiscent of the Latin words for "gadfly" (*asilus* and *tabanus*)[18]—a reminder of Juno's persecution of Io, the unfortunate mistress of Jupiter who was transformed into a cow and pursued relentlessly by a stinging fly sent by his jealous wife. Io is at the center of Turnus' shield (7.789-92).[19] Juno's persecution of the "bulls" is further reinforced by an echo of the bullfight simile in her final speech. She

18. Thomas (1982) 84.

19. Ross (1987) 160 observes that "it was not just coincidence that Io's frenzy occurred to Virgil more than once as he contemplated the actions of Turnus and Juno in the *Aeneid*, a frenzy summing up through suggestion the great themes of passion and its inevitable madness, conflict, historical causation, divine vengeance

declares petulantly that if she had her way, she would not be a mere spectator in the final battle, but an active participant:

> "sed flammis cincta sub ipsa
> starem acie traheremque *inimica in proelia Teucros.*"
> (12.811–12)
>
> "But girded with flames I would stand at the very line of fighting and draw the *Trojans into enemy battle.*"

The phrase *inimica in proelia* ("into enemy battle") occurs in Virgil's corpus only here and in the line *inimica in proelia tauri* (12.716) less than a hundred lines before. The echo, like the allusion to gadflies, reminds us of Juno's desire for bloodshed.[20] In Apollonius' boxing match, the fighters are compared to fighting bulls, then to sacrificial bulls; at the end of Virgil's boxing match, a bull is sacrificed; at the end of the *Aeneid,* Turnus is sacrificed. Juno's implicit presence in the bullfight simile takes on an added dimension when seen in this context. Virgil's poetry suggests that she represents the motivation for, and the recipient of, these sacrifices.

Turnus, then, plays a dual role in prefiguring Aeneas' death. The Italian hero represents the resentment of the Italian countryside, which will exact vengeance for Aeneas' intrusion; yet Turnus also is to become, like Aeneas, the victim of the gods' irresistible power. The next chapter explores the implications of that power both for Aeneas and for Rome.

---

and anger (Juno's)." He also notes that the references to Inachus, Io's father, in connection with Juno (7.286) and Turnus (7.372) reinforce the importance of the Io legend in Turnus' background.

There is a faint association of the bovine Io with the bull that is the prize for the boxing match in the unusual monosyllabic line-end *bos* used to describe the two (and appearing nowhere else in Virgil's works). Io is described, *iam saetis obsita, iam bos* ("now covered with bristles, now a cow," 7.790); the prize animal "falls to the ground" in the words *procumbit humi bos* (5.481).

20. Briggs (1980) 50 points out a verbal parallel that similarly reinforces the association between Turnus and sacrificial bulls. The line introducing Turnus in the catalogue of warriors, *Ipse inter primos praestanti corpore Turnus* ("Turnus himself among the first men, with outstanding body," 7.783), echoes the line describing the bulls that Aristaeus must sacrifice in the *Georgics, quattuor eximios praestanti corpore tauros* ("four excellent bulls with outstanding body," *Geo.* 4.538 = 550).

CHAPTER SIX

JUNO'S *HONORES*

Juno is savage (*saeva*, 1.4).[1] A happy resolution of the poem would seem to depend upon overcoming, decisively, the hostility and chaos that she represents.[2] Virgil chooses not to set our minds entirely at rest. Putnam's essay "Tragic Victory" ushered in a new era of Virgilian scholarship by posing the question, Does Juno actually win?[3] The "optimist" would say that she does not—that her *furor* and *ira* have been turned to the service of a higher good manifested in the will of Jupiter and Aeneas.[4] The "pessimist" would say that she does—that her *furor* and *ira* have penetrated the fabric of the universe and infected the will of Jupiter and Aeneas. The latter view seems better supported by the text: through Virgil's carefully crafted

---

1. On the appropriateness of this epithet, and the attempts of ancient commentators to explain it away, see Knox (1997).

2. Feeney (1991) 134: "What threatens the Trojan and Vergilian enterprise from the beginning is a multivalent frustrating negativity which finds actualization in one character, Juno, whose words and actions are powerfully represented through the medium of various authoritative reading conventions. Each manner of looking at 'Juno' gives something hostile and destructive: chaos threatens from all directions, from history, myth, and nature." Pöschl (1962) 18 characterizes the contrast between Jupiter and Juno as a symbol "of the struggle between light and darkness, mind and emotion, order and chaos, which incessantly pervades the cosmos, the soul, and politics."

3. Putnam (1965) 151–201.

4. See, e.g., Galinsky (1988); Stahl (1990); Hardie (1986) 176–80.

parallels, Aeneas' wrath toward Turnus at the end of the poem resembles Juno's wrath toward himself at the beginning.[5] But this is not the only way in which the sacrifice of Turnus represents a victory for Juno. She is pacified only by the promise of endless human sacrifices.

Virgil never tells us where Juno goes after her final interview with Jupiter, and certain details of the scene suggest that she will remain an active force after the poem's end.[6] One such detail is the parallel between her situation at the end of the poem and that of Aeneas in Book 4. Jupiter asks Juno the ostensibly rhetorical question,

> "*quid struis? aut qua spe* gelidis in nubibus haeres?" (12.796)
>
> "*What are you building? Or with what hope* do you cling in the icy clouds?"

When Aeneas was stalled from his mission by his affair with Dido, Jupiter asked his messenger Mercury a similar rhetorical question about Aeneas' behavior:

> "*quid struit? aut qua spe* inimica in gente moratur . . . ?" (4.235)
>
> "*What is he building? Or with what hope* does he delay among an enemy people . . . ?"

Mercury had dutifully repeated this question to Aeneas, with a variation:

> "*quid struis? aut qua spe* Libycis teris otia terris?" (4.271)
>
> "*What are you building? Or with what hope* do you waste your leisure in the Libyan land?"

The half-line "quid struis/t? aut qua spe" is one of only two from Jupiter's mouth that are repeated in the *Aeneid*, even though Mer-

5. See, e.g., Putnam (1965) 200–201, (1995) 4; Hardie (1993) 33–34; Boyle (1993) 93–94; Knox (1997) 231–33.

6. See Feeney (1984).

cury's speech is ostensibly a faithful rendition of Jupiter's words to him.[7] In addition, its first appearance (4.235) is a metrical anomaly, with the long *spe* before *inimica* "the only case in the *Aeneid* of a monosyllable in such a hiatus retaining its long quantity."[8] By repeating this memorable hemistich,[9] Virgil apparently wishes the reader to hear an echo of Jupiter's message to Aeneas in his chastisement of Juno. Jupiter's admonition spurred Aeneas to leave Carthage, ending one episode but beginning a new series of adventures. Juno's final action in the poem is to leave the cloud from which she has been observing the battle:

> adnuit his Iuno et mentem laetata retorsit;
> interea excedit caelo nubemque relinquit. (12.841–42)

> Juno agreed to these conditions, and, happily, wrenched back her mind; meanwhile, she leaves heaven and abandons the cloud.

Where does she go? After hearing that Juno "happily wrenched back her mind," the reader expects to hear that she went home, never to trouble Aeneas again.[10] We hear instead, in the puzzling present tense (*excedit, relinquit*) introduced by the puzzling adverb "meanwhile" (*interea*), that she leaves heaven and abandons her cloud.

---

7. The other is *tantarum gloria rerum* ("the glory of such great things," 4.232b = 272b). Heinze (1993) 316–17 and 363 observes that Mercury's speech is the only example in the *Aeneid* of "having an errand carried out in the same words with which it was given." Unlike Homer, however, Virgil employs *variatio* even in this pair of speeches, thus making the repetition of 4.235a the more remarkable. See Highet (1972) 334 for a list of Jupiter's speeches, Moskalew (1982) 194–245 for a list of repetitions in the *Aeneid*.

8. Pease (1935) ad 4.235, who also cites 4.271 and 12.796 as comparanda for *quid struit?*, without commenting further on thematic reasons for the echo.

9. The line has drawn much commentary; see Austin (1955) ad 4.235, who suggests that the pause is "as if Jupiter were musing over the possible reasons for Aeneas' behaviour, or trying to decide exactly how to refer to the Carthaginians."

10. Johnson (1976) 127 has an interesting suggestion for a secondary meaning of *adnuit his Juno et mentem laetata retorsit:* "The mild catachresis, *mentem retorsit*, is naturally taken as Lewis and Short take it, 'she changed her mind.' But suppose it means also, *his mentem retorsit*? That is, she openly assents to what Jupiter says, but, in her mind, she turns away from his words, rejects them?"

Logic would dictate that a god who leaves heaven must go to earth, as Athena does in the closest Homeric model for this scene (*Od.* 24.473–88). Virgil's silence about Juno's destination leaves open the possibility that her intervention in human affairs is far from ended. The parallel with Aeneas leaving Carthage hints that it may be just beginning.

Jupiter's final speech answers two of the crucial questions asked at the beginning of the poem. When Juno offers to stop persecuting Aeneas on the condition that the name of Troy be obliterated (12.808–28), Jupiter smilingly concedes:

> "es germana Iovis Saturnique altera proles,
> *irarum tantos volvis sub pectore fluctus.*
> verum age et inceptum frustra summitte furorem:
> do quod vis, et me victusque volensque remitto." (12.830–33)

> "You are the sister of Jupiter and the other offspring of Saturn, *such great floods of wrath do you roll beneath your heart!* Come now, and lay down your fury, taken up in vain: I grant what you wish, and, conquered, willingly, defer."

His admission that they are two of a kind in the "floods of wrath beneath their hearts" is all in good fun.[11] Nevertheless, coming from the highest authority in the universe, right before he proclaims ex cathedra the destiny of Rome, the jest has an ominous ring. When after his speech he summons a Dira to send to Turnus (12.845–54)—as Juno had summoned the Fury Allecto (7.323–40)—this conjugal similarity is confirmed.[12] There could be no clearer answer to the

---

11. On the Lucretian resonances in this scene, see Dyson (1997a) 454–56.

12. As Knox (1997) 228 notes, this is the only time in the poem that the adjective *saevus* is used of Jupiter (12.849). See Johnson (1976) 127; Lyne (1987) 90–94. It is a vexed question whether the Dirae are identical to the Furies, and in particular whether the Dira sent by Jupiter is in fact Allecto. Mackie (1992) 354–56 adduces inscriptional evidence from Southern Italian vase paintings to show that the Dirae and the Furies are probably the same group, consisting of Allecto, Megaera, and Tisiphone. He well summarizes the way in which scholars tend either to differentiate or to assimilate the groups "in accordance with more general perceptions of the poem" (353). He is right to point out that Virgil leaves the matter ambiguous.

question posed at the end of the proem, *tantaene animis caelestibus irae?* ("is wrath so great in celestial hearts?" 1.11).[13]

The second question answered by Jupiter has implications as chilling as the first. Juno's opening speech ends with the jealous fear that she will not receive due *honor,* here clearly meaning "sacrifice":

> "ast ego, quae divum incedo regina, Iovisque
> et soror et coniunx, una cum gente tot annos
> bella gero. et quisquam numen Iunonis adorat
> praeterea aut supplex aris imponet *honorem*?" (1.46–49)

> "But I, who stride as queen of the gods, and both sister and wife of Jupiter, wage war with one people for so many years. And does anyone adore the divinity of Juno anymore, or will he, suppliant, place a *sacrifice* on her altars?"

After describing the mingling of Aeneas' stock with that of the native Italians, Jupiter concludes with the assurance that the new race will honor Juno like no other:

> "hinc genus Ausonio mixtum quod sanguine surget,
> supra homines, supra ire deos *pietate* videbis,
> nec gens ulla tuos aeque celebrabit *honores*." (12.838–40)

> "The race that will arise hence, mixed with Ausonian blood, you will see go beyond men, beyond the gods in *piety*, nor will any people equally celebrate your *sacrifices*."

The last word of Jupiter, *honores,* responds to the last word of Juno's opening speech. His characterization of the future Romans, with its implicit equation of *pietas* and sacrifice to Juno, has dark and far-reaching implications. As Aeneas stands over the suppliant freshly killed, we see the truth of this equation. In the proem, the *ira* of Juno was a foil to the *pietas* of Aeneas (1.8–11); in the sacrifice of Turnus, *ira* and *pietas* have united in the service of revenge.[14]

---

13. See Feeney (1991) 130.

14. See Boyle (1999) 155: "Juno's wrath seems placated only when Aeneas becomes its agent."

For this union culminating in human sacrifice Virgil had a potent model in the events of his own day. Though the mature Augustus would have preferred to forget it, an incident from the uncertain early years of his principate could not be erased entirely from the memories of his fellow citizens. After the subjugation of Perusia in 40 B.C., historians tell us, he avenged his father by sacrificing 300 knights and senators at the altar of Divus Julius.[15] Whether he hoped that this act would restore the *pax deorum* we will never know. We do know that what followed was not peace but a decade of bloody civil war.[16]

♦ ♦ ♦

Most interpretations of the *Aeneid*, even "pessimistic" ones, view the sacrifice of Turnus as a painful but necessary means of furthering Roman imperial goals. Readers may disagree about whether that sacrifice is worth it, but most assume that, in some sense, it "works."[17] The purpose of the first half of this book has been to unsettle this assumption. Many of the *Aeneid*'s sacrifices, from the ritual slaughter of animals to the more symbolic offering of humans, are characterized by failures that in Roman practice would have demanded expiation. Repeated allusions to the tradition of Aeneas' death, images of priest-become-victim, and ominous links between Turnus and Aeneas foretell the sacrifice of the hero himself. The second part of this study approaches the theme of "sacrificial victory" from another angle: Virgil's sustained allusion to a mysterious Roman cult with reciprocal sacrifice at its center.

---

15. Kraggerud (1987) argues that this sacrifice may have been a figment of anti-Augustan propaganda rather than an actual event. But it does not follow that the alleged event had no bearing on Virgil's poetic imagination. Rumor can be as potent as reality. On ancient sources for and attitudes toward the incident, see Dyson (1996a) 284–85; Gurval (1995) 176–77.

16. See Lyne (1983) 334: "Unless . . . a victor is prepared to extend tactical forgiveness, a sequence of honour, dishonour, vengeance, and vengeance in return, may never end."

17. See, e.g., Hardie (1993) 28: "The successful sacrifice of Turnus brings to an end the series of misfortunes inaugurated by the failure to sacrifice Sinon." Otis (1964) 382 sees it as an advance in the progress of civilization: "Aeneas thus stands for a new idea in history, the idea that *violentia* and *superbia* can be controlled, that a just *imperium* can be established, that universal peace can be a fact as well as an ideal."

PART TWO

The Ghastly Priest

CHAPTER SEVEN

THE GOLDEN BOUGH

It is one of the ironies of intellectual and literary history that the monumental work entitled *The Golden Bough* has had no appreciable effect on Virgilian scholarship. This is partly because few who own Sir James Frazer's book actually read it.[1] The section most likely to be read, however—the first five pages or so—brings a startling religious and anthropological perspective to bear on a central passage of the *Aeneid*. Frazer's introduction is worth quoting at some length, for his words will convey most vividly the seductive elegance, faulty logic, and imperial chauvinism that have obscured the issue he treats.[2] His romantic portrait of the *Rex Nemorensis* is followed by his summary, nearly accurate, of the cult's key features:

---

1. Beard (1992) 223: "The success of *The Golden Bough* rests on the undeniable fact that it is so rarely read." This is the punchline of her trenchant analysis of Frazer's popularity; see especially 216–23 on the themes that contribute to the book's perennial appeal.

2. Frazer's place in the anthropological pantheon is summarized thus by Griffin (1998) 44: "Modern writers are careful to distance themselves from anything that seems to imply, as Frazer's book did, that some forms of religion are superior to others, or that some beliefs or practices are less rational, or less sophisticated; and denunciations of Frazer are *de rigueur* for modern anthropological writers. Sometimes, indeed, one could feel that these writers form a kind of tribe—we might call them the Anthropologi—for whom Frazer is a kind of evil spirit, whose influence must be kept away by constant ritual utterances: in fact by what is sometimes called apotropaic magic."

Who does not know Turner's picture of the Golden Bough? The scene, suffused with the golden glow of imagination in which the divine mind of Turner steeped and transfigured even the fairest natural landscape, is a dream-like vision of the little woodland lake of Nemi, "Diana's Mirror," as it was called by the ancients. No one who has seen that calm water, lapped in a green hollow of the Alban hills, can ever forget it. . . .

In antiquity this sylvan landscape was the scene of a strange and recurring tragedy. On the northern shore of the lake, right under the precipitous cliffs on which the modern village of Nemi is perched, stood the sacred grove and sanctuary of Diana Nemorensis, or Diana of the Wood. The lake and the grove were sometimes known as the lake and grove of Aricia. But the town of Aricia (the modern La Ricca) was situated about three miles off, at the foot of the Alban Mount, and separated by a steep descent from the lake, which lies in a small crater-like hollow on the mountain side. In this sacred grove there grew a certain tree round which at any time of the day and probably far into the night a strange figure might be seen to prowl. In his hand he carried a drawn sword, and he kept peering warily about him as if every instant he expected to be set upon by an enemy. He was a priest and a murderer; and the man for whom he looked was sooner or later to murder him and hold the priesthood in his stead. Such was the rule of the sanctuary. A candidate for the priesthood could only succeed to office by slaying the priest, and having slain him he held office till he was himself slain by a stronger or a craftier.

This strange rule has no parallel in classical antiquity, and cannot be explained from it. To find an explanation we must go farther afield. No one will probably deny that such a custom savours of a barbarous age and, surviving into imperial times, stands out in striking isolation from the polished Italian society of the day, like a primeval rock rising from a smooth-shaven lawn. . . .

> I begin by setting forth the few facts and legends which have come down to us on the subject. According to one story the worship of Diana at Nemi was instituted by Orestes, who, after killing Thoas, King of the Tauric Chersonese (the Crimea), fled with his sister to Italy, bringing with him the image of the Tauric Diana. The bloody ritual which legend ascribed to that goddess is familiar to classical readers; it is said that every stranger who landed on the shore was sacrificed on her altar. But transported to Italy, the rite assumed a milder form. Within the sanctuary at Nemi grew a certain tree of which no branch might be broken. Only a runaway slave was allowed to break off, if he could, one of its boughs. Success in the attempt entitled him to fight the priest in single combat, and if he slew him he reigned in his stead with the title of King of the Wood (Rex Nemorensis). Tradition averred that the fateful branch was that Golden Bough which, at the Sibyl's bidding, Aeneas plucked before he essayed the perilous journey to the world of the dead. . . .[3]

Frazer travels the world before returning to Nemi, explaining the barbarous rites of Diana Nemorensis by analogy with other societies. He argues that in many cultures the life of the community is magically bound to the life of the king, whose strength must never be allowed to fail; the sacred tree represents the spirit of the king, and the combat initiated by breaking the bough ensures that the younger and stronger will prevail. He observes that "tradition" (*publica opinio*) connected the branch in the Arician grove with Virgil's Golden Bough. Elevating this connection to an equation, and taking literally Virgil's simile comparing the Golden Bough to mistletoe on an oak tree, he conjectures that the bough on the sacred tree at Nemi must have been mistletoe. If the oak represented the king, the mistletoe represented the king's vulnerable "external soul." He ultimately explains the priest at Nemi by analogy with the Nordic god Balder, who was killed by a shaft of mistletoe.

3. Frazer (1890) 1–4.

Nearly all of Frazer's arguments are based on fanciful conjectures and false analogies, and most readers concur in rejecting any connection between Virgil's Golden Bough and the Arician cult.[4] Perhaps the most obvious flaw is his statement that the bough of the sacred tree at Nemi "was" the Golden Bough plucked by Aeneas. This equation is essential for his purposes (largely because of the mistletoe connection), but it is patently absurd to say that a tree at Nemi and a tree at Cumae are the same tree. To dismantle his theory one need go no further.

The ancient source from which Frazer derives the equation, however, does not say quite what he claims it does. Virgil's description of the Golden Bough leads Servius to describe a cult in which the breaking of a bough from a sacred tree precedes combat between an incumbent and a challenger (ad 6.136). Although Servius' comment also may be a mixture of fact and fancy, it is likely to be accurate on an essential point that Frazer glosses over:

> LATET ARBORE OPACA AVREVS licet de hoc ramo hi qui de sacris Proserpinae scripsisse dicuntur, quiddam esse mysticum adfirment, publica tamen opinio hoc habet. Orestes post occisum regem Thoantem in regione Taurica cum sorore Iphigenia, ut supra diximus, fugit et Dianae simulacrum inde sublatum haud longe ab Aricia collocavit. in huius templo post

4. For instance, Michels (1945) 59 considers it unlikely that "so eminently civilized a person as Vergil should introduce this literary and intellectual passage, and the teaching which it conveys, by a rather pointless allusion to a bloody survival of primitive ritual." Austin (1977) ad 6.138 f. says that the legend "has no definable relevance to Virgil: Servius does not identify the *aureus ramus* with the branch plucked from the tree at Aricia; he merely says that Virgil 'istum inde sumpsit colorem,' and that the legend accounted for the poet's association of the death of Misenus (149 ff.) with the finding of the Bough." Horsfall (1991) 23 sees no need for an allusion to "quei riti complicati e crudeli" ("those complicated and cruel rites"). West (1987) 228 labels Frazer's "parade of Scandinavian deities" as "Balderdash." The most comprehensive rebuttal to date is that of Smith (1978); see especially 220–21 for a list of the few scholars who have accepted Frazer's "identification" and the many who have "flatly rejected it." Beard (1993) 174 summarizes objections to Frazer's theses and evidence for Frazer's own second thoughts about equating Virgil's Golden Bough with the bough at Nemi. Notable exceptions are Merkelbach (1961) 86–90; Clark (1979) 202–203; and, most importantly, Green (2000).

mutatum ritum sacrificiorum fuit arbor quaedam, de qua infringi ramum non licebat. dabatur autem fugitivis potestas, ut si quis exinde ramum potuisset auferre, monomachia cum fugitivo templi sacerdote dimicaret: nam fugitivus illic erat sacerdos ad priscae imaginem fugae. dimicandi autem dabatur facultas quasi ad pristini sacrificii reparationem. nunc ergo *istum inde sumpsit colorem*. ramus enim necesse erat ut et unius causa esset interitus: unde et statim mortem subiungit Miseni: et ad sacra Proserpinae accedere nisi sublato ramo non poterat. inferos autem subire hoc dicit, sacra celebrare Proserpinae. de reditu autem animae hoc est: novimus Pythagoram Samium vitam humanam divisisse in modum Y litterae, scilicet quod prima aetas incerta sit, quippe quae adhuc se nec vitiis nec virtutibus dedit: bivium autem Y litterae a iuventute incipere, quo tempore homines aut vitia, id est partem sinistram, aut virtutes, id est dexteram partem sequuntur: unde ait Persius "traducit trepidas ramosa in compita mentes." ergo per ramum virtutes dicit esse sectandas, qui est Y litterae imitatio: quem ideo in silvis dicit latere, quia re vera in huius vitae confusione et maiore parte vitiorum virtus et integritas latet. alii dicunt inde ramo aureo inferos peti, quod divitiis facile mortales intereunt. Tiberianus "aurum, quo pretio reserantur limina Ditis."

IN THE SHADY TREE THE GOLD [BRANCH] LIES HIDDEN Although concerning this branch those who are said to have written about the rites of Proserpina assert that it is something related to the mysteries, yet the common opinion (*publica opinio*) holds the following. After the slaying of King Thoas in the Tauric region, Orestes fled with his sister Iphigenia, as we said above [ad 2.116], and placed the image of Diana that he had taken from there not far from Aricia. In her sanctuary, after the rite of sacrifices was changed, there was a certain tree from which it was not permitted that a branch be broken off. However, the power was given to fugitives that, if one had been able to carry off a branch from there, he would fight

> in single combat with the fugitive priest of the sanctuary: for the priest there was a fugitive, in imitation of the ancient flight. But this ability to fight was given as if to make reparation for the original sacrifice. Now, therefore, *he has taken thence this shade of meaning*. For it was necessary that the branch be the cause also of one untimely death: whence he also immediately puts next the death of Misenus: and it was not possible to approach the rites of Proserpina unless a branch had been carried away. Now to go down to the Underworld means this, to celebrate the rites of Proserpina. About the return of the soul, there is this: we know that Pythagoras of Samos divided human life in the manner of the letter Y, that is, because the first age is uncertain, in that it has as yet given itself neither to vices nor to virtues: but the branching of the letter Y begins from adolescence, at which time men pursue either vices, i.e., the left part, or virtues, i.e., the right part. Whence Persius says "he leads across anxious minds to branching crossroads." Therefore by means of the branch, which is the imitation of the letter Y, he says that virtues ought to be followed: which [branch] he says lies hidden in the forest on this account, that in actual fact in the confusion of this life and the greater part of vices virtue and integrity lie hidden. Others say that the Underworld is to be approached with a golden branch for this reason, that mortals are easily destroyed by riches. Tiberianus [says] "gold, by which price the threshold of Dis is thrown open."

We can probably reject what Servius says about the branch representing the crossroads of virtue and vice (any branch could do that), but his description of the Arician cult cannot so easily be discounted.[5] Servius is most reliable when his comments could not be derived simply from something in the text.[6] In the present instance,

---

5. For convenience, cult and players will be referred to in this work as "the Arician cult," "Rex," and "Challenger."

6. For an example of the opposite phenomenon (deriving a "tradition" from a clue in the text), see the discussion of *patrias obtruncat ad aras* (3.332) in chap. 4.

the breaking of a branch leads him to describe a cult that has no other obvious link to the *Aeneid* context. Though this comment is the only ancient source that connects the breaking of a bough with the Arician cult, Servius hardly could have made up this unusual feature. It is important to notice that, *pace* Frazer, Servius does *not* say that Virgil's Golden Bough "was" the bough of the tree at Nemi. He says that Virgil's Bough *alludes* to that cult, *istum inde sumpsit colorem*. Frazer's extravagant conjectures, paradoxically, have drawn attention away from the implications of this allusion for the *Aeneid*.[7]

It is shocking to see a connection between *pius* Aeneas and the "ghastly priest," in Macaulay's words, "the priest who slew the slayer, and shall himself be slain." The first part of this book, however, has been devoted to demonstrating just such a connection: Virgil casts Aeneas as a priest-king whose sacrifice of others will ultimately result in the sacrifice of himself. This theme is not confined to Aeneas, but embraces major and minor characters from beginning to end. The Golden Bough in the grove of Diana at the *Aeneid*'s center is indeed to be associated with the strange and barbarous cult of Diana Nemorensis; this "primeval rock" is one of the foundation stones in Virgil's temple to Augustus. The cult was both readily known to Virgil's ancient readers and thematically appropriate to the *Aeneid*, and Virgil's sustained allusion to it is a structuring principle of the poem.

This was the most prominent cult of one of the most important goddesses in the Roman world.[8] Aricia, the hometown of Augustus' mother, lay in the Alban Hills that were Rome's birthplace, less than twenty miles from Rome itself. Written and archeological evidence

---

Prompted by *patrias* ("paternal"), Servius cites a "tradition" that Pyrrhus had set up an altar to his father Achilles.

7. The present study does not attempt to explain all the distinguishing features of the Golden Bough, which is clearly a multivalent symbol. It may well be, as West (1987) 234 argues, that Virgil is alluding in part to the Eleusinian mysteries (though see objections in Zetzel [1989] 276–77). The fact that the Bough is "golden" is likely to be an allusion to the Meleager epigram in which Plato is called a "golden twig," as Michels (1945) argues. Yet neither of these theories adequately explains the violent *breaking off* of the Bough.

8. See Green (2000) 27–30.

indicates that the sanctuary did a thriving business in Virgil's day and beyond.[9] Just as Rome was referred to as simply *urbs*, "The City," so Diana's grove was referred to as *nemus*, "The Grove."[10] Amatory elegists attest that it was a notorious trysting spot. Propertius lists it first among the cult places to which Cynthia is likely to sneak off on the pretense of worshipping (*currere . . . in nemus et Triviae lumina ferre deae*, "to run off to The Grove and bring torches to the goddess Trivia," 2.32.9–10). In the *Ars Amatoria*, after advising his pupil about the wounds to the heart threatened by the sulphurous spas of Baiae (a fashionable watering-hole), Ovid warns of the similar dangers posed by the haunt of "suburban Diana" and her priest-king:

> ecce, suburbanae templum nemorale Dianae,
>   partaque per gladios regna nocente manu.
> illa, quod est virgo, quod tela Cupidinis odit,
>   multa dedit populo vulnera, multa dabit. (*A. A.* 1.257–60)

> Here is the woodland temple of suburban Diana, and the kingdom gained through swords by harmful hand. Because she is a virgin, because she hates the arrows of Cupid, she has given many and will give many wounds to the people.

In addition to serving as a rendezvous for lovers, Aricia was famous as the political and religious center of the Latin League, an alliance of communities in Latium that was active for more than a century and a half following the fall of the Roman monarchy (509 B.C.).[11]

---

9. See MacCormick (1983); Leach (1985); Blagg (1993); Horsfall (1999) ad 7.778.

10. See Ernout and Meillet (1931) s.v. *nemus*. Ancient writings and coins are inconsistent, calling the grove *nemus*, *nemus Aricinum*, or *lucus Dianae*; the phrase *nemus Dianae* does not seem to have been used. See Ampolo (1993) 162–63. As Pairault (1969) 428 notes, the phrase *lucus Dianae* always meant the *lucus Dianae Nemorensis*.

11. As Coarelli (1987) 167 notes, "Il culto di Diana nel *nemus* di Aricia ha attraversato, fin dalla sua origine, fasi alterne, determinate da vicende piuttosto politiche che religiose: la sua funzione di santuario della lega latina è stata in questo senso determinante, anche se non si tratta forse di una connotazione originaria." ("The cult of Diana in the grove of Aricia has passed through various phases since its origin, determined by events rather political than religious: its

Servius Tullius was said to have established on the Aventine a replica of the shrine of Diana Nemorensis.[12] An allusion to the cult would have seemed neither obscure nor improbable to the Romans, as Servius' reference to *publica opinio* also suggests.

One of Virgil's epic successors may confirm the potential impact of the cult on Latin poetry. In a provocative article entitled " 'The Necessary Murder': Myth, Ritual, and Civil War in Lucan, Book 3," Carin Green argues that an important model for Lucan's rivalry between Pompey and Caesar is to be found in the ritual combat of the Rex Nemorensis and his Challenger. This paradigm would explain "various puzzling choices Lucan has made elsewhere in the epic, as regards his narrative of events, his development of character, and the recurrent images of lightning, tree, and blood sacrifice owed to the gods."[13] Green summarizes as follows her argument about allusions to the Arician cult in Book 3:

> In particular, it is through the paradigm of the *rex nemorensis* that the relationship of the specific events of Book 3 can now be understood to make a related, dramatic whole. Pompey's abandonment of Rome, which has ended Book 2, opens the way for Caesar's triumphal advance through Latium to Rome. In turn, because he is retreating, because he is in eclipse, because he is the dying oak, Pompey loses strength, conviction, and power as he goes. The royal panoply of kings and armies who are catalogued in forces supporting Pompey simultaneously calls attention to his diminishing personal powers, as the surrounding vigorous forest calls attention to the leafless oak, and, by contrast, cast him ever more vividly as a king, and a leader among kings; for this is his role—Pompey is Rome's dying priest-king, bedecked with the ancient honors of

---

function as sanctuary of the Latin League was in this sense a deciding factor, even if it did not perhaps have to do with the cult's original connotation.") For ancient sources on "Rome and the Latins," see Beard, North, and Price (1998b) 11–17.

12. See Simon (1984) 792–95 (with bibliography) on the controversial issue of the relationship between Diana Aventinensis and Diana Nemorensis.

13. Green (1994) 205.

> his people. He is the oak, Caesar is the lightning; both lightning and oak are symbols of the power of Jupiter—and of Rome—and it is the very nature of that power to destroy and renew itself. All this is the preparation for Caesar's great act of sacrilege, when he cuts down an oak in the sacred grove outside Massilia. He claims the crime, for it is only through the crime that he can approach and challenge the reigning priest—Pompey.[14]

It is quite likely that Lucan, in this as in so many ways, has picked up a clue from Virgil.[15] Although modern commentators may state that the allusion Servius heard in the Golden Bough has "no definable relevance to Virgil," at least one of Virgil's best ancient readers apparently did not agree.

The cult was a rich source for poets, not only because of its ritual combat for kingship, but also because of its association with two Greek tragedies, the *Oresteia* and the *Hippolytus*.[16] Servius' comment on *Aeneid* 2.116, "with blood and a slaughtered maiden you pacified the winds" (*sanguine placastis ventos et virgine caesa*), transports us from the assembly of the Greek fleet at Aulis all the way to Orestes bringing the statue of Diana to Aricia (and beyond).[17] In

---

14. Green (1994) 231–32.

15. For an overview of Virgil's reception in antiquity, see Tarrant (1997), especially 65–67 on Lucan.

16. On the cult's dual association with Orestes and Hippolytus, see Montepaone (1993) 72–73.

17. On reasons for the connection of the Orestes/Iphigeneia myth with the cult of Diana at Aricia and elsewhere, see Graf (1979). Servius ad 2.116 (part):

> occiso Thoante, simulacrum sustulit absconditum fasce lignorum: unde et Facelitis dicitur, non tantum a face, cum qua pingitur, propter quod et Lucifera dicitur: et Ariciam detulit. sed cum postea Romanis sacrorum crudelitas displiceret, quamquam servi immolarentur, ad Laconas est Diana translata . . .

> After Thoas was killed, Orestes stole the statue [of Diana], hidden in a bundle (*fasces*) of wood: whence she is called "Facelitis," not only from the torch with which she is depicted, because of which she is also called "Lucifera": and he brought her to Aricia. But afterward, when the cruelty of her rites [of human sacrifice] displeased the Romans, although [only] slaves were being sacrificed, Diana was brought to the Laconians . . .

Servius' mind, the cult was bound up with the mythic cycle that we know mainly from Greco-Roman literature. Echoes of the *Oresteia*, of course, are important for the *Aeneid* regardless of their connection to Diana's grove.[18] But if a pattern of allusion to Diana Nemorensis can be established in other ways, it may add a dimension to our understanding of how Virgil transformed the poetic heritage of the *Oresteia* as it was transmitted in the verse of Aeschylus and Lucretius.

More explicitly linked to the Arician grove by Virgil himself is the story of Hippolytus, who was renamed "Virbius" after his resurrection. His is the longest entry in the catalogue of Italian warriors and the last before Turnus and Camilla:

> Ibat et Hippolyti proles pulcherrima bello,
> Virbius, insignem quem mater Aricia misit,
> eductum Egeriae lucis umentia circum
> litora, pinguis ubi et placabilis ara Dianae.
> namque ferunt fama Hippolytum, postquam arte novercae
> occiderit patriasque explerit sanguine poenas
> turbatis distractus equis, ad sidera rursus
> aetheria et superas caeli venisse sub auras,
> Paeoniis revocatum herbis et amore Dianae.
> tum pater omnipotens aliquem indignatus ab umbris
> mortalem infernis ad lumina surgere vitae
> ipse repertorem medicinae talis et artis
> fulmine Phoebigenam Stygias detrusit ad undas.
> at Trivia Hippolytum secretis alma recondit
> sedibus et nymphae Egeriae nemorique relegat,
> solus ubi in silvis Italis ignobilis aevum

---

18. See especially Hardie (1991) on the many thematic and structural similarities between the two works (e.g., cosmic sweep, ring composition, repeated motifs such as hunting and sacrifice, prevalence of Furies). As Mack (1999) 147 notes, however, Virgil's *Oresteia* "will have no transformation of Furies into Kindly Ones."

> exigeret versoque ubi nomine Virbius esset.
> unde etiam templo Triviae lucisque sacratis
> cornipedes arcentur equi, quod litore currum
> et iuvenem monstris pavidi effudere marinis.
> filius ardentis haud setius aequore campi
> exercebat equos curruque in bella ruebat. (7.761–82)

> The most beautiful offspring of Hippolytus also went to war, Virbius, outstanding warrior whom his mother Aricia sent, brought up in the groves of Egeria around watery shores, where the altar of Diana is rich and placable. For they say that Hippolytus, after he died by his stepmother's device and paid his father's penalty in blood, torn apart by his horses, came again to the etherial stars and the upper air, recalled by Paeonian herbs and Diana's love. Then the father omnipotent, resentful that any mortal should rise from the infernal shades to the light of life, himself cast down to the Stygian waves with his thunderbolt the inventor, Phoebus-born, of such medicine and art. But fostering Trivia hid away Hippolyus in her sacred seat and entrusted him to the nymph Egeria and her grove, where he might spend his life alone and ignoble in the Italian woods, and change his name to Virbius. Wherefore also horn-hooved horses are prohibited from the temple and sacred groves of Trivia, because on the shore they threw off chariot and youth, terrified at monsters from the sea. But his son, nonetheless, plied his horses on the surface of the field, and rushed to war with his chariot.

Virbius never appears again in the poem. Yet characteristics of this son of Theseus, dying through his stepmother's lust and treachery, resurrected to Jupiter's chagrin by Paeonian herbs, hidden in the woods to live out his days in obscurity, and of course dwelling in the Arician grove, will reappear many times—sometimes in surprising places. According to Pausanias, the Aricians considered the resurrected Hippolytus to be the one who consecrated the sacred precinct of their Artemis (Diana):

> χωρὶς δὲ ἀπὸ τῶν ἄλλων ἐστὶν ἀρχαία στήλη· ἵππους δὲ Ἱππόλυτον ἀναθεῖναι τῷ θεῷ φησιν εἴκοσι. ταύτης τῆς στήλης τῷ ἐπιγράμματι ὁμολογοῦντα λέγουσιν Ἀρικιεῖς, ὡς τεθνεῶτα Ἱππόλυτον ἐκ τῶν Θησέως ἀρῶν ἀνέστησεν Ἀσκληπιός· ὁ δὲ ὡς αὖθις ἐβίω, οὐκ ἠξίου νέμειν τῷ πατρὶ συγγνώμην, ἀλλὰ ὑπεριδὼν τὰς δεήσεις ἐς Ἰταλίαν ἔρχεται παρὰ τοὺς Ἀρικεῖς, καὶ ἐβασίλευσέ τε αὐτόθι καὶ ἀνῆκε τῇ Ἀρτέμιδι τέμενος, ἔνθα ἄχρι ἐμοῦ μονομαχίας ἆθλα ἦν καὶ ἱερᾶσθαι τῇ θεῷ τὸν νικῶντα· ὁ δὲ ἀγὼν ἐλευθέρων μὲν προέκειτο οὐδενί, οἰκέταις δὲ ἀποδρᾶσι τοὺς δεσπότας. (2.27.4)
>
> Apart from the others is an old slab; it says that Hippolytus dedicated twenty horses to the god [Asclepius]. The Aricians tell a story agreeing with this inscription, that Asclepius resurrected Hippolytus after he had died by the curses of Theseus. When he was living again, he did not deign to grant forgiveness to his father, but scorning his prayers went to Italy among the Aricians, and was king there and set up a sacred precinct for Artemis, where up to my day the prize for victory in single combat was for the victor to be priest of the goddess. The contest was open to no free man, but rather to slaves who had run away from their masters.

In fact, the association of Hippolytus/Virbius with the Roman cult probably dates from centuries after its foundation. Many modern scholars regard Virbius as a mysterious figure who happened to live in Diana's territory without necessarily participating in her cult.[19] Nevertheless, the testimony of Pausanias, which states that Hippolytus consecrated the precinct and then immediately describes its priesthood, suggests that his connection with the cult is more than geographical. Virgil depicts him as a fugitive, beloved of Diana, who lives *alone* in the Arician grove near her temple and her altar: even if he does not explicitly identify Virbius with the Rex Nemorensis, he makes such an identification probable and a close association

19. On the lack of evidence about Virbius, see Caviglia (1990) 556.

indisputable.[20] Whether he was regarded as such by the average Roman is less important than what Virgil's poetic fiction implicitly suggests.

♦ ♦ ♦

Three characteristics of trees render them particularly suited to Virgil's poetic strategies. First, they are naturally analogous to human bodies, as Latin shows even more clearly than English.[21] Foliage is *comae*, "hair"; branches are *bracchia*, "arms"; the tree-top is the *vertex*, often used of a human "head." One of Virgil's particularly evocative words is *truncus*, "trunk." As an adjective it gives us "truncated," but with more violent connotations in Latin of "mutilated, maimed, dismembered, lopped off, removed by chopping." As a noun, it gives us the "trunk" of a tree or of a human body, specifically the body "as separate from the head and/or limbs."[22] It is notable that Virgil uses it in this sense exclusively for decapitated corpses. Second, trees supply the material for many other mute but important objects in the *Aeneid*: ships, spears, houses, funeral pyres, scepters, and a horse pregnant with Greeks. As Virgil uses proper names of minor characters to suggest entire mythological and historical episodes,[23] so he uses the names of trees and provenances of wooden artifacts to link apparently disparate passages. Third, like rivers and streams, trees were thought to be inhabited by divine spirits easily angered if mistreated. To harm any part of a tree without proper propitiatory rites was a dangerous act of impiety that invited retribution, soon

---

20. Frazer sees Virbius as the original King of the Wood. Modern scholars of religion are more tentative about his role, especially since our knowledge of Virbius comes entirely from literary sources (Gordon [1934] 14). Dumézil (1970) 408 calls Virbius "a complete mystery." Latte (1960) 170–72 discusses the problem of connections among Diana, Virbius, Hippolytus, Egeria, and the Rex Nemorensis without coming to a conclusion. For his purposes, a "künstliche Kombination lehrt nichts" ("an artificial conflation tells us nothing," 170); for mine, it is essential.

21. See Weber (1995) 5.

22. *OLD* s.v. *truncus* [1], 1.a, 2.a, 2b; s.v. *truncus* [2], 1.a.

23. See chap. 11, n. 27.

or late, and Virgil often uses "tree violation" to suggest moral culpability.[24]

In his beautiful essay "Some Trees in Virgil and Tolkien," Kenneth Reckford writes that "a deep affinity exists between Virgil's mind and Tolkien's and may be observed in the way they perceive life, in their sense of the relation between heroic choice and achievement, on the one hand, and time, change, loss, sadness, uncertainty, and suffering, on the other. Or, more poetically, in the way they look at trees."[25] Poets of every age, and the ancients especially, have seen something numinous in trees, something that both parallels and transcends the human condition. Achilles springs up like a sapling, only to be cut down in his prime to gain "unwithering glory"; Odysseus is home and himself at last when he shares with Penelope the sign of the immovable olive that is their marriage bed. Many of the *Aeneid*'s most significant themes are intimately bound up with its numerous and memorable portraits of trees, from Troy the fallen ash to Aeneas the unshakable oak to Mezentius the mutilated trunk. Virgil's pervasive tree imagery radiates from the groves of Diana, at Nemi and at Cumae, with their sacred boughs marking the boundary between the living and the dead.[26]

---

24. See especially Thomas (1988b) on "Tree Violation and Ambivalence in Virgil." He begins by demonstrating that "[e]very piece of relevant evidence from Greece and Rome, as from numerous other societies, conspires to demonstrate that the cutting of trees is a hazardous act, stigmatized by society and divinity alike" (263). In particular, Aeneas' triple attempt to pull up the tree inhabited by the spirit of Polydorus (3.22–48), his "greedy pull" at the Golden Bough (6.210–11), and the Trojans' leveling of the sacred tree of Faunus (12.770–71) cast a pall over Aeneas' *pietas* and suggest that "the price in spiritual loss attending the advent of civilization may, in the last analysis, not be worth the result" (270).

25. Reckford (1974) 57–58.

26. See Weber (1995) for the intriguing theory that the Golden Bough is itself an allegorical representation of Aeneas' soul.

CHAPTER EIGHT

THE THREE FACES OF DIANA

"Why did Venus wear boots?"[1] Probably, as E. L. Harrison argues, because *cothurni* (1.337) were the buskins worn by tragic actors, and what follows her "prologue" will be a tragedy. A related question, with a more complicated answer, is, "Why do Venus and Dido both appear first as Diana the huntress?" To recall Homer's Nausicaa (*Od.* 6.102–109) and Apollonius' Medea (3.876–85), to emphasize the theme of hunting that pervades the Dido episode—and to introduce the goddess whose priest and victim Aeneas and others symbolically will become. Virgil's poetry fuses tragedy with cult, bringing both hunter and hunted into the realm of Diana Nemorensis.

The goddess we call "Diana" is actually an amalgam of at least three deities. Scholars disagree about her provenance and her (or their) original primary function, but by Virgil's time, her "three faces" had become relatively fixed: the Moon (Greek Selene), called Luna or Phoebe; Trivia (Greek Hecate), a goddess of the Underworld and of black magic; and Diana (Greek Artemis), goddess of the hunt and the young. Coins depicting Diana Nemorensis generally show three goddesses linked by a bar, representing the three aspects of the single goddess, with cypress trees in the background.[2] This triple

1. Harrison (1972–73).
2. Alföldi (1960).

identity complements the inherent paradox of her nature, and especially of her relationship to animals, for she both protects them and aids those who hunt them. To huntsmen as well she can be both nurturing and dangerous. Even Hippolytus, her favorite, found the salvation she brought him to be less than complete. The Hippolytus myth is important for the Dido episode and for Aeneas' catabasis; other aspects of Diana's cult emerge in the opening of the Italian War and in the adventure of Nisus and Euryalus.

The shifting nature of Diana is mirrored in the changes that Dido herself undergoes.[3] When Aeneas first lays eyes on Dido, she is likened to the huntress Diana with a band of nymphs and trademark quiver (1.498–504).[4] The joy and confidence of that persona will not last long. When she stoops to the black arts in desperation, after erecting a huge wooden pyre and crowning it with "funereal foliage" (*fronde . . . funerea*, 4.506–507)—which to the ancient reader would mean "cypress," Diana's tree—she invokes "tri-form Hecate, the three faces of the maiden Diana" (*tergeminamque Hecaten, tria virginis ora Dianae*, 4.511). When she appears to Aeneas for the last time, "wandering in the great wood" (6.451), she is like the moon, hidden by shadows (6.451–54).[5] The "three faces of Diana" could be said to represent the stages of Dido's tragic decline and partial resumption of heroic stature, as she passes from the mountains to the Underworld to the moon.

Dido also plays quite another role in the complex of mythology surrounding Diana. In his discussion of "The Tragedy of Dido," Harrison points out that "the structure of Virgil's 'tragedy' can be compared with that of Euripides' *Hippolytus*, where Venus' equivalent, Aphrodite, likewise delivers an opening prologue, and the

---

3. This idea is elaborated by Duclos (1969), who observes that *triformis Diana* "encompasses the whole psychological tragedy of Dido" (33).

4. The passage was censured in antiquity (and by Heinze), though modern readers have found more to admire and important associations with other parts of the poem. For a discussion of previous critical response and of associations with Penthesilea, see Pigoñ (1991). On similarities to Apollonius' Medea, see Briggs (1981) 964–67.

5. On moon imagery in the story of Dido, see Lee (1988) 10–11.

action similarly ends with an intervention by the goddess who opposes her, in this case Artemis."[6] This is but one of several ways in which Dido's tragedy resembles that of Phaedra. The counsel of Anna that dissolves Dido's *pudor* (4.31–55) is modeled on that of Phaedra's nurse, the archetype of a well-meaning adviser who encourages disastrous love.[7] The nurse claims that she can help Phaedra with "love charms" (*philtra . . . thelktêria / erôtos*, 509–10), in conjunction with which she requires a lock of hair or piece of clothing from Hippolytus (514). The nature of her sorcery is unclear: *philtra* normally refers to a "charm to produce love" but could be a charm to drive it away, and *thelktêria erôtos* could be either "to charm love away" or "to charm love into existence."[8] Dido gathers Aeneas' belongings (4.495–97, 507–508), presumably for some kind of sympathetic magic, but with similar ambiguity about whether she seeks to curse him or to lure him back.[9] She too employs a mysterious "love charm," with the word *amor* placed at the end of a striking half-line:[10]

> quaeritur et nascentis equi de fronte revulsus
> et matri praereptus *amor*. (4.515–16)
>
> A *love* (charm) is sought, torn from the forehead of a horse
> being born and stolen away from the mother.

Pease's comment establishes that the reference is to *hippomanes*, which Virgil in the *Georgics* connects explicitly with scheming stepmothers:[11]

> hic demum, hippomanes vero quod nomine dicunt
> pastores, lentum destillat ab inguine virus,

---

6. Harrison (1989) 8.

7. Harrison (1989) 11. Dido's unnecessarily stringent emphasis on her own *pudor* also bears a certain resemblance to that of Hippolytus; see Moles (1988) 154–55. Similarly, she is likened both to a Bacchant (4.300–303) and to Pentheus (4.469–70), the antagonists in Euripides' *Bacchae*. See Duclos (1971) 195.

8. Barrett (1964) ad 509–12.

9. Watson (1993) 846.

10. Austin (1955) ad 4.515f.: "the chance that has left the lines unfinished has added to their mysterious horror."

11. Pease (1935) ad 4.515.

> hippomanes, quod saepe malae legere novercae
> miscueruntque herbas et non innoxia verba. (*Geo*. 3.280–83)

> Finally, what shepherds with a true name call "horse-madness" (*hippomanes*), a sticky slime drips down from the loins, *hippomanes*, which often evil stepmothers have gathered and mixed in herbs and words not innocent.

Stepmothers in Greco-Roman literature typically either lust after their stepsons or hate them (or both). The combination of "herbs and words not innocent" could be employed in the service of either passion, for seduction or for murder. In the *Georgics* context, a long passage on *amor* and lustful mares, Virgil implies that the stepmothers employ *hippomanes* as an aphrodisiac rather than a poison.[12] The passage calls to mind the prototypical lustful stepmother, Phaedra. Dido's use of *hippomanes* thus alludes both to the Euripidean Phaedra, with her mysterious "love charm," and to Virgil's own use of that myth in the *Georgics*.

To cast Dido as Phaedra is to cast Aeneas, momentarily, as Hippolytus. Given the many allusions to Greek tragedy in the Dido episode,[13] it may seem that literary motivations are enough to account for these "roles." Yet Virgil goes to some length to connect the Hippolytus of tragedy with the Hippolytus of cult: the one time Hippolytus appears in the poem is as the resurrected Virbius, living alone in the Arician grove near Diana's temple and altar. As was shown in chapter 7, the nature of the relationship between Virbius and the Rex Nemorensis is unclear. The conjecture that Virbius was the original Rex is not unreasonable, however, and Virgil's description certainly allows and even implies that identification. Virgil

12. Watson (1993). The word *venenum*, usually translated as "poison," has an obvious resemblance to "Venus"; it is tempting to suppose that the Romans' instinct for wordplay and truth in etymology led them to see "poison" and "aphrodisiac" as connected. But see the cautionary words of O'Hara (1996) 106, who points out that "ancient awareness of the perhaps genuine connection between Venus and *venenum* is not clearly attested."

13. See Hardie (1997a) 321–22. On tragic elements in the *Aeneid* more generally, see Quinn (1968) 323–49.

associates Aeneas with the Rex Nemorensis by creating a parallel between Hippolytus/Virbius, father of Virbius (Junior), and Aeneas, father of Silvius.

Hippolytus, like his father Theseus, shares with Aeneas the distinction of a sojourn in the Underworld. Aeneas himself calls attention to the parallel between his fate and that of Theseus, who, like Orpheus, Pollux, and Hercules, descended alive to the Dead (6.119–23). The parallel extends further: as Theseus abandoned Ariadne and was cursed by her, so Aeneas is cursed by the abandoned Dido. The mural on the temple of Apollo near the entrance to the Underworld reminds the reader of this abandonment and curse, for the scenes described imply that the missing scene Aeneas would have "read," if the Sibyl had not interrupted him, is that of Theseus abandoning Ariadne.[14] Aeneas implies that Theseus is one who entered the Underworld alive and returned from it, but the Sibyl later points to Theseus among the sinners, "unhappy Theseus, who sits there and always will sit there" (*sedet aeternumque sedebit / infelix Theseus*, 6.617–18). This apparent inconsistency troubled Virgil's ancient readers enough to be listed by the Augustan commentator Hyginus among the errors the poet undoubtedly intended to correct (Aul. Gell. 10.16.11–13).[15] Servius' comment on these lines indicates that the presence of Theseus in the Underworld is a surprise to the reader:

> AETERNUMQUE SEDEBIT INFELIX THESEUS contra opinionem, nam fertur ab Hercule esse liberatus: quo tempore eum ita abstraxit, ut illic corporis eius relinqueret partem. frequenter enim variant fabulas poetae: Hippolytum Vergilius liberatum ab inferis dicit, Horatius contra "neque enim Diana pudicum liberat Hippolytum."

14. Casali (1995).

15. See Zetzel (1989) on the pattern of inconsistencies in *Aeneid* 6, among which the presence of Theseus in the Underworld is an "anomaly of a piece with the rest" (270).

> AND UNHAPPY THESEUS WILL SIT THERE ETERNALLY contrary to opinion, for he is said to have been freed by Hercules: at which time he dragged him away in such a way that he left part of his body there. For poets often give variant stories: Virgil says that Hippolytus was freed from the Underworld, while Horace, on the other hand, says, "For neither does Diana free chaste Hippolytus [*Odes* 4.7.25–26]."

This comment points to yet a third possibility, the intermediate position that Theseus was *partially* freed but part of his body remained there. It is perhaps possible to reconcile the conflicting versions of Theseus' fate more casually by supposing that Aeneas and the Sibyl are referring to different times, that is, that Theseus was rescued once from the Underworld (as Aeneas implies) but then returned after his death to eternal punishment (as the Sibyl says). Whether or not the apparent inconsistency can be smoothed over, it remains a shock to hear that Theseus is in the Underworld after Aeneas has referred to him as one who escaped. Like Orpheus, whose catabasis led to a second loss of his wife followed by his own dismemberment, Theseus is hardly an auspicious role model for a mortal about to make the awful descent.

Servius' comment emphasizes that Theseus and his son Hippolytus are similar in the partial success of their exits from the Underworld. Was Hippolytus in fact recalled by Paeonian herbs and the love of Diana, as Virgil claims (7.769)? Or is he doomed to remain, as Horace implies?[16] Or is there something in between, a sort of life-in-death, where (like Theseus) only part of him remains? Servius describes something like this intermediate state in his comment on

---

16. In the same poem, Horace makes Aeneas his first exemplum of one who is simply *dead* as we all shall be:

> nos ubi decidimus
> quo pater Aeneas, quo Tullus dives et Ancus,
> pulvis et umbra sumus. (*Odes* 4.7.14–16)

> When we have gone down to where father Aeneas, where rich Tullus and Ancus [are], we are dust and a Shade.

the word "ignobilis" (776), which characterizes the life of Hippolytus after his resurrection:

> IGNOBILIS non vilis, sed ignotus: quamquam possit etiam ad illud referri quod dicunt quibusdam artibus posse hominum vitam ultra fata protendi, ita tamen, ut solam habeant vitae imaginationem; videntur enim omnia facere nec faciunt.
>
> IGNOBLE not "contemptible," but "unknown": although it also could refer to the fact that they say the life of men can by certain arts be prolonged beyond fate, in such a way, however, that they have only the appearance of life; for they seem to do everything, but they do not do it.

Whether Hippolytus/Virbius is officially alive or dead, this ghostly state can hardly be considered a triumph over the powers of darkness. Other elements in Virgil's description of Hippolytus/Virbius also imply that his exit from the land of the Dead was less than completely successful. Though Jupiter does not prevent Hippolytus from being revived, he vents his anger upon the one who put him together again (7.770–73) and remains resentful, *indignatus*, that a mortal should emerge from the infernal shades. The word *indignor* connotes anger temporarily contained but potentially resurgent; in particular, the phrase *indignatus ab umbris* (7.770) anticipates the last words of the poem, in which Turnus' life flees indignantly to the shades, *indignata sub umbras*.[17] The divine displeasure incurred by Hippolytus' resurrection, and his consequent need to live in the woods incognito, make his departure from the Underworld as problematic as his father's. In fact, the dual fates of Theseus and his son resemble the duality of Aeneas' fate discussed in the first half of this book. Both the glory of apotheosis and the horror of drowning belong to the tradition, and Virgil's poetry keeps both possibilities in tension.

---

17. See Mitchell (1991) 231–32: the echo also provides a link between Turnus and Hippolytus, "young male virgins whose virginity in some way destroys them" (231).

Another strange allusion associates Aeneas with the death of Hippolytus. The four warriors whom Aeneas encounters first during his Achillean rampage, Magus, Haemonides, Anxur, and Tarquitus (10.521–60), each share some feature of Aeneas' own fate. One other warrior in this section exhibits an odd similarity to Hippolytus:

> quin ecce Niphaei
> quadriiugis in equos adversaque pectora tendit.
> atque illi longe gradientem et dira frementem
> ut videre, *metu* versi retroque ruentes
> *effundunt*que ducem rapiuntque ad *litora currus*. (10.570–74)

> But look, he heads for the four-horse chariot and opposing breast of Niphaeus. And as they [the horses] saw him taking large strides and growling terribly, turning and rushing backward *in fear* they *throw off* their leader and seize the *chariot* away to *the shore*.

In theme and word, this scene echoes Virgil's own description of Hippolytus' death:

> unde etiam templo Triviae lucisque sacratis
> cornipedes arcentur equi, quod *litore currum*
> et iuvenem monstris *pavidi effudere* marinis. (7.778–80)

> Wherefore also horn-hooved horses are prohibited from the temple and sacred groves of Trivia, because *on the shore* they *threw off chariot* and youth, *terrified* at monsters from the sea. But his son, nonetheless, plied his horses on the surface of the field, and rushed to war with his chariot.

Though the similarities are strong—horses spooked by monstrous figures throw their driver from his chariot near a shore—most commentators do not mention the Hippolytus myth in connection with Aeneas and Niphaeus. Such an association seems at first glance to have little point. Yet if it is true that Aeneas in this episode kills a series of "doubles" of himself, and that the parallel between

Aeneas and Hippolytus is sustained in other ways, then it is appropriate for Aeneas to kill a Hippolytus figure in this scene.[18]

The similarity between Aeneas and Hippolytus extends to their sons, Silvius and Virbius, respectively. We learn from the shade of Anchises that Aeneas' dynasty will be carried on, not through Ascanius, but through a second son born after Aeneas' death:

> ille, vides, pura iuvenis qui nititur hasta,
> proxima sorte tenet lucis loca, primus ad auras
> aetherias Italo commixtus sanguine surget,
> Silvius, Albanum nomen, tua *postuma proles,*
> quem tibi longaevo serum Lavinia coniunx
> *educet silvis regem* regumque parentem,
> unde genus Longa nostrum dominabitur Alba. (6.760–66)

> That youth—you see—who leans upon a headless spear holds by lot the next place in the light; he will rise first to the etherial breezes, mingled with Italian blood—Silvius, an Alban name, your *posthumous offspring*, whom for you in your old age, late, your wife Lavinia *will rear in the woods a king* and the father of kings, whence our race will reign in Alba Longa.

Though Anchises does not dwell on this point, the reader may well wonder why, if Silvius is to be a king and the father of kings, he will be raised in a wood. What Anchises does not say is that there will be a conflict between Ascanius and his stepmother that will force her to go into hiding and raise her son in a wood (Dion. Hal. 1.70). Similar elements are prevalent in the description of the Virbii: Hippolytus is said to have died by his stepmother's device, his afterlife in the woods is explicitly for the purpose of hiding, and Virbius junior is "brought up in the woods" (*eductum . . . lucis,* 7.764). Silvius is called a "posthumous offspring" (*postuma proles,* 6.763), and Virbius junior is even more so, a son not only born but even conceived after his father's death. (How the notoriously chaste

18. For Virgil's final allusion to the death of Hippolytus in reference to Aeneas, see the end of chap. 12.

Hippolytus who lived alone in the woods managed to father a son is another question. Servius is right to call the whole thing *fabulosum.*[19]) Finally, the momentary ambiguity of the phrase *educet silvis regem* raises the specter of the Rex Nemorensis. The line ultimately may be construed to read "she will raise him in the woods, (though he is to be) a king and the father of kings." But the first reading suggests, "she will raise him in the woods a king"—that is, "a king in the woods," and in the *Alban* woods, at that, for he is introduced as an "Alban name." Silvius gets his name from being raised in the woods; Virgil chooses not only to emphasize this through wordplay but immediately to juxtapose the word "king" in such a way as to conjure up the King of the Wood.[20]

To associate Silvius with the King of the Wood has profound implications for Roman history. The first group of named descendants of Aeneas begins with Silvius and ends with Silvius Aeneas (6.763–69), and the Silvii were the ruling dynasty of Alba (*Albani patres,* 1.7), the mother city of Rome. Romulus, the next descendant named, was the son of a priestess called "Ilia" in this passage (6.778) but more commonly known as Rhea Silvia.[21] To implicate Silvius in the rites of the Rex Nemorensis, however obliquely, is to implicate the hereditary monarchy that gave rise to the founder of Rome. Green argues that the single combat of Rex and Challenger reenacts in ritual what Romulus and Remus enact in myth, the fratricide that haunts all of Roman history.[22] The succession of Silvii from Aeneas to Romulus would provide an additional link between the ritual and the myth.[23]

---

19. See Caviglia (1990) 554 on responses to this problem. Horsfall (1999) ad 7.761 characterizes *Hippolyti proles* ("the offspring of Hippolytus") as "[s]tartling; indeed an oxymoron."

20. See Merkelbach (1961) 89. Frazer (1922) 164 conjectures that the King of the Wood was the "lawful successor and representative of the ancient line of the Silvii or Woods," noting also the crown of oak leaves worn by the Silvii (6.772).

21. There is perhaps a slight hint of the parallel between Silvius and Romulus in the repetition of *educet* at line beginning (6.765, 779).

22. Green (1994) 216.

23. Servius Tullius, who brought Diana's cult to Rome, is conspicuously absent from Anchises' list of Rome's kings (6.773–818).

Furthermore, another member of Virgil's catalogue of Italian warriors in Book 7 links Rhea Silvia indirectly with Diana Nemorensis. The catalogue consists of an (almost) alphabetical list framed by two pairs of "important" characters, Mezentius/Lausus and Turnus/Camilla.[24] The last in the alphabetical list is Virbius. The first is a putative son of Hercules named Aventinus who seems to be Virgil's invention and who, like Virbius, never appears again in the poem.[25] The circumstances of his birth sound suspiciously like those in a familiar legend:

> collis Aventini *silva* quem *Rhea sacerdos*
> *furtivum partu* sub luminis edidit oras,
> *mixta deo mulier* . . . (7.659–61)

> Whom the *priestess Rhea,* in a *wood* on the Aventine hill, brought *secretly in birth* up to the shores of light, *a woman mingling with a god* . . .

The Romans could hardly have failed to see a similiarity to the mother of Romulus and Remus, also a *priestess* named *Rhea* who gave birth *secretly* to children begotten by a *god*.[26] The collocation *silva . . . Rhea sacerdos* provides an additional reminder of Rhea *Silvia*—never called by that name in the *Aeneid,* interestingly enough, but referred to in Jupiter's prophecy as *regina sacerdos*

24. See O'Hara (1989) on the one anomaly in this alphabetical sequence.

25. Three characters in the catalogue of Italian warriors do not reappear in the poem: Aventinus, Virbius, and one Oebalus, whom Virgil (wryly?) introduces with the statement, "Nor will you depart from our poem unsung" (*nec tu carminibus nostris indictus abibis,* 7.733). Brotherton (1931) 199–200 summarizes as follows the parallels between Aventinus and Virbius: "Against these two leaders [Mezentius and Turnus], throwing them into even stronger relief, are set the two shadowy figures of legend, Aventinus and Virbius. Their rôle as indicated in the later action of the *Aeneid* is the same: they do not appear. But their value for the picturesqueness of the catalogue is high. Their nature, as men of myth, as well as their failure to appear in the action, reinforces their likeness. Again, both are equipped with chariot and horses (655–657, 781 f.). That they are a balanced pair is obvious." See also Caviglia (1990) 553.

26. Horsfall (1999) ad 7.659 notes, "Rhea was a Vestal, the mistress of a god, and her offspring were reared in the wild: V. therefore, by his choice of name, positively flaunts the rather banal origin of the details here related!"

("royal priestess," 1.273). Since the Aventine Hill was particularly associated with Remus, who in some traditions founded there his rival city Remuria,[27] it seems clear that Virgil's invented warrior Aventinus is intended to recall the legendary birth of Rome's most infamous twin brothers. Another strong association of the Aventine, however, was with Diana: sometimes called the Hill of Diana (*Collis Dianae*),[28] it housed the cult of Diana supposedly transplanted by Servius Tullius and regarded as a duplicate of the one at Nemi.[29] Thus the first and last "alphabetical" warriors in the catalogue (Aventinus and Virbius) are associated with the two most important cult centers of Diana.[30]

The legend of Silvius' birth is also alluded to in the beginning of Virgil's war in Italy, with all its connotations of civil war.[31] Dionysius says that after Aeneas' death, Lavinia, pregnant and fearing harm from her stepson Ascanius, entrusted herself to the royal herdsman Tyrrhenus (some editors read "Tyrrhus"). He hid her and her baby in the woods, naming the baby "Silvius" accordingly (Dion. Hal. 1.70). Virgil gives the royal herdsman Tyrrhus a daughter named "Silvia" (7.485–87). Fordyce, after quoting Servius' comment that this is an appropriate name for a *puella rustica*, notes that "it is perhaps surprising that Virgil should have used for a minor character a name so prominent in the legendary pedigree of the Kings of Rome."[32] To name a royal herdsman Tyrrhus would itself recall the legend of Lavinia and Silvius. It is unlikely that Virgil would have named Tyrrhus' daughter "Silvia" if he had not wished to bring this legend to the fore.

---

27. See Wiseman (1995) 90–91.

28. Scullard (1981) 174.

29. Green (1994) 210–13 discusses the connection of the Servius legend with the Arician cult.

30. Montepaone (1993) 72 refers to the difficulty of elucidating the traditions of Diana Nemorensis in light of the "confronto/confusione/rivendicazione delle tradizioni della Diana Aventinensis" ("confrontation/confusion/claim of the traditions of Diana of the Aventine").

31. *Pace* Cyril Bailey, whose *OCD* entry s.v. "Silvius" says that the legend was "unknown to Virgil."

32. Fordyce (1977) ad 487.

Silvius and Silvia, then, are associated with Diana Nemorensis in various ways: through wordplay, parallels with Virbius, invention of a doublet of Rhea Silvia, and allusions to the tradition of Silvius hiding in the woods. The association becomes more direct when Ascanius shoots Silvia's pet deer. Deer were the special province of Diana, and she is often depicted holding, riding, hunting, or standing beside them. Silvia's is the third in a series of wounded deer that begins with the seven killed by Aeneas on his arrival in Carthage,[33] is pathetically elaborated in a simile for the lovesick Dido, and culminates in a simile for the fleeing Turnus.[34] While wounded deer are inevitably associated with Diana the huntress, the deer wounded by Aeneas and Ascanius are connected even more precisely with the rites of Diana Nemorensis.

One reminder of the Grove arises from associating these deer with trees, especially cypress trees. The leaders of the herd killed by Aeneas are said to have "*tree*-like antlers" (*cornibus arboreis,* 1.190). At least one ancient reader took this image as more than a casual metaphor, for it reaches a comic extreme in Ovid's portrait of the deer of Cyparissus:

> ingens cervus erat lateque patentibus altas
> ipse suo capiti praebebat cornibus umbras. (*Met.* 10.110–11)
>
> There was a huge stag, and he himself with his wide-spreading antlers provided high shade for his own head.

As Catherine Connors remarks, "With his portable '*locus amoenus,*' Cyparissus' stag, like Orpheus who summons up a shady grove with his song, can procure himself pastoral shade anywhere."[35] The deer shot by Aeneas and the deer shot by his son come together in the stag of Ovid's Cyparissus, who drapes his pet's tree-like antlers with garlands like those worn by Silvia's stag (and necklaces

33. On the sacrificial overtones of the number "seven," see Lee (1992); Dyson (1996b).

34. The similes are discussed in chap. 12.

35. Connors (1992) 9.

and earrings, again amplifying Virgil's hint).[36] Silvia's stag probably derives from a Hellenistic source treating the story of Cyparissus, who turns into a cypress tree in his grief over the wounding of his stag.[37] If such a model does indeed lie behind Silvia's wounded deer, then tree-like antlers would call to mind not only trees in general but the trees most closely associated with Diana Nemorensis. Even without reference to Cyparissus, the connection between "deer violation" and "tree violation" unites two elements within Diana's sphere.

The natives' response to the wounding of Silvia's stag creates even clearer associations among wounded trees, wounded deer, and the Grove of Diana. Silvia's cry rouses the Italian farmers from their occupation of chopping wood:

> olli (pestis enim tacitis latet aspera *silvis*)
> improvisi adsunt, *hic torre armatus obusto,*
> *stipitis hic gravidi nodis*; quod cuique repertum
> rimanti telum ira facit. vocat agmina Tyrrhus,
> quadrifidam *quercum cuneis ut forte coactis*
> scindebat rapta spirans immane securi. (7.505–10)

> They arrive unexpectedly (for the harsh plague lies hidden in the silent *woods*), *this one armed with a half-burnt brand, that one with the knots of a heavy stick*; wrath makes a weapon of whatever each finds in his search. Tyrrhus calls the troops—as by chance he was splitting an *oak* in four *with a wedge driven in*—snatching up his axe and breathing heavily.

The plague is in the woods; the weapons snatched by the farmers are all tree branches; Silvia's father is splitting an oak tree.[38] As the native Italians are no strangers to war (despite assertions to the

36. Makowski (1996) 34: "Seeing the potential for comedy, Ovid presents his own 'improvement' on [Silvia's] deer with a congeries of details that overwhelms."

37. Connors (1992) 4–12.

38. The phrase *cuneis coactis*, "with a wedge driven in," later appears in the battle narrative of "massed wedges of troops" (12.457), in a simile comparing Aeneas to a storm that will "spread ruin to trees and destruction to crops" (*dabit ille ruinas / arboribus stragemque satis*, 453–54). See Fordyce (1977) ad 7.509, Conington (1883) ad 10.396 for phrases repeated with different meanings.

contrary),[39] so, it seems, they are no strangers to tree violation. The clearest signal pointing to Diana Nemorensis, however, is the reference to her sacred grove and lake four lines later (515–16). When Allecto sounds her horrible bugle call to begin the war, the "whole grove trembled and the deep woods resounded" (*omne / contremuit nemus et silvae insonuere profundae*, 7.514–15). Servius understands this *nemus* to mean our Nemi, "a place not far from Aricia, in which there is a lake which is called Diana's mirror" (*locus haud longe ab Aricia, in quo lacus est, qui speculum Dianae dicitur*, ad 7.515). Whether or not he is correct in this interpretation of *nemus*, the reference in the next line to "the far off lake of Diana" (*Triviae longe lacus*, 516) almost certainly means the lake in the Arician grove (as Servius also notes). This detail is not merely a "romantic" circumlocution for "South."[40]

In addition to these opening scenes of the Italian War, Virgil several times alludes to Diana in omens, epiphanies, and invocations of other deities that mark points of decision for Aeneas and Turnus. The first and most obvious of these is the incident mentioned above in which Venus appears to Aeneas dressed as a huntress (1.314–401). Aeneas wonders whether she is "the sister of Phoebus" (1.329) and declares that "many a victim will fall at your altars by my right hand," *multa tibi ante aras nostra cadet hostia dextra* (334). A more subtle "transference" between Venus and Diana occurs after Aeneas lands in another strange country, receives the famous omen of his men "eating their tables" (while picnicking under a tall tree, 7.108), and knows that he has reached the promised land. He prays last to his "two parents in heaven and hell" (*duplicis caeloque Ereboque parentis*, 7.140). This strange reference to Venus and Anchises recalls the formula with which he invoked the deity of the Avernan wood, "Hecate, powerful in heaven and hell" (*Hecaten caeloque Ereboque potentem*, 6.247), before entering the Underworld.

Aeneas is not the only one to address another deity with a title also appropriate to Diana. When Iris appears to Turnus as he sits

39. See O'Hara (1994).
40. Fordyce (1977) ad 514 ff.

perplexed in a sacred grove (9.3–4), he calls her *decus caeli*, "the glory of heaven" (9.18). Both of the comparanda cited by Hardie are phrases applied to Diana, *decus caeli* in Horace's Secular Hymn (1–2) and *astrorum decus* ("glory of the stars") in Nisus' prayer later in the book (9.405). Turnus then claims, "I see the middle of heaven parting and the stars wandering in the sky" (*medium video discedere caelum / palantisque polo stellas*, 9.20–21). These lines recall both a Lucretian passage about heavenly bodies (2.1031–32) and a Homeric simile comparing the Trojans' watchfires to stars "around the shining moon" (8.555):[41]

> οὐρανόθεν δ' ἄρ' ὑπερράγη ἄσπετος αἰθήρ,
> πάντα δὲ εἴδεται ἄστρα. (*Il.* 8.558–59)

> the endless ether breaks forth from the heavens, and all the stars are seen.

Commentators note the similarity with the slightly apologetic caveat that Homer is describing a night scene and Virgil is not.[42] Rather than faulting Virgil for the inappropriateness of his echo, we should ask why he chose to recall one of antiquity's most memorable descriptions of the night sky, having just made Turnus address the goddess of the rainbow with a phrase naturally belonging to the goddess of the moon. We may well wonder whether Turnus is "seeing things"[43]—seeing, in fact, one of the faces of Diana.

In the episode of Nisus and Euryalus, Diana plays a more overt role. Hunting is an important theme in Book 9, the book most concerned with the "initiation" of adolescents, and it is fitting that Nisus should pray to the goddess of the hunt.[44] But Virgil also takes pains, by means of a puzzling geographical parenthesis, to bring in

41. Hardie (1994) ad 9.18–19, 19–21.

42. Page (1929) is the most reluctant to admit *Iliad* 8.559 into the comparison (choosing instead to draw attention to *Iliad* 16.300, which = 8.558), noting, "but the time is night and the passage difficult." Conington (1893) cites the Homeric lines and adds, "where however the conditions are different, as it is a night scene."

43. Hardie (1994) ad 19–21.

44. See Hardie (1994) 14–18; Petrini (1997) 93.

specifically the cult of Diana Nemorensis. Euryalus has lost his way, baffled by the "shadows of branches" (*tenebrae ramorum*, 384). Virgil interrupts the narrative with an apparently gratuitous piece of antiquarian nostalgia:

> Nisus abit; iamque imprudens evaserat hostis
> *atque locos qui post Albae de nomine dicti*
> *Albani* (tum rex stabula alta Latinus habebat),
> ut stetit et frustra absentem respexit amicum:
> "Euryale infelix, qua te regione reliqui?
> quave sequar?" (9.386–91)

> Nisus goes off; and now, imprudently, he had evaded the enemy *and the places that afterward were called "Alban" from the name of "Alba"* (at that time, King Latinus had his high stalls [there]), when he stopped and looked back in vain for his absent friend: "Unhappy Euryalus, in what region have I left you? Or where shall I follow you?"

Where indeed? Nisus' question about the location of his friend is mirrored in the perplexity of commentators about his own. Various emendations of *atque locos* have been proposed, such as *ac lucos* (the reading of some ninth-century manuscripts) and *atque lacus*, but these do not really help.[45] The two friends started out from the Trojans' camp at the Tiber mouth, and "the *lacus Albanus, mons Albanus*, and the site of Alba Longa, are all an improbably long way for Nisus to have run."[46] The more incongruous a digression, the more likely that Virgil intends a poetic point. Here he has improbably transported the youths thirty miles east of the Tiber's mouth to a dark grove in the region of Alba—to what can only be the Grove of Diana in the Alban Hills.

It is with this in mind that we should read the subsequent prayer of Nisus to the goddess. He reminds her of past sacrifices by his father Hyrtacus and himself:

---

45. See Hinds (1987b) on paronomasia involving *locus*, *lacus*, and *lucus* ("place," "lake," and "grove").

46. Hardie (1994) ad 387-8.

ocius adducto torquet hastile lacerto
suspiciens altam Lunam et sic voce precatur:
"tu, dea, tu praesens nostro succurre labori,
astrorum decus et *nemorum Latonia custos*.
si qua tuis umquam pro me *pater Hyrtacus* aris
dona tulit, si qua ipse meis venatibus auxi
suspendive tholo aut sacra ad fastigia fixi,
hunc sine me turbare globum et rege tela per auras."
dixerat et toto conixus corpore ferrum
conicit. hasta volans noctis *diverberat* umbras
et venit aversi in tergum Sulmonis ibique
frangitur, ac *fisso* transit praecordia *ligno*.
volvitur ille *vomens calidum de pectore flumen*
frigidus et longis *singultibus* ilia pulsat. (9.402–15)

Swiftly he draws back his arm and winds his spear, looking up at the high Moon, and thus prays out loud: "You, goddess, you be present and aid our labor, glory of the stars and *Latonian guardian of groves*. If my *father Hyrtacus* ever brought any offerings to your altars on my behalf, or if I myself with my own hunting magnified any or hung them from your shrine or fixed them to your gables, allow me to confound this crowd and direct my weapons through the breezes." He had spoken, and straining with his whole body hurls the iron. The flying spear *splits apart* the shadows of night *and comes into the back of Sulmo, facing away*, and there is shattered, and traverses his chest *with the wood split*. He rolls around *vomiting a hot stream from his chest*, himself cold, and convulses his guts with long *sobs*.

A scene from the Funeral Games in Book 5, to which the Night Raid continually looks back,[47] contains a clearer reference to the violation of a "tree" in a parallel context. Nisus shares with an archery

47. Harrison (1995) 157 notes that "no two books of the *Aeneid* have a closer relationship than 5 and 9." See also Harrison (1984) 224 for a list of correspondences between these two books.

contestant not only the patronymic Hyrtacides (as his prayer reminds us), but also the rare verb *diverberat*[48] and the phrase *et venit adversi/aversi*:

> primaque per caelum nervo stridente sagitta
> Hyrtacidae iuvenis volucris *diverberat* auras,
> *et venit adversique infigitur* ***arbore*** *mali*. (5.502–504)

> And through the sky the first arrow from the whizzing bowstring of the young *son of Hyrtacus splits apart* the winged breezes, *and comes and is fixed in the* ***tree*** *of the facing mast*.

These verbal correspondences are so close as to suggest that we should read Nisus' bowshot in light of the earlier one. Nisus has just prayed to Diana the "guardian of the woods," *nemorum custos*, in what must be the grove presided over by the Rex Nemorensis. His arrow traverses the chest of his enemy Sulmo "with the wood split," *fisso ligno*, a whispered allusion to the wounding of the sacred tree. The arrow of the earlier Hyrtacides, fixed in the "*tree* of the mast" (arbore *mali*), makes this whisper more audible.

These allusions to Diana Nemorensis add force to various other hints of sacrifice and fratricide earlier in the episode. During the nocturnal slaughter, Nisus decapitates—that is, turns into a *truncus*—a man who happens to be named Remus:[49]

> tris iuxta famulos temere inter tela iacentis
> armigerumque Remi premit aurigamque sub ipsis
> nactus equis ferroque secat pendentia colla.
> tum caput ipsi aufert domino *truncum*que relinquit
> *sanguine singultantem*; atro tepefacta cruore
> terra torique madent. (9.329–34)

---

48. The verb *diverberare* (which appears eleven times in extant Latin literature) occurs elsewhere in the *Aeneid* only when Aeneas in the Underworld is about to attack the *elm tree* full of ghostly monsters (6.294). On the Lucretian flavor of this line, see Dyson (1997a) 453–54.

49. Some commentators prefer *Remum* to *Remi*: see Hardie (1994) ad 9.330.

> He attacks three servants nearby, lying haphazardly among their weapons, and the arms-bearer of Remus, and his charioteer, catching him right under his horses, and severs their drooping necks with his sword. Then he carries off the head of the master [Remus] himself and leaves him a *trunk, sobbing with blood;* the earth and couches are wet and warm with black gore.

"Remus" would surely bring to any Roman mind the most famous loser in a single combat for kingship, and the word *truncus* conjures up the equation of human and tree that characterizes the Arician cult. The image of this Remus "sobbing with blood" (*sanguine singultantem*) anticipates a similar image of Sulmo (quoted above), who vomits a river of blood "with long sobs" (*longis singultibus,* 9.415). The words *singultus* and *singultare,* which appear in the *Aeneid* only here, further unite the two victims of Nisus who are assimilated to trees. Certain elements of the Night Raid, however, cast Nisus himself in the role of sacrificial victim.[50] Nisus is compared to a lion ravaging a flock "mute with dread" (*mutumque metu,* 9.341), a phrase used of the Lucretian Iphigeneia before she is sacrificed (*muta metu, DRN* 1.92). But another echo of that famous Lucretian passage implicitly casts Nisus (and Euryalus) in the role of Iphigeneia (9.226 ≈ *DRN* 1.86). Like all who attack the sacred tree of Diana, Nisus is both priest and victim. The reversal comes quickly.

The *Aeneid* presents a web of allusions to the myth and cult of Diana. As the goddess is the savior of both hunter and hunted, so these allusions often suggest the shifting roles of many of the *Aeneid*'s characters. Dido can be alternately Diana and Phaedra; the wounding of Silvia's deer leads into the natives' attacks on trees; Nisus passes quickly from sacrificer to sacrificed. One group of characters is particularly prone to such transformations: human kings associated with the violation of trees.

---

50. Dyson (1996a) 282–83. See also Wigodsky (1972) 105, 134.

CHAPTER NINE

DYING KINGS

ac veluti summis antiquam in montibus ornum
cum ferro accisam crebrisque bipennibus instant
eruere agricolae certatim, illa usque minatur
et tremefacta comam concusso vertice nutat,
vulneribus donec paulatim evicta supremum
congemuit traxitque iugis avulsa ruinam. (2.626–31)

> As when farmers press on competitively to uproot an ancient ash on a mountaintop, slashed with iron and frequent axe-blows, it keeps threatening and totters, with trembling hair and shaken head, until gradually, conquered by wounds, it groans its last and crashes down, torn away from the ridge.

Aeneas watches in horror as Troy comes crashing down like a tree. Much of the power and pathos of this simile derive from the tree's human qualities;[1] comparison to a tree, in turn, often creates sympathy for a human character. A similar symbolic equation between human and tree seems to have characterized the Arician cult, in which an attack on the sacred tree necessarily preceded an attack on the Rex himself.[2] Virgil metaphorically equates human kings and

---

1. See Reckford (1974) 64–66; Briggs (1980) 33; Thomas (1988b) 272–73; Lyne (1989) 121–23.
2. Green (1994) 221: "The priest-king and his tree are one."

violated trees.[3] This would be a powerful theme even without reference to the rites of Diana Nemorensis, but the cultic implications appear to have been present in Virgil's mind and serve to enrich his many allusions to human "trees." Moreover, several passages point specifically to the goddess and her cult.

Bernard Knox's classic article "The Serpent and the Flame" demonstrates how those two symbols form defining motifs for the fall of Troy.[4] The same could be said of trees. The proximate cause of Trojan destruction (the Horse) is a wooden object with humans inside its "womb" who personify the indwelling spirit of a tree. The Trojans ascribe Laocoön's death to his wounding of the "sacred wood/oak," *sacrum robur* (230). The Greeks begin their attack when Pyrrhus takes an axe to the beams of Priam's wooden house:

> ipse inter primos correpta dura *bipenni*
> limina perrumpit postisque a cardine vellit
> aeratos; iamque *excisa trabe* firma cavavit
> *robora* et ingentem lato dedit ore fenestram. (2.479–82)

> He himself [Pyrrhus] among the forefighters, snatching an *axe*, breaks through the hard threshold and tears the bronze doors from their hinge; and now, *with the beam cut out*, he has hollowed the rigid *wood* and made a huge window with broad mouth.

Axes feature again in the climactic simile quoted above describing the final destruction of Troy (627). Immediately after this simile, Aeneas returns home and has a conversation with his father, whose metaphors continue the imagery of violated trees. Anchises refuses to follow his son into exile "with Troy cut out," *Troia excisa* (637), the same participle and grammatical construction (ablative absolute) applied to the wooden beam in Priam's house (*excisa trabe*, "with the beam cut out," 481). He bequeaths arduous exile to the young,

3. On the importance of kings and kingship theory in the *Aeneid*, see Cairns (1989), especially 1–28. On the Rex Nemorensis as a paradigm of kingship, see Green (2000) 49–53.

4. Knox (1950).

whose strength, literally, "stands solid in its wood," *solidaeque suo stant robore vires* (639). Translations rarely capture the double meaning of *robur* as "(hard oak) wood" and "strength," yet the metaphor is vital.[5] Anchises concludes his speech with the complaint that he has been drawing his life out uselessly ever since Jupiter "blew on me with the winds of his thunderbolt and touched me with fire," *fulminis adflavit ventis et contigit igni* (649). Though lightning does sometimes strike humans (such as Oilean Ajax, 1.44), the prime targets for thunderbolts are trees. Anchises' complaint hints that, in comparison with the woody youth, he sees himself as a burned out tree.[6]

The life of Troy is tied to that of its dying king. The aftermath of Priam's death finds him lying like a fallen and mutilated tree with his head "torn away" (*avulsum*), the same participle used of the mountain ash that will symbolize Troy (*avulsa*, 2.631):

> iacet ingens litore truncus,
> *avulsum*que umeris caput et sine nomine corpus. (2.557–58)

> The huge *trunk* lies on the shore, a head *torn away* from its shoulders and a body without a name.

Chapter 3 posits that the placing of Priam's corpse on the "shore," in an unexpected and inconsistent conflation with the account in which he is dragged to the Sigean promontory, alludes to the fate of Aeneas' corpse. It is equally surprising to hear that Priam has been decapitated, another feature of the alternate version, because Aeneas has just told us that Pyrrhus "plunged the sword in his *side* up to the hilt" (lateri *capulo tenus abdidit ensem*, 553).[7] Priam is the

5. See Hexter (1989–90) 119–20 on the extension of the meaning of *robur* from "oak" to "hardwood" to "strength": "Vergil often conveys the richest ambiguities precisely by using the most traditional of metonymies" (120).

6. Lucan's use of trees and thunderbolts would support seeing such an implication in Anchises' speech. Green (1994) 222 observes that Lucan's comparison of Pompey to a sacred oak (1.135–43) and Caesar to the lightning that (implicitly) soon will strike it (1.151–57) "introduce . . . the imagery of the ancient Latin rite [i.e., of the Rex Nemorensis] into Lucan's epic."

7. Servius comments that the decapitated corpse of the fallen ruler of Asia lying on the shore "alludes to the story of Pompey" (*Pompei tangit historiam*, ad

first human in the *Aeneid* to be referred to as a *truncus*, in implicit comparison to a mutilated tree. He will not be the last.

As Priam represents the life of Troy, so an ancient tree is at the religious heart of his household. Priam's laurel overshadows the altar around which his family huddles in fear:

> aedibus in mediis nudoque sub aetheris axe
> ingens ara fuit iuxtaque veterrima laurus
> incumbens arae atque umbra complexa penatis.
> hic Hecuba et natae nequiquam altaria circum,
> praecipites atra ceu tempestate columbae,
> condensae et divum amplexae simulacra sedebant. (2.512–17)

> In the middle of the house, under the naked pole of heaven, there was a huge altar and near it a very ancient laurel leaning over the altar and embracing the *penates* with its shade. Here Hecuba and her daughters in vain around the altar, like fleeing doves in a black storm, were sitting huddled together and hugging the images of the gods.

Pyrrhus has no respect for Priam's altar or for his supplication: the tree merely forms a pathetic backdrop when Priam is dragged by the hair and slain "before the very altar" (*altaria ad ipsa*, 550). As discussed in chapter 4, Pyrrhus, "who slays the father at the altar" (*patrem qui obtruncat ad aras*, 663), receives retribution when Orestes "slays him at his father's altar" (*patrias obtruncat ad aras*, 3.332). The slaying of a king symbolically figured as a "tree" at an altar that stands before a sacred tree presents a clear parallel to the Arician cult, for the loser in the duel between Rex and Challenger probably was killed at an altar in front of Diana's tree. Orestes' role as (one) putative founder of the Arician cult may have been part of Virgil's motivation for depicting his retributive sacrifice of Pyrrhus.

2.557): see Hinds (1998) 8–10. Conversely, it is possible that Lucan's picture of that tragic general as an oak, doomed to fall (*casura*, 1.141), which "makes a shadow with its *trunk*, not its foliage" (trunco, *non frondibus, efficit umbram*, 1.140), alludes to Virgil's tragic king. See Green (1994) 222–23.

The recurring allusions to felled trees in Book 2 are particularly important in light of Virgil's mirroring of the sack of Troy in the second half of the poem, where Latinus' city is besieged by Trojans playing the role of attacking Greeks. In particular, the raging Aeneas resembles Pyrrhus.[8] The parallel between Priam and Latinus is supported by the ancient laurel trees in the center of the households of the two aged kings. Latinus' laurel, personified like Priam's and similarly regarded with religious awe, is beset by an enemy of a different kind:

> sed variis portenta deum terroribus obstant.
> laurus erat tecti medio in penetralibus altis
> sacra comam multosque metu servata per annos,
> quam pater inventam, primas cum conderet arces,
> ipse ferebatur Phoebo sacrasse Latinus,
> Laurentisque ab ea nomen posuisse colonis.
> huius apes summum densae (mirabile dictu)
> stridore ingenti liquidum trans aethera vectae
> obsedere apicem, et pedibus per mutua nexis
> examen subitum ramo frondente pependit.
> continuo vates "externum cernimus" inquit
> "adventare virum et partis petere agmen easdem
> partibus ex isdem et summa dominarier arce." (7.58–70)

> But the portents of the gods with manifold terrors stand in the way [of Turnus marrying Lavinia]. There was a laurel in the middle of the house, deep in its inward rooms, with sacred hair and preserved with dread through many years, which father Latinus himself was said to have discovered and consecrated to Phoebus when he was first building the citadel, and to have given the name "Laurentians" from it to his colonists. Dense bees, carried across the clear ether with huge screeching, occupied its top (amazing to say!), and with feet mutually interwoven the sudden swarm hung from a leafy

8. See chap. 4, n. 24.

> branch. At once the soothsayer said, "We see that a foreign man arrives and his army seeks the same parts from the same parts and wins control in the highest citadel."

This portent should well be a source of "terrors." The bees' *stridor*, "screeching," is an ugly word, used elsewhere of *wrathful* bees (12.590), of a whizzing arrow (11.863), and of a Dira who flies like a poisoned one (12.869). *Stridor* is also used for the iron chains of sinners (6.558), for ships' ropes in a storm (1.87), and for the north winds that batter the oak tree to which Aeneas is compared (4.443). In a metaphor with military overtones, the bees "occupy" or "besiege" (*obsedere*) this tree. The bees hang from a branch of the sacred tree: the vatic utterance that the foreigner's army will head for "the same parts" (*partes easdem*), and gain control over the citadel, conceals and reveals (as vatic utterances often do) a truth about the manner of Aeneas' victory. Commentators and characters in the poem may interpret the "same parts" to mean simply "the citadel," but Aeneas will also assault various real and metaphorical trees. Pyrrhus' attack on the timbers of Priam's house and his transformation of the king himself into a *truncus* render ominous the parallel between the laurels of Priam and Latinus. If the prophecy suggests that the foreign invader, like the bees, will attack the sacred tree, the subsequent resemblance of Aeneas to Pyrrhus reinforces this suggestion.[9]

Latinus himself is never described with arboreal metaphors. His citadel, however, with its parade of his ancestral *imagines*, is densely populated by forests, trees, wooden artifacts, and sylvan mythology. The place is "bristling with woods and with the *religio* of fathers" (*horrendum silvis et religione parentum*, 172). The effigies of ancestors are made "of ancient cedar," *antiqua e cedro* (178). Latinus' palace is said to have belonged to "Laurentian Picus" (171),[10] who was changed into a woodpecker (*picus*) by Circe's wand (*virga*) and

9. Merkelbach (1961) 88–89 interprets the portent in light of Aeneas' symbolic status as Rex Nemorensis, somewhat more optimistically than I.

10. Fordyce (1977) ad 7.171 observes that "Virgil has forgotten that in 61 he makes Latinus himself found the town and bestow the name *Laurentes*." The inconsistency may suggest rather that Virgil wants to associate Picus with the laurel tree.

poisons (190). There are only two other objects called *virga* in the *Aeneid*, the wand used by Mercury to lead souls into and out of the Underworld (4.242–43)[11] and the Golden Bough (6.409). Picus is thus doubly connected to tree violation: his avian occupation is to wound trees, and his metamorphosis was facilitated by an object similar to the Bough broken off by Aeneas.[12]

It is Latinus' scepter (173), however, that has the most important association with the Golden Bough. There is an inherent similarity between the two objects: both are branches, one metal and the other encased in metal. A clever verbal echo reinforces this similarity. The scepter takes center stage near the beginning of Book 12, when Latinus swears an extravagant oath to ratify the terms of the duel between Turnus and Aeneas:

"nec me vis ulla volentem
avertet, non, si tellurem effundat in undas
diluvio miscens caelumque in Tartara solvat,
ut sceptrum hoc" (*dextra sceptrum nam forte gerebat*)
"numquam fronde levi fundet virgulta nec umbras,
cum semel in silvis imo de stirpe recisum
matre caret posuitque comas et bracchia ferro,
olim arbos, nunc artificis manus aere decoro
inclusit patribusque dedit gestare Latinis." (12.203–11)

"Nor will any force turn me away willing, not if it should pour the earth into the waves, mingling it in the flood, and dissolve the sky into Tartarus; *as this scepter"* (*for by chance he was carrying a scepter in his right hand*) "never will give forth branches with light foliage nor shade, since at one time, in the woods, cut back from the depth of the stem, it lacks its

11. See Davidson (1992) 368 on Mercury's sinister *virga*.

12. Most commentators take *aurea* in line 7.190 as an ablative singular modifying *virga*, so that *aurea percussit virga* would mean "she struck him with her golden wand." This would bring Circe's wand even closer to the Golden Bough. Weber (1999) 325–26 recently has argued, however, that *aurea* should be read as a nominative singular modifying Circe (from the previous line), so that we should read "golden Circe struck him with her wand."

mother, and has put away its hair and arms through iron—once a tree, now the hand of the craftsman has enclosed it in beautiful bronze and given it to Latin fathers to carry."

The Sibyl reveals her trump card to the ferryman in these words:

> "si te nulla movet tantae pietatis imago,
> *at ramum hunc*" (*aperit ramum qui veste latebat*)
> "agnoscas." (6.405–407)

> "If no image of such great piety moves you, *yet this branch* (*she reveals the branch which lay hidden in her clothing*) you may recognize."

The echo here is the more artful in that the two italicized lines (12.206 and 6.406) have not a word in common, yet the parallels in syntax and sound are unmistakable.[13] Moreover, the introduction of the scepter recalls the Golden Bough at the moment when it is used to gain Aeneas admission to the Underworld, an image of descent into hell not unlike that in Latinus' oath. The violent imagery describing the cutting of the scepter, which "lacks its mother, and has put away its hair and arms through iron," recalls the resistance of the Bough strangely "hesitant" as Aeneas "greedily breaks it off" (*avidusque refringit / cunctantem*, 6.210–11). If the Golden Bough indeed recalls the bough on Diana's sacred tree in the Arician grove, then the scepter and the "Latin fathers" who wield it are drawn implicitly into the realm of the Rex Nemorensis.

---

13. Wills (1996) 336–37 cites this syntactical self-reference to "demonstrate the way Augustan poets enliven what might be seen as the academic Callimachean poetics of parenthesis," observing that "[e]xcept for the demonstrative, not a word is echoed between the two passages and yet formally the allusion is clear." Tarrant (1998) 156–57 notes that these are Virgil's only two instances of this kind of parenthesis, though it becomes a mannerism in Ovid: see Fantham (1998) ad *Fasti* 4.691. As Wills demonstrates throughout, important allusions in Latin poetry often involve parallels of sound and syntax rather than exact verbal repetition. For another nice example of syntactical allusion, see Thomas (1988) ad *Geo.* 3.454, in which Virgil's *alitur vitium vivitque tegendo* ("the fault is nourished and lives through covering") alludes to Lucretius' *ulcus enim vivescit et inveterascit alendo* ("the ulcer comes to life and grows inveterate through nourishing," *DRN* 4.1068).

Like his grandfather Picus, Latinus' father Faunus is closely associated with trees.[14] Faunus is also the father of Tarquitus,[15] one of the four characters who become a *truncus* (10.555). He is the son of "*forest-dwelling* Faunus and the nymph *Dryope*" (silvicolae *Fauno* Dryope *quem nympha crearat*, 10.551), a name that puns on the Greek word for "oak tree."[16] Evander, "founder of the Roman citadel" (8.313), begins his antiquarian catalogue with various arboreal beings:

> "haec *nemora* indigenae *Fauni* Nymphaeque tenebant
> gensque virum *truncis et duro robore* nata." (8.314–15)
>
> "These *woods* the indigenous *Fauns* and Nymphs used to possess, and a race of men born *from tree-trunks and hard wood*."

Whereas Latinus comes from a line of woodpeckers and wood spirits, the aborigines of Italy, born from trees, share the woods with multiple Fauni. Most importantly, the temporary revenge of Faunus' sacred tree is the final obstacle in Aeneas' pursuit of Turnus (12.766–90).

One minor king named Aulestes, who appears only in a catalogue and in his death scene, exemplifies clearly the association of kingship with both tree violation and human sacrifice. Messapus violates the peace treaty by killing him at an altar, declaring, "this is a better victim offered for the great gods" (*haec melior magnis data victima divis*, 12.296). Other details of his brief entrance and exit suggest a specific connection, not merely with human sacrifice, but with the cult of the Rex Nemorensis in particular. When Aulestes is

---

14. See Mannhardt (1905) 113–27.

15. See the end of chap. 3 on the parallel between Tarquitus' watery death and Aeneas' own fate.

16. Harrison (1991) ad 10.551 notes that the derivation of Dryope's name makes her an appropriate bride for *silvicola Faunus*. See Weber (1990) 209–10 for an Ovidian pun on *dryops*, "woodpecker," in the epithet *Dryopeius* applied to the tree-violator Erysichthon. The line describing Latinus' parentage similarly puns on tree names: he is "born of Faunus and the Laurentian nymph Marica" (*Fauno et nympha genitum Laurente Marica*, 7.47). The connection between "Laurentian" and "laurel" is made explicit in the episode immediately following (and Virgil has again used the adjective "Laurentian" somewhat anachronistically); "Marica" resembles two trees, the *myrica* (tamarisk) and the *marisca* (fig).

introduced, he is said to be led to the sea by the river Mincius "in a hostile pine" (*infesta . . . pinu*, 10.206) and to "beat the flood with a hundred trees" (*centenaque arbore fluctum / verberat*, 10.207–208). The reference to "oars" as "trees" here is unique.[17] When he is killed, it is with a "spear like a tree-trunk" (*telo . . . trabali*, 12.294); the word *trabalis* ("like a tree-trunk") appears nowhere else in Virgil's works.[18] It is remarkable that *three* synecdochic uses of "tree," two of them unique and all associated with violence, should attach to a character spotlighted so briefly. Moreover, Aulestes in his death scene is called "a king, and wearing the emblem of a king" (*regem regisque insigne gerentem*, 12.289). The repetition of "king" and the focus on his insignia implies that Aulestes' thematic significance depends upon his regal status, just as the priesthood of Haemonides (whom Aeneas sacrifices) is emphasized in a line devoted to his priestly regalia. Two other features of Aulestes also are worth noting. The first is the phrase *insigne gerentem* ("wearing the emblem"), which anticipates the poem's final human sacrifice: Aeneas is enraged to see that Turnus "*was wearing the emblem* of the enemy on his shoulders" (*umeris inimicum* insigne gerebat, 12.944). The other is that, according to Servius Auctus (ad 10.198), Aulestes was the founder of Perusia, the town whose leaders the fiery young Octavian was said to have sacrificed at the altar of Divus Julius.[19]

Several kings, Priam, Latinus, Latinus' ancestors, and Aulestes, are associated metaphorically with trees and, specifically, with the violation of trees. There is one king in the *Aeneid*, however, whose final assimilation to a tree is overt. It was conventional for Romans victorious in battle to set up a *tropaeum*, a tree trunk draped with

---

17. Harrison (1991) ad 10.207–208.

18. Indeed, the voyage itself seems to suggest Virgil's ignorance of or indifference to the geographical position of his own hometown. As Harrison (1991) ad 10.206 notes (with mild apology), "This would imply that the Mantuans have sailed down the Mincio into the sea and circumnavigated the Italian peninsula to join Aeneas, a highly improbable voyage, but the poet is not over-concerned with logistics here." On Virgil's manipulation of tradition in his catalogues of warriors, see Zetzel (1997) 194–95.

19. On the Perusine sacrifice, see the end of chap. 6.

the arms of the conquered enemy, obviously meant as an effigy of the fallen warrior himself.[20] Nowhere in the *Aeneid* is the analogy between human and tree more prominent than in the oak upon which Aeneas places the arms of Mezentius, declaring plainly, "this is Mezentius by my hands" (11.16). This *tropaeum* is the fulcrum of a series of arboreal allusions that have characterized Mezentius from the beginning.

The transformation of Mezentius from a loathesome to a sympathetic character is expressed by his changing relationship to trees. He first appears "brandishing an Etruscan pine" (*quassabat Etruscam / pinum*, 9.521–52). As Hardie notes, this may mean either a spear or a torch, but "[e]ither way there is a hint of the gigantic warrior wielding a whole tree, like Polyphemus (3.659 *trunca manum pinus regit* ["a broken-off pine directs his hand"]), to whom Mezentius is related in other ways."[21] As several scholars have shown, Mezentius resembles the Cyclops so closely and that we should "understand the Polyphemus episode as a kind of baseline for the interpretation of the encounter between Aeneas and Mezentius."[22] In addition to wielding a tree as a walking-stick, Polyphemus and the other Cyclopes are compared to trees in the only simile of Book 3:[23]

> cernimus astantis nequiquam lumine torvo
> Aetnaeos fratres caelo capita alta ferentis,
> concilium horrendum: quales cum vertice celso
> aeriae quercus aut coniferae cyparissae
> constiterunt, *silva alta Iovis lucusve Dianae*. (3.677–81)

> We see the Aetnaean brothers standing by in vain with fierce eye, carrying their high heads to the sky, a horrid assembly: as when lofty oaks or coniferous cypresses stand on a high peak, *the tall forest of Jupiter or the grove of Diana*.

---

20. See Malavolta (1990) 296–97.

21. Hardie (1994) ad 521–22.

22. Hardie (1986) 267. See Glenn (1971); La Penna (1980) 14–16; Hershkowitz (1991) 75.

23. Williams (1962) 3.

To compare gigantic beings to trees seems natural, but to specify the *sacred* groves of particular deities is rather shocking. (Servius' explanation that trees in sacred groves grow highest because they are protected is clever but not quite convincing.) The mention of the "forest of Jupiter" ironically underscores the Cyclopes' absolute impiety: the contempt of these man-eating monsters for Zeus/Jupiter, guardian of hospitality, was one of their identifying features (as at *Odyssey* 9.275–78). But why the "grove of Diana"?

This strange detail admits several possible explanations. Cypresses are linked with death, the Underworld, and Diana in her manifestation as the witch Hecate/Trivia—dark associations that arguably have some relevance to the wicked Cyclopes. The oak of Jupiter and the cypress of Diana would represent the Olympian and the chthonic, respectively. Yet it is not immediately obvious what the point of such a contrast would be; it would be easier to explain a comparison to either one of these deities than to both together. One reason for mentioning the groves of both deities could be to bring to mind a particular location associated with the two of them together. Since Diana tended to be associated with the "periphery" and Jupiter with the "center," their shrines were not often found in close proximity. The Alban Mount was one exception. The shrine of Jupiter Latiaris, patron god of the ancient Latins, was on the top of that mountain, not far from the shrine of Diana Nemorensis in the Alban Hills. When Valerius Flaccus (first century A.D.) mentions the goddess Diana's impending transplantation from Tauris to Aricia, he refers to Jupiter Latiaris as a would-be neighbor summoning her:[24]

> dixerat. ille procul trunca fugit anxius alno,
> Taurorumque locos delubraque saeva Dianae
> advenit. hic illum tristi, dea, praeficis arae
> ense dato; mora nec terris tibi longa cruentis.

24. This scene occurs after the women of the island of Lemnos, maddened by Venus, have killed almost all of the males. Hypsipyle alone hides her father Thoas (*ille*) and helps him to escape.

> iam nemus Egeriae, iam te ciet altus ab Alba
> Iuppiter et soli non mitis Aricia regi. (*Arg*. 2.300–305)

> She had spoken. He flees anxiously in a broken-off alder,[25] and arrives at the region of the Tauri and the savage temple of Diana. Here, goddess, you put him in charge of the grim altar, giving him a sword; nor is there long delay for you in these bloody lands. Now the wood of Egeria, now high Jupiter summons you from Alba [i.e., from high on Mount Alba] and Aricia, ungentle to its king [i.e., the Rex Nemorensis] alone.

It is possible that Virgil's collocation of the "forest of Jupiter" with the "grove of Diana" is meant to bring to mind these neighboring cult centers.[26] Even without reference to Jupiter, however, the most famous "grove of Diana," for the Romans, was the one near Aricia. The parallel between Polyphemus and Mezentius, who "becomes" a mutilated tree, suggests that the rites of tree violation in this grove may have contributed to Virgil's motivation in employing the strange simile.

A simile applied to Mezentius himself reinforces his association with Cyclopes, with trees, and implicitly with Diana. He is likened to the enormous hunter, Orion:

> quam magnus Orion,
> cum pedes incedit medii per maxima Nerei
> stagna viam scindens, umero supereminet undas,
> aut summis referens annosam montibus *ornum*
> ingrediturque solo et caput inter nubila condit,
> talis se vastis infert Mezentius armis. (10.763–68)

> As great Orion, when he goes on foot through the greatest pools of the middle of the ocean, cleaving his way, stands out

25. I translate the phrase *trunca . . . alno* literally. Presumably the "alder" refers to a ship made of alder wood, but it is not clear what the force of the adjective *trunca* is here—is the ship "oarless" or otherwise "broken"? It is tempting, though possibly far-fetched, to suppose that Valerius is alluding to the tree violation associated with Diana's cult, and/or the flight of the statue of the goddess in a bundle of wood.

26. On the political implications of this proximity, see Coarelli (1987) 167.

> above the waves with his shoulder, or carrying back an old *ash* from the highest mountains both walks on the ground and hides his head among the clouds, so Mezentius bears himself with his vast arms.

Though Orion was proverbially said to stride across the sea, Virgil, uniquely, has him carry a tree.[27] As noted above, Polyphemus, similarly, uses a whole tree as a staff, a *trunca pinus* ("lopped-off pine," 3.659), with all the nuances of mutilation attaching to the adjective *truncus*. While Polyphemus is compared to a tree in Diana's grove, Orion traditionally is killed by Diana (Artemis) for attempting to rape either her or her follower Opis (Apollodorus 1.4.3–5). Virgil makes this nymph the avenger of Camilla, perhaps as a reminder of the punishment that follows the violation of one in Diana's retinue.

The affinity between Polyphemus and Mezentius is strengthened also by the linking of both with Polydorus, whose spirit inhabits the bleeding tree assaulted by Aeneas and who is the paradigmatic victim of "tree violation."[28] The similarity in the names "Polydorus" and "Polyphemus," and the position of their episodes at the beginning and end of Book 3, might lead us to expect some sort of "ring composition"[29] between these scenes. In addition to the repeated injunction to Aeneas in both scenes to "flee, flee!" (*fuge . . . fuge*, 3.45; *fugite . . . fugite*, 3.639), the figuring of both Polydorus and Polyphemus as "trees" creates such a thematic correspondence. The trees that ultimately deck the altar for Polydorus are cypresses (3.64), one of the two used in the simile for Polyphemus. More important, however, is the association between Polydorus and Mezentius, both humans who become "trees" violated by Aeneas. The announcement of Lausus' death finds Mezentius washing his wounds in the

---

27. Part of the point of the simile is surely to "remythologize" the Lucretian *adunaton* ("impossibility") of men so enormous they can stride across the sea (*DRN* 1.200–201); see Gale (1994) 182–83.

28. On Aeneas' religious obtuseness in the Polydorus episode, see chap. 1.

29. Ancient authors were fond of this compositional technique, in which the end of a work (or self-contained section) in some way resembles its beginning. Compare the insightful remark of Hardie (1993) 1: "The epic strives for totality and completion, yet is at the same time driven obsessively to repetition and reworking."

Tiber and leaning on the trunk of a tree, his helmet hanging on the branches (10.835–36). His grief at Lausus' death, his self-recrimination, and his speech to his beloved horse have gone far toward changing this sometime monster into an object of pity.[30] When the battle begins, he circles Aeneas three times on horseback, hurling a "forest" of spears into the Trojan's shield, which Aeneas carries around with him in an impressively spondaic silver line:[31]

> *ter* secum Troius heros
> immanem aerato circumfert tegmine *silvam.*
> inde ubi tot traxisse moras, tot spicula taedet
> *vellere* . . . (10.886–89)

> *Three times* the Trojan hero carries around with him an enormous *forest* in the bronze covering. Then, when it irks him to have drawn out so many delays, to *pluck out* so many darts . . .

In the Polydorus episode, Aeneas attempts, three times, to "pluck out a forest" (*convellere silvam,* 3.24) that turns out to be a "crop of spears" (*telorum seges,* 46) bleeding with the human blood of the murdered Trojan.[32] Both of these figurative uses of *silva* (10.887 and 3.24) are odd enough to catch the reader's attention. The additional similarities of the *three* attempts and of Aeneas trying to *pluck out* the forest of spears suggest that Virgil intended the parallel to be noticed.

Human kings are especially likely to be victims or perpetrators of tree violation in the *Aeneid*. Priam is slain before a sacred tree, and himself becomes a *truncus,* moments before his city comes crashing down like a mountain ash. The apian attack on Latinus' sacred laurel, and his provenance from a "woodpecker" (Picus) and a wood spirit (Faunus), lend significance to the association of

---

30. See Gotoff (1984).

31. That is, a line consisting of all spondees (two long beats, except for the fifth foot) and exhibiting the relatively rare syntactical pattern "adjective$_1$ adjective$_2$ verb noun$_2$ noun$_1$."

32. On images of a "crop of swords" see Lyne (1989) 142–43.

his ancestral scepter with the Golden Bough. Aulestes beats the water with "trees" and is sacrificed by means of a trunk-like spear. But it is Mezentius who becomes a mutilated tree through the actions of Aeneas. That spectacle, and its implications for the end of the poem, will be the subject of the next chapter.

CHAPTER TEN

The *Tropaeum*

ingentem quercum decisis undique ramis
constituit tumulo fulgentiaque induit arma,
Mezenti ducis exuvias, tibi magne tropaeum
bellipotens; aptat rorantis sanguine *cristas*
*tela*que trunca viri, et bis sex *thoraca* petitum
perfossumque locis, *clipeum*que ex aere sinistrae
subligat atque *ensem* collo suspendit eburnum.
tum socios (namque omnis eum stipata tegebat
turba ducum) sic incipiens hortatur ovantis:
"maxima res effecta, viri; timor omnis abesto,
quod superest; haec sunt spolia et de rege superbo
primitiae manibusque meis Mezentius hic est." (11.5–16)

A huge oak tree, with its branches everywhere cut off, he set up on the mound and clothed in gleaming arms, the booty of the leader Mezentius, a trophy to you, O great powerful-in-war [Mars]; he fastens on the *crest* dripping with blood and the broken spears of the man, and the *corselet* sought and dug through in twice six places, and ties the *shield* of bronze beneath the left and hangs the ivory *sword* from the neck. Then he encourages his cheering allies (for the whole packed crowd of leaders was thronging him), beginning thus: "The

> greatest thing has been accomplished, men; for what remains, let all fear be gone; these are the spoils and the first-fruits from the proud king, and this is Mezentius by my hands."

The metaphor of the decapitated *truncus* that began with Priam comes to fruition in this tree of death.[1] The grim portrait exploits the analogy between tree and human that was explicit in the Polydorus episode, where Aeneas unwittingly commits an act of impiety (3.42) even as he attempts to perform the pious act of decking his altar with boughs (3.25). Here too he is "fulfilling his vows to the gods" (*vota deum . . . solvebat*, 11.4). Although no audible voice (from tree or narrator) condemns him, the language used and details emphasized create a sense of desecration. The first item mentioned, Mezentius' "crest dripping with blood" (*rorantis sanguine cristas*), resembles two particularly gruesome objects that "drip with blood" (*rorare sanguine*) in the *Aeneid*: the heads that Turnus places on stakes (*capita . . . rorantia sanguine*, 12.512) and the bushes depicted on Aeneas' shield that drip with blood from the dismembered limbs of Mettius Fufius (*rorabant sanguine vepres*, 8.645). Mezentius' weapons are *trunca*, "broken," with the suggestion of the shorn tree trunk on which they are hung (*decisis undique ramis*, "with its branches everywhere cut off").[2] The breastplate with its twelve holes suggests not only a warrior's brave death, but also the malice of the enemy mocking his corpse.[3] Mezentius' plea for burial has fallen on deaf ears. Aeneas exults that his own hands have turned his enemy into the horrible tree, *manibusque meis Mezentius hic est*. This image casts its shadow over the final lines of the poem: Turnus is

1. Reckford (1974) 78: "The landscape we are shown here is that of Hell."

2. Gransden (1991) ad 11.9.

3. Lyne (1989) 113 notes that *perfossum* ("dug through") is a strong and unusual metaphor: "The action described here has important implications; Vergil has an ulterior motive in composing a striking phrase for it. This damage was not done to Mezentius' breastplate during the battle, so far as we can judge (10.783-6, 856 f., 893 ff.). It is presumably due to posthumous mutilation. Aeneas did not therefore comply with Mezentius' request at 10.904 f." As Anderson (1999) 198 observes, "[Mezentius'] armor undeniably tells us exactly how Aeneas rejected his appeal" for decent burial. On Mezentius' death-rush on horseback and frontal wounds as reminiscent of Roman *devotio*, see Leigh (1993) 95–101.

sacrificed partly because he has symbolically transformed himself into a living *tropaeum*. Some readers have mentioned or hinted at this idea,[4] but in fact it is an essential theme to which Virgil devotes a range of allusive strategies.

One means of associating Turnus with both sacrifice and *tropaeum* is through parallels with other characters in whom these themes are explicit. The first mention of a *tropaeum* in the *Aeneid* follows the death of Haemonides,[5] a priest-become-victim discussed in chapter 4. Aeneas' friend Serestus gathers the fallen priest's arms to be a trophy for Mars Gradivus, a cult title that appears elsewhere in the *Aeneid* (3.35) only during the Polydorus episode (that is, in the context of tree violation):

> *immolat* ingentique umbra tegit, arma Serestus
> lecta refert umeris tibi, rex Gradive, *tropaeum*. (10.541–42)

> [Aeneas] *sacrifices* [Haemonides] and covers him with a huge shadow; Serestus gathers the arms and brings them back on his shoulders to you, king Gradivus, as a *trophy*.

The technical term *immolare* ("sacrifice") is used twice in Book 10, once of Haemonides and once of the predicted sacrifice of eight youths to the shade of Pallas (*inferias quos immolet umbris*, "which he would sacrifice as funeral-offerings to the shades," 10.519). During Pallas' funeral procession in Book 11, these youths appear in company with tree trunks wearing enemy arms:

> vinxerat et post terga manus, quos mitteret umbris
> inferias, caeso sparsurus sanguine flammas,
> indutosque iubet *truncos* hostilibus armis
> *ipsos ferre duces* inimicaque nomina figi. (11.81–84)

> And he had tied their hands behind their backs, those he would send as funeral offerings to the shades, and sprinkle

4. See especially Traina (1994) 29, 35–36. For an analysis of the *tropaea* in Books 10 and 11, see Nielson (1983).

5. This is the first appearance of the word *tropaeum* in the poem. There are seven altogether (10.542, 10.775, 11.7, 11.172, 11.224, 11.385, 11.790).

> the flames with their slaughtered blood; and he commands *trunks* clothed in enemy arms *to bear [the identities of] the leaders themselves* [or: commands *the leaders themselves to bear trunks* clothed in enemy arms] and the names of the foes to be attached [on them].

A meaningful grammatical ambiguity here further confuses men with trees: the two accusatives make it unclear whether Aeneas commands "the leaders to bear the trunks" or "the trunks to bear the (spoils and hence identities of the) leaders," as the trunk with which the book opens "is" Mezentius. Servius prefers the latter interpretation (ad 11.84), which would emphasize the equation of man and tree.[6] In any event, the juxtaposition of these two couplets creates a parallel between the sacrificial youths and the tree trunks. The youths and Haemonides, who share the distinction of the verb *immolare*, are also alike in their close association with *tropaea*. The only other appearance of *immolare* in the poem is in Aeneas' sacrifice of Turnus (12.949). We are encouraged to expect a *tropaeum* in that scene as well.

Another parallel between Turnus and trophy depends upon a subtext in the trophy for Mezentius. The description of Aeneas fastening Mezentius' armor and weapons onto the tree grotesquely parodies the arming of an epic warrior. Clausen notes the highly formulaic nature of Iliadic arming scenes, in which "the warrior's gear is described piece by piece: greaves, corselet, sword, shield, helmet, spear(s)—always the same six pieces and, whether simply or elaborately, in the same order."[7] The *tropaeum* receives five of these six items, crest, spears, corselet, shield, and sword (*cristae, tela, thorax, clipeum, ensis*; see the quotation at the beginning of this

6. See Narducci (1990) 306. Servius' interpretation probably is not the "correct" one, that is, it is not the most natural way of understanding the Latin. But his reading indicates that the phrase would have been at least *temporarily* ambiguous to a native speaker, and such temporary ambiguity is often significant; see Dyson (1997b). Perhaps many disputes about what a problematic Latin phrase really means would be better framed in terms of whether a given ambiguity is "temporary" or "permanent."

7. Clausen (1987) 95.

chapter). For obvious reasons of arboreal anatomy, greaves (shin-guards) are not a possibility. Unlike Homer, who places an arming scene before the *aristeia* of every warrior except Diomedes, Virgil describes such scenes rarely, and never directly before an *aristeia*.[8] Turnus (11.486–89) and Aeneas (12.430–32) each receive a few lines whose brevity merely emphasizes the heroes' impatience to get on with the battle. The only scene elaborated in Homeric detail is the arming of Turnus near the beginning of Book 12:

> ipse dehinc auro squalentem alboque orichalco
> circumdat *loricam* umeris, simul aptat habendo
> *ensem*que *clipeum*que et rubrae cornua *cristae*,
> ensem quem Dauno ignipotens deus ipse parenti
> fecerat et Stygia candentem tinxerat unda.
> exim quae mediis ingenti adnixa columnae
> aedibus astabat, validam vi corripit *hastam*,
> Actoris Aurunci spolium, quassatque trementem
> vociferans . . . (12.87–95)

> He himself then places the *corselet* stiff with gold and white mountain-copper around his shoulders, and fastens for handling the *sword* and *shield* and the horns of the ruddy *crest*, the sword which the god powerful in fire himself had made for Daunus his father and had dipped white-hot in the Stygian wave. At once he violently seizes the strong *spear*, which stood in the middle of his house leaning on a huge column, the spoil of Aruncan Actor, and brandishes it as it trembles, shouting . . .

The same verb for "fasten" (*aptat*) appears in the "arming" of the *tropaeum* and of Turnus (11.8, 12.88), and the five items mentioned are essentially the same, with three exact matches (*cristae, clipeum, ensis*, "crest, shield, sword") and two semantic equivalents (*tela* ≈ *hasta* "spear," *thorax* ≈ *lorica* "corselet"). Turnus follows precisely the Homeric order (*lorica, ensis, clipeum, cristae, hasta*), a signal that the

8. Clausen (1987) 94–95, 164.

reader is meant to notice the absence of greaves, the first Homeric item. Even Virgil's two abbreviated arming scenes, though they omit most of the Homeric items, show the warriors enclosing their shins in gold. The conspicuous absence of shin-guards in the most elaborate arming scene corresponds to their necessary absence in the "arming" of the tree that is Mezentius. By the five items he includes and the one item he omits, Virgil creates a parallel between Turnus—the only warrior with a full arming scene—and the *tropaeum* for Mezentius.

It is Mezentius himself who in even clearer terms introduces the idea of a man becoming a living *tropaeum*. Before the death of Lausus leads him to repent, the exiled king speaks a blatantly impious prayer that foreshadows his own doom:

> dextra mihi deus et telum, quod missile libro,
> nunc adsint! voveo praedonis corpore raptis
> *indutum spoliis* ipsum te, Lause, *tropaeum*
> Aeneae. (10.773–76)

> Let my right hand now be present for me as a god, and the spear, which I brandish to hurl! I vow you yourself, Lausus, *clothed in spoils* snatched from the body of the robber, as a *trophy* of Aeneas.

Aeneas, in his own words, succeeds in turning a tree into a human (*Mezentius hic est*). Mezentius desires but fails to turn a human into a tree. His wish to make his son a living trophy, arrogating to himself the offerings due to the gods, is the sort of perversity one might expect from a *contemptor deum* who prays to his own right hand. Mezentius was famous for commanding his people to give to him rather than to the gods the offering of "first-fruits," *primitiae*; Virgil alludes to this tradition when he has Aeneas (incorrectly) call the *tropaeum* the "first-fruits" (*primitiae*, 11.16).[9] However gruesome

9. See Burke (1974) 29: "It is impossible to explain otherwise the selection of Mezentius' arms as the first offerings to Mars since the Etruscan king, after three full books of war, is far from being the first enemy killed." Macrobius (*Sat.* 3.5.10) relates

the mutilated tree with broken and bloody armor may appear, we are meant to see in it a certain poetic justice. Mezentius' punishment resembles the doom he sought to inflict on others. Trees, not humans, are meant to be clothed in spoils.

Turnus' failure to recognize this is his fatal error. Virgil makes it clear that the swordbelt Turnus strips from Pallas will be his downfall. After describing the evocative scene depicted on the belt (the fifty Danaids killing their husbands on their wedding night), the narrator intrudes with a unique prophetic statement:[10]

> nescia mens hominum fati sortisque futurae
> et servare modum rebus sublata secundis!
> Turno tempus erit magno cum optaverit emptum
> intactum Pallanta, et cum spolia ista diemque
> oderit. (10.501–505)

> The mind of men, ignorant of fate and of the future and of how to maintain moderation when elated by favorable circumstances! There will be a time for Turnus when for a great price he will have desired to have bought Pallas untouched, and when he will hate those spoils and that day.

This heavy foreshadowing, however, does not make it clear *why* the spoils will prove deadly to Turnus. There is nothing immoral or unusual in taking a foe's armor. The arming scene quoted above (12.87–95) conspicuously omits any mention of the swordbelt; only in the poem's final lines is it revealed that Turnus is *wearing* the armor of Pallas. It is that climactic moment of recognition that causes Aeneas to kill him. Turnus' fatal and impious mistake, we

---

the legend of the *primitiae* and aptly calls Aeneas' taunt a *pia insultatio* ("just insult"). Nielson (1983) 28 notes that the "horror of becoming a living trophy, wearing the accoutrements of the dead warrior, is also reminiscent of Mezentius' practice of lashing the living to the dead."

10. The narrator occasionally does comment philosophically on the action (e.g., 12.503–504), but only here does he give an elaborate prediction of the future in his own voice. See Heinze (1993) 295–97; Harrison (1991) ad 10.501–505; Barchiesi (1984) 43–52.

find out at last, consists in clothing *himself* in the spoils that should have been hung on a tree.[11]

Though the vows of Pallas and Mezentius are never fulfilled, both have bearing on this aspect of the death of Turnus. Pallas prays to the god Tiber (*Thybris*) for a successful spear-cast (10.421–22) and promises that "your oak will have these arms and the man's booty" (*haec arma exuviasque viri tua quercus habebit*, 423). As Harrison notes, "Pallas' promise of dedication contrasts with Turnus' ill-omened keeping of his spoils."[12] The contrast is even more pointed than this note implies: Turnus not only keeps the spoils, but hangs them on himself as if he were a tree. Pallas' prayer also contrasts sharply with that of Mezentius, discussed above, in which the king prays to his right hand and vows to turn his son into a *tropaeum* "clothed in spoils" (*indutum spoliis*, 10.775). On *indutum spoliis*, Harrison refers the reader to 12.947 and offers no further comments. Yet the implications of this repetition are momentous. Although "spoils" appear frequently in the *Aeneid*, the only other appearance of the phrase "clothed in spoils" is in the reproachful last words of Aeneas:

> ille, oculis postquam saevi monimenta doloris
> *exuvias*que hausit, furiis accensus et ira
> terribilis: "tune hinc *spoliis indute* meorum
> eripiare mihi? Pallas te hoc vulnere, Pallas
> immolat et poenam scelerato ex sanguine sumit." (12.945–49)

> Aeneas, after he drank in with his eyes the reminder of savage pain and the *booty*, enflamed with fury and terrible in his wrath—"Are you to be stolen hence from me, *clothed in the spoils* of my own people? Pallas, Pallas with this wound sacrifices you and exacts the penalty from your accursed blood."

Aeneas had "clothed" the *tropaeum* of Mezentius in arms referred to as "booty" and "spoils" (*induit*, 11.6; *exuivias*, 7; *spolia*, 15), a disturbing spectacle, but consistent with Roman religious practice.

---

11. See Horsfall (1995) 212, 176.
12. Harrison (1991) ad 10.423.

The echo of Mezentius' prayer in Aeneas' last words should remind us that Turnus has placed on his own body the offerings due to the gods. He has become the *tropaeum* that Mezentius hoped to make of his own son. Aeneas' "savage pain" upon seeing the swordbelt of his friend is not without righteous indignation at a grave, even cosmic, impiety.[13]

The motive behind Aeneas' sacrifice of Turnus is a vexed question that looms large in the modern debate between "optimists" and "pessimists." The first half of this book argues that this sacrifice of Turnus belongs to the *honores* craved by Juno and promised by her husband. Yet as "optimists" from Servius (ad 12.940) on have stated, it is important to recognize the role of Evander's plea to Aeneas to avenge his son's death. Clausen's essay on "The Death of Turnus" emphasizes the *pietas* implicit in Aeneas' final act:[14]

> But Turnus cannot be spared, however moving his appeal, for there is the pressing emotional debt that Aeneas owes to Evander, a debt of gratitude originally, now become with Pallas' death a sacred obligation, as both Aeneas and Evander recognize. "Go," says Evander, in a scene of extreme pathos, to the Trojans who have returned his son's body, "go, and remember to take this message to your king":
>
> "quod vitam moror invisam Pallante perempto
> dextera causa tua est, Turnum gnatoque patrique
> quam debere vides." (11.177–79)

13. Hornsby (1966) 356: "Under the old dispensation, heroes lived for themselves, not for the good of society as a whole, and from the point of view of the civilized life Aeneas is bringing to the West, they were selfish, concerned only with their own glory. Such a motive the mission of Aeneas is to purify so that the valor or strength of the hero can be used for society. Arms are now dedicated to the gods, to the divine powers in whose care, hopefully, the state rests, just as Aeneas dedicates Mezentius' arms to the gods." Harrison (1998) 228–29 suggests that Turnus' religious transgression in failing to dedicate the armor parallels the transgression depicted on that armor, the Danaids' murder of their husbands. Huskey (1999) examines a parallel instance of Turnus' impiety in moving a boundary stone (so as to hurl it at Aeneas, 12.896–907), an act with dire legal and religious ramifications.

14. Clausen (1987) 100.

> "If I abide this hateful life, with Pallas dead, it is because you see that your right hand owes Turnus to son and father."

Evander's speech does more, however, than place upon Aeneas an obligation to kill his son's killer. As Evander imagines a suitable punishment, he wishes that his son's "(hard-wood) strength" (*robur*) had been able to transform Turnus, too, into a "trunk":

> "magna tropaea ferunt quos dat tua dextera leto;
> tu quoque nunc stares immanis *truncus* in arvis,
> esset par aetas et idem si *robur* ab annis,
> Turne. sed infelix Teucros quid demoror armis?
> vadite et haec memores regi mandata referte:
> quod vitam moror invisam Pallante perempto . . ."
> (11.172–77)

> "Those whom your right hand gives to death bear great trophies;[15] you, too, would now stand as an enormous *trunk* in the field,[16] Turnus, if [Pallas'] age and *strength* from years were equal. But why do I in my unhappiness delay the Trojans from arms? Go, and mindfully bring back these orders to your king: If I abide this hateful life, with Pallas dead . . ."

Like so many curses in ancient literature, Evander's wish comes true in a way that he does not anticipate. *Mezentius hic est*: Turnus, like the *tropaeum*, is now no more than the spoils he wears. Aeneas no longer sees the pleading eyes and hands (930) of his opponent. As Evander might have hoped, Turnus has become a "trunk," and it is "Pallas" (12.948) who kills him.

The *tropaeum* is an inherently ambiguous symbol. The poet's choice of language and imagery can color it positively or negatively,

---

15. The translation of *ferunt* ("they bear") is problematic; see Gransden (1991) ad loc. The difficulty may be intentionally reminiscent of the ambiguity of *ferre* in 11.84, discussed above.

16. The reading *in arvis* ("in the field") is Bentley's emendation of *in armis* ("in arms"), in order to avoid repetition (with 11.175). See Gransden (1991) ad loc. (who prefers the manuscripts' *in armis*).

can make it a symbol of piety or impiety—or both. The *tropaeum* represents piety toward the gods, because the arms of the defeated warrior are being duly dedicated to them. Yet at the same time it can recall the impiety inherent in tree violation and the sadness of a once living creature becoming mutilated and encased in bronze. It can represent the triumph of the powerful Olympian gods to whom it is dedicated over the lowlier divinities closer to the spirit of the tree.[17] There also can be an element of cruel mockery in it. In short, it gives play to the full range of Virgil's poetic dexterity.

Aeneas is the one to dedicate the only *tropaeum* in the poem that is given a full description. But Turnus as well deserves his reputation for creating trophies (11.224), with all that that implies.

17. See the discussion of Faunus' sacred tree at the end of chap. 12.

CHAPTER ELEVEN

IDA AND ALBA

Eastern ancestry posed difficulties for the Romans. Aeneas was a useful progenitor to claim, because Homer prophesied that his descendants would rule the world; but he was also a problematic one, because Troy was associated with the effeminate Orient. This tension is reflected in the Romans' ambivalent attitude toward Cybele, the "Berecynthian Mother" whose sacred grove on Mount Ida supplies the wood for Aeneas' ships.[1] The eunuch priests of her orgiastic rites form the climax of Numanus Remulus' vituperation of the Trojans (9.617–20). The prototype of these priests was Attis, a mortal lover or votary of Cybele, who in some versions of the myth castrates himself. When Attis appears among the arboreal audience hastening to hear the song of Orpheus in Ovid's *Metamorphoses*, he

1. Wiseman (1984) 119 well summarizes this ambivalence: "To the superstitious crowd, Cybele was an awesome power, a worker of miracles; to the rationalising philosopher, she was an allegory of mother Earth; to the Roman statesman, she was the first of the deities annually honoured by the aediles' games. But many Romans in Virgil's lifetime thought of her in terms of madness and high camp—a sinister alien goddess served by a priesthood of contemptible half-men." North (1976) 8 wryly observes, "the Romans, having spent long years casting their net wider and wider, finished the [third] century by pulling in a larger fish than they expected or wanted in the cult of Cybele, the Great Mother, who brought with her a new and alien religious tradition from the East." See Wilhelm (1989) on the role of Cybele in the Augustan program.

has been transformed into the shape often assigned him by tradition: a pine, Cybele's sacred tree (*Met.* 10.103–105).[2]

Readers ancient and modern have noted that the relationship between Cybele and Attis resembles in key respects the relationship between Diana and Hippolytus/Virbius.[3] In the *Aeneid*, the parallel between Attis and Virbius—sexually inactive priestly consorts associated, even identified, with their goddesses' sacred trees—belongs to a larger pattern of symmetry between Cybele and Diana. Virgil carefully develops this symmetry. The mountains that held the most prominent cults of these goddesses have similar functions:[4] when Juno watches the battle from Diana's Mount Alba (12.134–35), she resembles the gods of the *Iliad* watching from Cybele's Mount Ida.[5] Both goddesses interrupt the narrative with flashbacks about the history of beings sacred to them and now endangered, incidents that Virgil apparently has invented.[6] Most importantly, representatives of the two goddesses mount real or symbolic attacks on one another's priests and trees. In the symbolic clash between Cybele and Diana, Virgil interweaves the themes of East versus West and the tree violation that precedes the combat of Rex and Challenger.

---

2. See Hexter (1989–90) 128, who quotes Servius ad 2.31: *pinus in tutela quidem est matris deum* ("pine of course is under the guardianship of the mother of the gods"). Martial (13.25.1) refers to *nuces pineae* ("pine cones" or "pine nuts") as "Cybele's apples" (*poma . . . Cybeles*). A century after Virgil (and possibly earlier), a pine tree decked out with ribbons and bearing an effigy of Attis was carried in procession during Cybele's festival on 22 March. See Wissowa (1912) 321; Vermaseren (1977) 115.

3. Servius calls Virbius a "divinity conjoined with Diana, like Attis with the Mother of the Gods" (*numen coniunctum Dianae, ut matri deum Attis*, ad 7.761). Vermaseren (1977) 94 remarks, "As Hippolytos dedicates himself with self-sacrificing love to Artemis, so the lover Attis turns into the worshipping Attis, who in the end even lacks the faculty of physical intercourse." Horsfall (1999) ad 7.761–82 and 776 notes the many points of contact between the Virbius of *Aeneid* 7 and the Attis of Catullus 63.

4. He uses similar techniques to associate the Italian Tiber/Numicus with the Trojan Xanthus/Simois; see chap. 2.

5. Conington (1883) ad 12.134 compares *Iliad* 14.292: "The Alban mount is for Virg.'s battles here what Ida is for Homer's."

6. See Fantham (1990) 104 on this similarity of narrative technique.

It is thematically fitting for Aeneas, as a foreigner and a precursor of Roman imperialism (for good or ill), to attack Italian trees. It would not be fitting for the native Turnus to be shown doing so. But if it is true that Virgil casts the combat between Turnus and Aeneas in terms of Rex and Challenger, then we might expect that Turnus will not to be entirely innocent: the Rex will have obtained his office by violating a sacred tree himself. As with the "traces" of *devotio* in the *Aeneid*,[7] Virgil suggests this allusively, never forcing his epic characters into impossibly confining religious moulds. Lucan can imply that Pompey is the Rex Nemorensis without showing how he obtained the office; Virgil might have done the same with Turnus. It is therefore remarkable that Virgil goes to some length, apparently inventing episodes and relationships absent from the Aeneas legend as he found it, to show Turnus doing violence to Trojan trees. Since Turnus cannot go to Mount Ida, Virgil makes the trees of Mount Ida come to him.

A character's first appearance often foreshadows some important aspect of his role in the poem. If Dido comes onstage like Diana, and Mezentius like a Giant brandishing a tree, Turnus' debut (7.413–74) recalls a notorious violator of trees, Erysichthon. In the Hymn to Demeter (6.31–119), Callimachus shows the blasphemer wickedly and willfully hacking at Demeter's sacred grove, despite the pained cries of tree nymphs. When the goddess appears in the form of her priestess Nikippe and warns him to stop, he threatens to hack at her too. Enraged, she appears in her real form, with feet on the ground and head reaching Olympus, and punishes him with insatiable hunger. The parallels between Turnus' confrontation with Allecto disguised as Juno's priestess Calybe and Erysichthon's confrontation with Demeter disguised as the priestess Nikippe are well summarized by A. S. Hollis. As he points out, "The differences are meant to be noticed as much as the similarities, but in the end we may feel that there is at least a touch of Erysichthon in Turnus."[8]

7. See Leigh (1993).
8. Hollis (1992) 270–73 (quote from 270).

This is a fair assessment. Virgil's gods (and demons) work with human emotions already latent, magnifying rather than supplanting.[9] But it is not simply Erysichthon's wickedness in general that Virgil wishes us to compare with Turnus: it is his violation of trees in particular. Moreover, whereas Allecto invades Amata with poisonous snakes, she invades Turnus with a torch (7.454–55), the weapon with which he will attempt to attack the sacred trees of Cybele.[10] Turnus' first appearance thus assimilates him both to a violator of trees and, more subtly, to a violated tree himself.

The initial allusion to the prototypical violator of trees (Erysichthon) is amplified in Book 9, where Turnus twice attacks "trees" from the sacred grove of Cybele. The first incident, in which Turnus tries to torch Aeneas' ships only to watch them transformed into nymphs, appears to be Virgil's invention and has drawn reproach as incongruous[11]—two signals that it is likely to be thematically important. Cybele's flashback narrative of the history of her trees begins much like other excursuses on sacred trees (such as the laurels of Priam and Latinus),[12] but with a twist:

> pinea silva mihi multos dilecta per annos,
> lucus in arce fuit summa, quo sacra ferebant,
> nigranti picea trabibusque obscurus acernis.
> has ego Dardanio iuveni, cum classis egeret,
> *laeta dedi*; nunc sollicitam timor anxius angit. (9.85–89)

> A pine wood beloved to me for many years, there was a grove on the top of the citadel, to which they used to bring

9. See Lyne (1987) 66–71; Feeney (1991) 169–71; Horsfall (1995) 158–60.

10. Fire imagery in connection with human passions is ubiquitous. It is perhaps worth noting, however, that torchlight processions were a distinguishing feature of the cult of Diana Nemorensis (e.g., Statius *Silv.* 3.1.56), and Servius tells us that the goddess was depicted with a torch (ad 2.116).

11. See Hardie (1994) ad 9.77–122; Hinds (1998) 106–107; Fantham (1990) 102–103; Wilhelm (1989) 89–90; Wiltshire (1999) 164–65. Servius ad 3.46 lists the metamorphosis of the ships as one of the episodes for which Virgil was criticized because it was too fantastic. The others are the "crop of spears" that grew up around Polydorus, Aeneas' descent to the Underworld by means of the Golden Bough, and the cutting of Dido's lock by Iris.

12. Hardie (1994) ad 9.85. On the parallel between these laurels, see chap. 9.

> offerings, dark with black spruce and maple trunks. These *I gave happily* to the Dardan youth when he needed a fleet; now anxious fear tortures me with worry.

When we hear of a sacred grove that will soon be cut down, it is surprising to learn too that the goddess herself gave the trees happily. This has not been Aeneas' experience with trees so far.[13] But it is an important point. Virgil (or Aeneas, the narrator) is reticent about the religious implications of Aeneas' shipbuilding at the beginning of his wanderings. Aeneas says simply, "we build our fleet under Antandrus and the mountains of Phrygian Ida" (*classemque sub ipsa / Antandro et Phrygiae molimur montibus Idae,* 3.5–6). Especially in light of the tree violation that follows (the Polydorus episode, 3.22–68), this leaves open the possibility, to say the least, that there is an impious element to their building. Aeneas' unadorned statement makes Cybele's later statement that she gave the fleet to him "happily" all the more impressive.[14] We might say that the grove goes to Aeneas with the spontaneous willingness that the Golden Bough does not. It is Turnus who will have trouble when he attacks Cybele's "sacred pines" (*sacras pinus,* 9.116).

Or are they pines? Ambiguity about the material of the ships connects this incident to the nexus of tree violation pervading the Fall of Troy. Cybele says in the space of three lines that her grove contains pines, spruces, and maples, which along with a certain grammatical awkwardness has led some commentators to suppose that the passage lacks Virgil's final touch. Hardie compares the "similar confusion about the material of the Wooden Horse in *Aen.* 2.16 [fir], 112 [maple], 258 [pine]."[15] The "confusion" is in fact so similar that a parallel must be intended.[16] Though the dominant tree metaphor in Book 2 is that of the Greeks led by Pyrrhus attacking various sorts of trees—Priam's wooden house with its central

13. On Aeneas' repeated violation of trees, see Thomas (1988b).
14. See Fantham (1990) 109–13.
15. Hardie (1994) ad 9.85–87.
16. See Hexter (1989–90) on the shifting composition of the Horse as a comment on the nature of the *Aeneid* itself.

laurel, the king himself as a *truncus,* Troy the fallen ash—these acts are preceded by Laocoön's spear-cast at the *sacrum robur* (2.230) of the Wooden Horse. Turnus and Laocoön both launch unsuccessful attacks on wooden artifacts referred to as "trees."[17] The Horse and Cybele's grove both consist of maple (*acer*), pine (*pinus*), and another evergreen. The Horse contains fir (*abies*), and the grove contains spruce (*picea*)—but the full name of spruce is "pitchy fir," *abies picea*. Finally, the Horse repeatedly is described with vocabulary and metaphors appropriate to a ship.[18] These instances of *reciprocal* tree violation, with the defender's abortive attack on the invader's "sacred wood" followed by the invader's counterstrike, fit the paradigm of Rex and Challenger: the stronger prevails, but both at some time must have attacked the sacred tree.

In addition to his assault on Cybele's sacred trees as ships, Turnus also joins battle with her "trees" in the form of men. While the metamorphosis of the ships has been called more suitable to Ovidian "fairy tale" than to Virgilian dignity,[19] Pandarus and Bitias, young Trojan giants from the woods of Mount Ida, would be even more at home in a silver epic. These brothers are about as close to trees as humans can be. The "wood-nymph Iaera brought them up in the grove of Jupiter" (*Iovis eduxit luco silvestris Iaera,* 9.673), they are "equal to their ancestral firs" (*abietibus . . . patriis . . . aequos,* 674), and they are compared to twin oak trees by river banks:

---

17. As Harrison (1995) 148 notes, Cybele's speech "keeps her trees rather than Trojan ships to the fore." He also observes that Cybele's appeal should have made more of the inviolability of her sacred trees, "[f]or the Trojan ships will then possess a sacrosanctity comparable to that of the Argo or the Wooden Horse."

18. On the Horse-as-ship motif, see Losada (1983) 305–10 (with bibliography). Losada discusses more fully the similarities between the "trees" of the Horse and those of Cybele's grove, including a clear verbal echo of a phrase used of the Horse, *trabibus contextus acernis* ("woven with maple trunks," 2.112), in Cybele's description of her grove, *trabibusque obscurus acernis* ("and dark with maple trunks," 9.87). He concludes that "Virgil has explicitly linked together the horse-ship and Aeneas' own fleet" (310).

19. Fantham (1990) 102, quoting J. W. Mackail, *The "Aeneid"* (Oxford, 1933), p. 335.

quales aëriae liquentia flumina circum
sive Padi ripis Athesim seu propter amoenum
consurgunt *geminae quercus* intonsaque caelo
attollunt capita et sublimi vertice nutant. (9.679–82)

As *twin oaks* rise high in the air around clear rivers, on the banks of the Po or near pleasant Athesis, and raise their unshorn heads to the sky and nod with lofty crown.

The first warriors they fight are Quercens and Aquiculus (684): this "pair seems to pun on the oak-trees [*quercus*] and waters of the preceding simile." Pandarus hurls at Turnus a spear "rough with knots and crude bark" (*rudem nodis et cortice crudo*, 743)—a "spear for the giant from the mountain forests." This continual association with mountain trees serves to cast the brothers as Giants in battle with a Turnus who here resembles Jupiter.[20] But the sustained emphasis on their tree-like nature goes far beyond the Homeric model (a simile comparing Greek sentinels to trees, *Iliad* 12.132–34). The associations are also more complex, for the confusions and reversals in this episode are similar to others elsewhere in the poem. They "are" *quercus*, but they fight with Quercens. Turnus hurls a missile like a thunderbolt (*fulminis . . . modo*, 706), but ultimately he is thrust out by *fulmineus Mnestheus* (812).

In the close of Book 9, Virgil's allusiveness makes identifying the forces of good and evil especially problematic. As noted in chapter 5, Turnus' plunge with full armor into the Tiber would undoubtedly have reminded the Romans of Horatius Cocles, the quintessential patriotic hero. Immediately before Turnus jumps into the river, a "pitchy stream" flows down his own body:

tum toto corpore sudor
liquitur et *piceum* (nec respirare potestas)
flumen agit, fessos quatit aeger anhelitus artus.
tum demum praeceps saltu sese omnibus armis
in fluvium dedit. (9.812–16)

20. Hardie (1994) ad 9.684, 743, 672–755.

> Then sweat pours down from all over his body and drives a *pitchy stream* (nor is he able to breathe), sickly panting shakes his exhausted limbs. Then, finally, headlong with a jump he gave himself to the river with all his arms.

The verbal resonances of this *piceum flumen* are manifold. Lucretius (*DRN* 6.256–59) refers to a black cloud that looks like a "stream of pitch" (*picis . . . flumen*, 6.257) and brings a storm pregnant with thunderbolts, traditionally the trademark weapon of Jupiter. Virgil's Jupiter swears to Cybele by the banks of the river Styx "seething with pitch" (*pice torrentis*, 9.105)—not perhaps the most tactful turn of phrase, given her fear that her own pines will be ignited.[21] Finally, Turnus' pinewood torch throws "pitchy light," *piceum . . . lumen* (9.75), which rhymes with *piceum flumen*.[22] It would seem that the weapons of heaven and hell are indistinguishable.[23] As his exploits in Book 9 make Turnus both source and victim of figurative thunderbolts (9.706, 812), so they make him both agent and victim of figurative forest fires. After a hellish agent (Allecto) attacks him with pinewood torches (*taedae*, 7.457), he attempts to assault pine (ships) with pine (torches) and ends by sweating pitch, like a burning pine.

Virgil's strategy of presenting his characters alternately—sometimes even simultaneously—as trees and as violators of trees is a powerful means of eliciting complex emotions. Tree violation generally places a character in a negative light, and though Turnus (unlike Aeneas) never attacks a live tree, he is repeatedly shown attacking men who are tree-like. In Book 12, a final instance of symbolic tree violation by Turnus occurs at what is arguably his moral nadir in the poem. The Italians have spontaneously broken the

---

21. On Jupiter's response (especially his oath) to Cybele as a deliberate snub, see Harrison (1995) 149–150.

22. Hardie (1994) ad 9.813–14.

23. Hardie (1994) ad 9.105: "Jupiter's heavenly authority rests on hellish guarantees; his final agent in the poem is a Fury (12.843–68). Here Jupiter's burning black pitch is the talisman that frustrates the black pitch torches of the 'hellish' Turnus (74-6)."

truce (12.266); Aeneas stands bareheaded in the midst of the warring factions, imploring them to contain their wrath (311–15); unarmed, he is wounded by an anonymous arrow and leaves the field (318–24). By contrast, Turnus, instead of attempting as Aeneas did to repair the treaty, takes advantage of his absence and fights with fiery zeal (324–25). It is appropriate that the last warrior whom Turnus kills (12.371–82), before the scene shifts to Aeneas (383), has a name that means "oak-man," Phegeus (Greek *phêgos* = oak tree).[24] True to his name, Phegeus is the fourth and final character in the poem to be turned into a *truncus* (12.382).

Earlier in Book 12, however, Turnus' words remind us that he will himself be the subject of symbolic tree violation. His response to Latinus' plea to surrender quietly illustrates the way his bravado is wedded to a tragic lack of self-knowledge. Boasting in words that convey a fatal second meaning unknown to himself, Turnus declares that "blood follows also from my [lit. "our"] wound," *et nostro sequitur de vulnere sanguis* (12.51). The ambiguity of "my wound" is obvious to the reader, who knows that while Turnus intends to say "the wound inflicted *by* me," his words will instead come true when a wound is inflicted *on* him. An echo from the *Aeneid*'s first and fullest example of tree violation increases the irony and pathos of Turnus' boast. When Aeneas tries for the second time to pluck up a tree from the forest of Polydorus, he finds that "black blood follows also from the other's bark," *ater et alterius sequitur de cortice sanguis* (3.33). The promise of this ominous echo will be fulfilled in the poem's final lines, when Turnus becomes a living *tropaeum*.

The portrayal of Turnus as a violator of Trojan "trees," then, whether ships (Cybele's sacred pines) or men (Pandarus and Bitias, Phegeus), is countered by his assimilation to a tree himself (Allecto's torch, the "pitchy stream," the echo of Polydorus). Turnus also

24. See Hardie (1994) ad 9.765. We have seen the name twice before in the *Aeneid*, in each case conjoined with that of a man named for a river in Asia minor (in 5.263 with Sagaris; in 9.765 with Halys). Turnus in this scene also does away with Chloreus, the poem's most conspicuous Attis figure (12.363).

mounts symbolic attacks on Cybele's priestly consort Attis, who is closely associated with and sometimes takes the form of a pine tree. Virgil suggests Attis obliquely in several minor characters. The only one named "Atys" (a variant of "Attis")[25] in the poem is a participant in the Troy Game (5.545–603), in which three bands of Trojan boys engage in mock equestrian battles:

> una acies iuvenum, ducit quam parvus ovantem
> nomen avi referens Priamus, tua clara, Polite,
> progenies, auctura Italos; quem *Thracius albis*
> *portat equus bicolor maculis*, vestigia primi
> *alba* pedis frontemque ostentans arduus *albam*,
> alter Atys, genus unde Atii duxere Latini,
> parvus Atys pueroque puer dilectus Iulo. (5.563–69)

> There is one battle-line of youths which little Priam leads as it cheers, recalling the name of his grandfather, your illustrious offspring, Polites, destined to increase the Italians; him *a Thracian horse carries, dappled with white spots*, displaying with high bearing *white* marks at the tip of his foot and a *white* forehead; the other, Atys, whence the Latin Atii have traced their family, little Atys, a boy beloved to the boy Iulus.

Little Priam, grandson of Priam and son of the Polites killed before Priam's eyes,[26] rides a Thracian horse with white spots, *Thracius albis . . . maculis*. The emphatic repetition of forms of *albus*, especially in such an overtly etiological context, is a reminder of Alba Longa; at the end of the episode, Ascanius is said to have taught the game to his people when he girded Alba Longa (597). Aside from being called the progenitor of the *gens Atia*—the family of Augustus' mother—Atys receives little attention, and it may seem that there is no reason to connect him with the mythological Attis.

---

25. Herodotus' story of Atys son of Croesus (1.34–45) is an adaptation of the Attis myth. See Vermaseren (1977) 88–90.

26. On dark aspects of little Priam's role in the Troy Game, see Petrini (1997) 95–96.

Yet this collocation of the two boys, like many details of the Funeral Games, gains significance in the second half of the poem. It is on a Thracian horse with white spots, *maculis . . . Thracius albis* (9.49), that Turnus attempts to break into the Trojan camp presided over by Iulus (Aeneas is absent throughout Book 9) before deciding to attack Cybele's pines (9.47–76). As in the Troy Game, the Thracian horse's rider fights against both Iulus and "Attis." The *maculi albi* may provide a hint of the clash between Ida and *Alba*.

In the midst of Turnus' second attack on the Trojan camp, Cybele is suggested by the names of two of his victims, Sagaris and Idas (9.575).[27] Idas bears obvious resemblance to Ida, Cybele's mountain, and Sagaris is a variant of "Sangarius," a river that played a role in the myth of Cybele and Attis.[28] In Ovid's version (*Fasti* 4.223–44), Sagaritis, daughter of the river Sagaris, is a tree nymph whose illicit affair with Attis enrages Cybele and leads to Attis' self-castration. Ovid emphasizes the fact that Cybele kills Sagaritis by "wounding" and cutting down the tree that is central to her being:

> Naida volneribus succidit in arbore factis,
> illa perit: fatum Naidos arbor erat. (*Fasti* 4.231–32)

> [Cybele] cuts down the Naiad by wounds made to her tree, and she [Sagaritis] perishes: the fate/death of the Naiad was her tree.

The equation of human (or nymph) and tree seems to have been a stock feature of the Attis myth. In some versions he is born from a tree, in others he becomes one, and here he falls in love with one.

Although Turnus is the most frequent attacker of pine trees and figures otherwise connected with the cult of Cybele, the poem's most obvious Attis figure is a priest named Chloreus who is nearly

---

27. Names of minor warriors are a rich source of Alexandrian allusions. See, e.g., Noonan (1993) 116 on the story of Gyges and Candaules (told by Herodotus) recalled by the names of Turnus' victims "Gyges" and "Halys" (9.762–65), and Hollis (1992) 275 on the story of Tereus and Harpalyce (told by Euphorion) recalled by Camilla's victims "Tereus" and "Harpalycus" (11.675).

28. Hardie (1994) ad 9.575.

attacked by Camilla.[29] Chloreus' lavish gold and purple costume causes Camilla to "burn with a woman's love of booty and spoils" (*femineo praedae et spoliorum ardebat amore*, 11.782):

> Forte sacer Cybelo[30] Chloreus olimque sacerdos
> **insignis** longe Phrygiis fulgebat in **armis**
> spumantemque agitabat equum, quem pellis aënis
> in plumam squamis auro conserta tegebat.
> ipse peregrina **ferrugine clarus** et ostro
> spicula torquebat Lycio Gortynia cornu;
> aureus ex umeris erat arcus et aurea vati
> cassida; tum croceam **chlamydemque** sinusque crepantis
> carbaseos fulvo in nodum collegerat auro
> **pictus acu** tunicas et barbara tegmina crurum.[31] (11.768–77)

---

29. The emasculated priests of Cybele were called *Galli*; this happens also to be the word for the inhabitants of Gaul. Virgil wittily exploits this lexical coincidence. On the Shield of Aeneas, the invading Gauls are embossed in gold in a way that anticipates the golden raiment of the "Gallus" Chloreus:

> *aurea* caesaries ollis atque *aurea* vestis,
> virgatis lucent sagulis, *tum* lactea colla
> *auro* innectuntur. (8.659–61)

> *Golden* their hair and *golden* their raiment, they gleam with striped cloaks; *moreover*, their milky necks are woven with *gold*.

30. Some editors read *Cybelae*, which would make Chloreus "sacred to Cybele" rather than "sacred to Cybelus," but *Cybelo* is preferable since it is the *lectio difficilior*. The difference in meaning between *Cybelo* and *Cybelae* is not significant. Mount Cybelus (on Crete) was a favorite haunt of Cybele, who in 3.111 is called the *mater cultrix Cybeli* ("the mother who lives on Cybelus"), and the description of Chloreus leaves no doubt that he is meant to be seen as one of her priests.

31. The phrases in boldface are shared by a minor warrior identified only as the son of Arcens:

> sta*bat* in egregiis Arcentis filius **armis**
> **pictus acu chlamydem** et **ferrugine clarus** Hibera,
> *insignis* facie, genitor *quem mis*erat *Arcens*
> *eductum* matris *luco* Symae*thia circum*
> flumina, *pinguis ubi et placabilis ara* Palici. (9.581–85)

> The son of Arcens stoo*d* there in conspicuous **arms, with chlamys embroidered with needlepoint** and **brilliant** in Iberian **rust,** *outstanding* in appearance,

By chance Chloreus, sacred to Cybelus and once a priest, **outstanding**, was gleaming far in his Phrygian **arms** and driving his foaming horse, who was covered by a skin plumed with bronze scales and clasped with gold. He himself, **brilliant** with foreign **rust** and purple, used to hurl Gortynian darts from Lycian bow; the prophet had a golden bow [hanging] from his shoulders and a golden helmet; moreover, he had gathered his saffron **chlamys** and rustling linen folds into a knot with tawny gold, his tunic and the barbarian coverings of his legs **embroidered with needlepoint**.

The readiness with which Camilla succumbs to the temptations of Eastern luxury provides an unflattering comment on both the nature of women and the (alleged) hardy simplicity of the native Italians.[32] The encounter between the priest of Cybele and the votary of Diana also contributes to the carefully developed parallel between the two goddesses. Diana's flashback explaining how Camilla came to serve her (11.532–94), as mentioned earlier, interrupts the narrative in a manner similar to Cybele's flashback history of her sacred pines (9.80–106). Both goddesses appear in person only here. Like Cybele's story, Diana's prepares us for the retribution that will follow the violation of one sacred to her.

---

whom his father *Arcens* had *sent, brought up* in his mother's *grove around* the Symaeth*ian* streams, *where the altar* of Palicus *is rich and placable.*

The italicized words in this description are shared by the younger Virbius:

Ibat et Hippolyti proles pulcherrima bello,
Virbius, *insignem quem* mater Aricia *misit,*
eductum Egeriae *lucis* umen*tia circum*
litora, *pinguis ubi et placabilis ara* Dianae. (7.761–64)

The most beautiful offspring of Hippolytus also wen*t* to war, Virbius, *outstanding* warrior *whom* his mother *Aricia sent, brought up* in the *groves* of Egeria *around* water*y* shores, *where the altar* of Diana *is rich and placable.*

The son of Arcens appears to be a strange hybrid of the consorts of Cybele and Diana.

32. On Chloreus as representative of Trojan decadence, see West (1985) 22.

These parallels are especially important in light of Camilla's many specific points of contact with the Arician cult. Camilla's father Metabus was a fugitive (*fugiens*, 541) who sought refuge in the isolated groves (*solorum nemorum*, 545). When in his flight he encountered a swollen river and found himself unable to swim across holding the infant Camilla, he decided to tie the baby to his spear and a piece of bark and hurl her across:

> telum immane manu valida quod forte gerebat
> bellator, *solidum nodis et robore cocto,*
> huic natam *libro et silvestri subere* clausam
> implicat atque habilem mediae circumligat hastae;
> quam dextra ingenti librans ita ad aethera fatur:
> "alma, tibi hanc, *nemorum cultrix, Latonia virgo,*
> ipse pater famulam voveo; tua prima *per auras*
> tela tenens supplex hostem fugit. accipe, testor,
> diva tuam, quae nunc dubiis committitur auris."
> (11.552–60)

> An enormous weapon which by chance the warrior was carrying in his strong hand, *sturdy with knots and seasoned wood*—to this he binds his daughter, enclosed *in bark and cork from the woods*, and ties her handily to the middle of the spear; poising it with his huge hand he speaks thus to the ether: "O kindly *guardian of the groves, Latonian maiden*, I myself as father devote this girl to you to be your servant; she flees the enemy *through the breezes* holding your weapons first, a suppliant. I bear witness: goddess, receive your own, who now is committed to the doubtful breezes."

Servius informs us that the fugitive Orestes hid the statue of Artemis in "a bundle of wood," *fasce lignorum* (ad 2.116); little Camilla is similarly "enclosed in bark," resembling both the statue of the goddess and a tree inhabited by a divine spirit. Metabus prefaces his spear-cast with a prayer to Diana of the Groves (*nemorum cultrix, Latonia virgo*, 11.557): Nisus offers a prayer to the same goddess (*nemorum Latonia custos*, 9.405) before he sends his shaft through the air in the Alban woods. The name "Camilla," which means "attendant at a sacrifice," associates her with the goddess's rituals.[33] Diana states that "whoever violates the sacred body with a wound," *quicumque sacrum violarit vulnere corpus*, will forfeit his life (11.591–92); similar consequences attend violation of her sacred tree. She then affirms that she herself will carry away Camilla's body. This is something the goddess does for only one other character in the mythological tradition: Hippolytus.

Turnus attacks the "trees" of Cybele, whether the pinewood of ships or various human manifestations of "Attis." Camilla, closely associated with Diana and with the Arician cult in particular, meets her downfall because of her clash with an Attis figure. The previous two chapters discuss the importance of tree violation with regard to Mezentius, who "stars" in the end of Book 10 as Turnus does in Book 9 and Camilla does in Book 11. All of these books are a fitting prelude to the final combat between Aeneas and Turnus.

---

33. The name of her attacker, Arruns, belongs also to an Etruscan who was killed in a battle against the Aricians (Livy 2.14.5–9). But there are too many historical figures named Arruns to make it certain that Virgil or his readers would have had this one in mind.

CHAPTER TWELVE

THE KING OF THE WOOD

ac velut annoso validam cum robore quercum
Alpini Boreae nunc hinc nunc flatibus illinc
eruere inter se certant; it stridor, et altae
consternunt terram concusso stipite frondes;
ipsa haeret scopulis et quantum vertice ad auras
aetherias, tantum radice in Tartara tendit:
haud secus adsiduis hinc atque hinc vocibus heros
tunditur, et magno persentit pectore curas;
mens immota manet, lacrimae volvuntur inanes. (4.441–49)

And as when Alpine north winds strive among themselves with blasts now here, now there, to overturn an oak strong with ancient wood; a screech goes up, and the high branches strew the earth when the trunk is shaken; the tree itself holds fast to the cliff, and stretches as far to the etherial breezes with its crown as to Tartarus with its root: not otherwise is the hero battered by constant speeches here and there, and feels sorrows deep in his great heart; his mind remains unmoved, tears roll down in vain.

Like Troy, Aeneas is compared in an elaborate simile to a tree under assault. Unlike Troy, Aeneas does not fall. This famous portrait of the hero exemplifies for C. S. Lewis the "Virgilian note": Homer's heroes act on their emotions and self-interest, Virgil's obey a higher calling.[1] Like the tree, Aeneas is destined for heaven and hell at once—an allusion to his apotheosis and catabasis, and also perhaps to the dualities that characterize his own nature (long-suffering compassion that can shift to Achillean brutality).[2] The image of the battered oak conveys all this. It also brings Aeneas into the equation of human and tree that contributes to Virgil's sustained allusion to the Arician cult. The single combat between Turnus and Aeneas, toward which the entire poem has been leading (12.710–952), allusively reenacts the ritual duel between the Rex Nemorensis and his Challenger.[3]

Chapter 5 discusses the simile of fighting bulls and suggests that Virgil plays on the theme of sacrificial bulls. There is one element of this simile that points also to the Arician cult. In the *Georgics* model, the bulls fight over a heifer; in the *Aeneid* (though the sexual element is implicit), they fight over kingship. The herd stands there gossiping about who the new leader will be:

ac velut ingenti Sila *summove Taburno*
cum duo conversis inimica in proelia tauri
frontibus incurrunt, pavidi cessere magistri,
stat pecus omne metu mutum, mussantque iuvencae
quis nemori imperitet, quem tota armenta sequantur;
illi inter sese multa vi vulnera miscent
cornuaque *obnixi* infigunt et sanguine largo
colla armosque lavant, gemitu *nemus omne remugit*:
non aliter Tros Aeneas et Daunius heros
concurrunt clipeis, ingens fragor aethera complet.
(12.715–24)

And as on huge Sila or the *top of Taburnus* when two bulls rush together into enemy battle with foreheads opposed, the

1. Lewis (1942) 37–38.
2. See Reckford (1974) 68–70.
3. See Merkelbach (1961) 88; Clark (1979) 203; Green (2000).

> fearful herders have withdrawn, the whole herd stands mute with dread, and the cows mutter about *who is to rule the wood*, whom the whole flock is to follow; the bulls mix wounds between themselves with much violence, and *butting* they drive in their horns and wash their necks and flanks with much blood, *the whole wood bellows back* with groaning: not otherwise do Trojan Aeneas and the Daunian hero clash with their shields, a huge crash fills the ether.

On line 719, Conington comments, "The victorious bull is king of the wood"—a perfectly natural translation of *quis nemori imperitet*, years before Frazer's *Golden Bough* brought the King of the Wood into the limelight. It is also no coincidence that Turnus is compared earlier to a bull "butting against a tree trunk," *arboris obnixus trunco* (12.105 = *Geo*. 3.233), an appropriate "prelude" (*proludit*, 106) to this scene in which they are "butting" (*obnixi*, 721) against each other. To complete the assimilation of bull, man, and tree, Virgil needed only to glance at the Catullan simile that describes Theseus slaying the Minotaur, the man-bull who falls like a tree on "Mount Bull":

> nam velut in *summo* quatientem bracchia *Tauro*
> quercum aut conigeram sudanti cortice pinum
> indomitus turbo contorquens flamine robur
> eruit (illa procul radicitus exturbata
> prona cadit, late quaeviscumque obvia frangens),
> sic domito saevum prostravit corpore Theseus
> nequiquam vanis iactantem cornua ventis. (64.105–11)

> For as *on the top of Taurus* an untamed whirlwind wrenching wood with its blast overturns an oak shaking its arms, or a coniferous pine with sweating bark (the tree falls headlong, utterly shaken up from its roots, breaking everything in its way far and wide), so Theseus laid low the savage one, his body broken, tossing his horns in vain to the empty winds.

Virgil's decision to situate his bullfight simile on a mountaintop (*summo . . . Taburno*, 715) may owe something to Catullus' simile, in which a tree is uprooted "on the top of Taurus" (*summo ... Tauro,* 64.105). But even without reference to Catullus' association of tree and bull, the two bull similes of *Aeneid* 12 show Turnus attacking a tree that stands in for his opponent (104–106), then Turnus and Aeneas locked in a mortal struggle to determine who will be "king of the wood" (715–24). There is an obvious parallel with the Challenger's attack on the tree followed by combat with the Rex.

Several elements in the ensuing narrative have even stronger overtones of the Arican grove. The Augustan geographer Strabo's description of Aricia's landscape underscores some of the cult's salient features:

> μετὰ δὲ τὸ Ἀλβανὸν Ἀρικία ἐστὶ πόλις ἐπὶ τῇ ὁδῷ τῇ Ἀππίᾳ· στάδιοι δ' εἰσὶν ἐκ τῆς Ῥώμης ἑκατὸν ἑξήκοντα· κοῖλος δ' ἐστὶν ὁ τόπος, ἔχει δ' ὅμως *ἐρυμνὴν ἄκραν*. ὑπέρκειται δ' αὐτῆς τὸ μὲν Λανούιον, πόλις Ῥωμαίων, ἐν δεξιᾷ τῆς Ἀππίας ὁδοῦ, ἀφ' ἧς ἔποπτος ἥ τε θάλασσά ἐστι καὶ τὸ Ἄντιον, τὸ δ' Ἀρτεμίσιον, ὃ καλοῦσι Νέμος, ἐκ τοῦ ἐν ἀριστερᾷ μέρους τῆς ὁδοῦ τοῖς ἐξ Ἀρικίας ἀναβαίνουσιν. τῆς δ' Ἀρικίνης τὸ ἱερὸν λέγουσιν ἀφίδρυμά τι· τῆς Ταυροπόλου· καὶ γάρ τι *βαρβαρικὸν* κρατεῖ καὶ *Σκυθικὸν* περὶ τὸ ἱερὸν ἔθος. καθίσταται γὰρ ἱερεὺς ὁ γενηθεὶς αὐτόχειρ τοῦ ἱερωμένου πρότερον *δραπέτης* ἀνήρ· *ξιφήρης οὖν ἐστιν ἀεί, περισκοπῶν τὰς ἐπιθέσεις*, ἕτοιμος ἀμύνεσθαι. τὸ δ' ἱερὸν ἐν ἄλσει, πρόκειται δὲ *λίμνη πελαγίζουσα, κύκλῳ δ' ὀρεινὴ συνεχὴς ὀφρὺς περίκειται καὶ λίαν ὑψηλὴ* καὶ τὸ ἱερὸν καὶ τὸ ὕδωρ ἀπολαμβάνουσα ἐν κοίλῳ τόπῳ καὶ βαθεῖ. (*Geog.* 5.3.12)

> After the Alban Mount is the city Aricia, on the Appian Way, a hundred and sixty stadia [about 18 miles] from Rome. The place lies in a hollow, but it has nevertheless a [natural] *fortified citadel*. Lanuvium, a city of the Romans, lies above it, on the right of the Appian Way, from which both the sea and Antium are visible; and the Artemisium, which they call "Nemus" ["The Grove"], is on the left part of the Way as you go up from Aricia. They call the temple of the Arician [Artemis] a copy of that of the Tauropolan; for something *barbaric,* and

> *Scythian,* predominates in the sacred custom. For they set up as priest a *runaway* slave who has killed by his own hand the one formerly consecrated; *so he is always armed with a sword, looking around for attacks,* ready to ward them off. The temple is in a grove, and a *lake like the sea lies before it, and in a circle a continuous and very high mountain-brow lies around it,* enclosing both the temple and the water in a place hollow and deep.

The surroundings and actions of Turnus resemble those of the Arician priest-king:

> postquam arma dei ad Volcania ventum est,
> mortalis mucro glacies ceu futtilis ictu
> dissiluit, fulva resplendent fragmina harena.
> ergo amens *diversa fuga petit aequora* Turnus
> et nunc huc, inde huc incertos implicat orbis;
> undique enim densa Teucri *inclusere corona*
> atque hinc *vasta palus,* hinc *ardua moenia cingunt.*
> (12.739–45)

> After [the contest] had come to the Vulcanian arms of the god, the mortal blade shattered like fragile ice at his blow, the fragments gleam on the tawny sand. Thus Turnus, beside himself, *heads for different parts of the plain in flight,* and weaves uncertain circles now here, now there; the Trojans have *enclosed him* on all sides with a dense *wreath,* and here the *vast swamp,* there the *high walls encircle him.*

Turnus' physical setting—he is encircled by high walls and a "wreath" of Trojans and trapped against the "vast swamp" (which has not hitherto been mentioned)—resembles the Arician grove, with its huge lake encircled by a "fortified citadel" of mountains. As the combat draws to a close, the amphitheatrical setting is emphasized in the landscape that echoes the Rutulians' groans:

> consurgunt gemitu Rutuli totusque remugit
> *mons circum* et vocem late *nemora alta* remittunt. (12.928–29)

> The Rutulians rise with a groan, and the whole *mountain all around* bellows in reply and the *deep groves* far and wide send back the sound.

At Allecto's bugle call signaling the beginning of the war, the *nemus* trembled and the lake of Trivia heard (7.515–16); at the end, the groves and encircling mountain respond again to the sounds of battle.

The swordfight, absent from the Homeric model, was also an invariable feature of the Arician cult. Strabo asserts that the Rex was armed constantly with a sword, and Ovid refers in passing to the "kingdom" obtained by this means:

> ecce suburbanae templum nemorale Dianae,
> partaque *per gladios* regna nocente manu. (*A. A.* 1.259–60)

> Here is the woodland temple of suburban Diana, and the kingdom gained *through swords* by harmful hand.

It is noteworthy that when Aeneas takes the oath to engage in single combat, he prays "with drawn sword" (*stricto ense*, 12.175). Servius' comment, "according to some custom or other of swearing oaths" (*iuxta quendam iuris iurandi morem*), is tantamount to an admission that neither he nor his sources have any idea why Aeneas does this.

Though the precise significance of flight during the cultic combat is not clear, several sources mention the fugitive status of the contestants as a defining feature. Statius refers to Aricia as the home of *profugi reges*, "fugitive kings" (*Silv.* 3.1.55). Ovid calls them *fortes manibus pedibusque fugaces* (*Fasti* 3.271), "strong of hand and prone-to-flee of foot." The *OLD* classifies this instance of *fugax* as "(of slaves) runaway" (1.c); only fugitive slaves were eligible for the office in historical times. Since Ovid's *fortes manibus* undoubtedly refers to the actual combat, it would be attractive to take *pedibusque fugaces* as referring not only to the fugitive status of the contestants but also to some element of flight in the ritual itself.[4] Whether or

4. The *Rex Sacrorum* (one of the chief priests in Rome) participated in a ritual chase called the *Regifugium* or "Flight of the King"; after performing a sacrifice, the "King" would flee the forum as fast as he could. See Scullard (1981) 81; Basanoff (1943).

not the ritual combat involved a chase, it certainly involved runaways, and both Aeneas and Turnus are portrayed as "fleeing" or "fugitive."[5] The first adjective applied to Aeneas in the poem is *profugus* (1.2), the word that Statius applies to the Rex Nemorensis in the line cited above. The phrase describing Turnus' flight from Aeneas, *diversa fuga petit aequora*, plays on the ambiguity of *aequor*, which means "a smooth or level surface" and can refer to either "sea" or "plain." In the *Aeneid*, only three of the forty-two instances of the plural form *aequora* refer to "plains," and the other thirty-nine refer to "seas" or "the sea."[6] The theme of the first half of the *Aeneid* is Aeneas' flight across the seas (1.29, *iactatos aequore toto*, "tossed on the whole sea," and 1.32, *errabant acti fatis maria omnia circum*, "driven by the Fates, they wandered around all the seas"). Aeneas' pursuit of Turnus at the end thus is assimilated momentarily to Juno's pursuit of Aeneas at the beginning.[7] It should also be noted that Turnus is frequently referred to as *rex* (9.327, 369, 728, 10.267), even though his father is still alive. Both heroes could be said to reenact, like the *profugi reges*, the flight of Orestes.

By means of two allusions to the *Georgics*, Virgil associates the shattered sword and consequent flight of Turnus even more specifically with the barbaric rites of Diana. Putnam observes that when Turnus' sword "shatters" (*dissiluit*) like fragile ice, this recalls "the dire effects of the chilling cold on life among the Scythians" in *Georgics* 3.363–65, where "bronze shatters everywhere" (*aeraque dissiliunt vulgo*) and everything is turned to ice. A few lines later, Turnus is compared to a hunted deer:

---

5. See Merkelbach (1961) 88.

6. The *Aeneid*'s other instances of *aequora* as "plains" are both from the catalogue of Italian warriors (7.728, 738). Except for 12.742 (Turnus *diversa fuga petit aequora*), all of Virgil's conjunctions of *aequora* with either *diversa* (1.376, 3.325) or *fuga* (2.176, 5.219, *Geo.* 3.201) refer to seas. See Austin (1971) ad 1.376 on Virgil's many reminiscences of Catullus 101.1, *multas per gentes et multa per aequora vectus* ("borne through many nations and many seas").

7. On similarities betweeen Aeneas and Juno, see the beginning of chap. 6.

inclusum veluti si quando flumine nactus
cervum aut *puniceae* saeptum *formidine pennae*
venator cursu canis et latratibus instat; . . . (749–51)

As when a hunter, coming across a deer closed in by a river or trapped *by the scare of a crimson feather*, presses on with the running and barking of the dog . . .

This simile echoes the description of the Scythians' hunting methods, especially in the memorable phrase *puniceae . . . formidine pennae* ("by the scare of a crimson feather," *Geo*. 3.372, *Aen*. 12.750), reinforcing the allusion to the Scythians in the shattered sword.[8] Strabo's reference to the "barbaric, and *Scythian*, element" of the Arican cult indicates that the Romans considered the human sacrifice demanded by Diana Nemorensis to be a survival of that demanded by the Scythian Diana.

The Romans' instinct for significant wordplay provided a link between fugitive deer and fugitive slaves in the context of Diana's cult. As A. B. Cook notes, "Runaway slaves were called with grim humour *cervi* ["deer"], not *servi* ["slaves"]; and Diana, who had under her protection the stags of the woodland, would also shelter the human quarry in her sanctuary."[9] The grammarian Festus implies that this connection between *cervi* and *servi* was in the mind of Servius Tullius when he founded the temple of Diana on the Aventine:

servorum dies festus vulgo existimatur Idus Aug., quod eo die Ser. Tullius, natus servus, aedem Dianae dedicaverit in Aventino, cuius tutelae sint cervi, a quo celeritate fugitivos vocent cervos. (p. 343 Müller)

The festival day of slaves (*servi*) is held to be the Ides of August, because on that day Servius Tullius, born a slave, dedicated on the Aventine a temple to Diana, under whose

8. Putnam (1965) 196–98.
9. Cook (1902) 378.

> protection are deer (*cervi*), wherefore because of [their] swiftness they call fugitive slaves "deer."

Hunted deer and fugitive humans alike bring Diana to mind. Turnus is both. The allusions to the Scythians in this context provide an additional reminder that the goddess did not always allow deer to be substituted for humans on her altars.

This is the last of the poem's four depictions of hunted deer, and its significance can be appreciated best in light of the others. Two of these depictions—the seven deer killed by Aeneas in Carthage and Silvia's deer shot by Ascanius—are indirectly associated with tree violation and with Diana Nemorensis.[10] The same can be said of the simile comparing Dido to a deer wounded by a shepherd's arrow in the Dictaean woods:

> uritur infelix Dido totaque vagatur
> urbe furens, qualis coniecta cerva sagitta,
> quam procul incautam nemora inter Cresia fixit
> pastor agens telis liquitque volatile ferrum
> nescius: illa fuga silvas saltusque peragrat
> Dictaeos; haeret lateri letalis harundo. (4.68–73)

> Unhappy Dido burns and wanders throughout the city in a frenzy, like a doe at an arrow shot, which a shepherd, working busily with his weapons, has unknowingly pierced from afar amid the Cretan woods when she is off her guard: she wanders in flight through the Dictaean forests and groves; but the lethal shaft clings to her side.

Recently, two scholars have again brought to light what was for centuries a standard interpretation of one aspect of this simile.[11] The scene is located in the *Dictaean* forests, not merely because Cretans are notoriously treacherous, but also because wounded goats proverbially seek *dictamnum*, "dittany," the magic herb that can expel arrows

---

10. See chap. 8.
11. Morgan (1994) 67–68; Connors (1992) 14–16.

and which derives its name from the Cretan Mount Dicte, where it is said to grow. The cypress, Diana's tree, was the tree most characteristic of the "Cretan woods."[12] In addition to *dictamnum*, Virgil's *Dictaeus* probably alludes to *Dictynna*, a Cretan goddess associated with Diana or an epithet of Diana herself.[13] Servius (ad 2.116) calls the Taurian Diana—that is, the one who demands human sacrifice—"Dictynna Diana." Ovid in the *Fasti* refers to Diana as "Dictynna" once: as she is placing Hippolytus/ Virbius in the Arician grove (6.755). Hunted deer belong to Diana's realm in any case, and the Cretan woods (with their cypresses) and Dictaean forests (reminding us of Dictynna) bring the goddess more specifically into the simile's landscape.

Dittany appears in Book 12 in an incident remarkably similar to several instances of tree violation. Aeneas has been shot by an arrow from an unseen hand. The doctor Iapyx, "girded in the manner of Paeon [i.e., Apollo the Healer]" *(Paeonium in morem . . . succinctus*, 12.401), finds both herbs and forceps powerless to remove the arrow (12.400–406). Venus brings dittany all the way from Cretan Ida, which Virgil elsewhere refers to as the characteristic location of cypresses (*Geo*. 2.84, *Idaeis cyparissis*):

> Hic Venus indigno nati concussa dolore
> *dictamnum* genetrix Cretaea carpit ab Ida,
> puberibus caulem foliis et flore comantem
> purpureo; non illa feris incognita capris
> gramina, cum tergo volucres haesere sagittae.
> . . .
> iamque secuta manum *nullo cogente* sagitta
> excidit, atque novae rediere in pristina vires. (12.411–15, 423–24)

12. See Connors (1992) 14–15 on the connection of cypresses with Crete.

13. P. Valerius Cato, a neoteric poet of the generation before Virgil, wrote a poem that Suetonius (*Gramm*. 11) calls "Diana" but that the poet Cinna (as Suetonius also tells us) called "Dictynna." See Connors (1991) on the adjective *Dictaeus* in *Ciris* 300 as a learned allusion to *dictamnum*, in the context of a nymph's transformation into "Dictynna." Dictynna, *dictamnum*, and Dictaeus are also etymologically related to the Greek *dictuon* or "net." See O'Hara (1996) 32, 235–36.

> Here Venus the mother, shaken by the undeserved pain of her son, plucks *dittany* from Cretan Ida, a stalk hairy with downy leaves and purple flower; that grass is not unknown to wild goats, when winged arrows have stuck in their back. . . .
> And now the arrow fell out, following [the doctor's] hand *with no one forcing it*, and his strength returned anew to its former state.

This episode plays off of several scenes that are associated directly or indirectly with Diana Nemorensis. The use of a magic herb at a goddess's instigation recalls the miraculous healing (or revivification) of Hippolytus, "recalled by Paeonian herbs and Diana's love" (*Paeoniis revocatum herbis et amore Dianae*, 7.769).[14] Virgil signals this similarity by his use in both passages (7.769, 12.401) of the rare adjective *Paeonius*, which occurs in his poetry nowhere else.[15] We think also of Dido the wounded deer searching in vain for the medicinal herb that is given to Aeneas. Finally, the healing of Aeneas is the second incident in the *Aeneid* involving a wooden object whose removal is said to be impossible. In the first, the Sibyl tells Aeneas that the Golden Bough either will follow his hand willingly or will be impossible to pluck:[16]

> namque ipse volens facilisque sequetur,
> si te fata vocant; aliter *non viribus ullis*
> vincere nec duro poteris convellere ferro. (6.146–48)

> for it will follow willingly and easily of itself if the fates are calling you; otherwise, *not with any strength* will you be able to conquer it nor tear it off with hard iron.

---

14. Bronzini (1990) 242.

15. Ovid uses the word *Paeonius* only once, in reference to the healing of Hippolytus (*Met.* 15.535)—a passage that carefully "rewrites" Virgil's account.

16. Harrison (1990a) compares Virgil's dittany with Homer's *moly* (*Od.* 10.302–305), noting that, unlike dittany, *moly* "is carried as a prophylactic and primitive magical charm in the manner of the Golden Bough in *Aeneid* 6." On other similarities between *moly* and the Golden Bough, see Clark (1992) 175–76.

Like the Bough (as the Sibyl describes it), the arrow shares the strange property of inextricability without supernatural aid and pliancy only with such aid.[17] The arrow in Aeneas' flesh, in this respect, is analogous to the Golden Bough on its host tree, an analogy that associates the wounded Aeneas momentarily with a violated tree. Yet he bears an even closer resemblance to a violated deer: the analogy between the metaphorical arrow wound of Dido and the real wound of Aeneas is clear, and the further link of the dittany invites us to compare them. At one of his most sympathetic moments in the poem, Aeneas is symbolically the subject of both tree violation and deer violation—at the same time that Turnus is turning the "oak-man," Phegeus, into a *truncus*.[18]

After Aeneas is healed and returns to battle, however, he is transformed from the victim to the agent of tree violation. The sacred tree of Faunus is the poem's third host to a wooden object said to be unremovable but ultimately removed with divine assistance. In light of the references in the combat of Aeneas and Turnus—and indeed in the entire poem—to the cult of the Rex Nemorensis, this incident clearly belongs to the *Aeneid*'s thematic core. The Trojans had cut down Faunus' tree in order to level their battlefield, and Aeneas' subsequent actions create a sort of reprise of all the tree violations that have occurred previously:

> *Forte sacer* Fauno foliis *oleaster* amaris
> hic steterat, nautis olim venerabile lignum,
> servati ex undis ubi figere dona solebant
> Laurenti divo et votas suspendere vestis;
> sed stirpem Teucri nullo discrimine sacrum
> sustulerant, puro ut possent concurrere campo.

---

17. The healer Iapyx's brother, as Lee (1981) 209 points out, is none other than Palinurus (each is referred to as "son of Iasus," 5.843, 12.392); the Bough is parallel not only to the arrow, but also to Palinurus, who like the Bough "hesitates" before his fall (5.856 [Palinurus] *cunctanti*, 6.211 [Bough] *cunctantem*). It should also be noted that Virgil, perhaps in order to signal the latter parallel, makes Sleep's weapon against Palinurus a "*bough* wet with the dew of Lethe" (ramum *Lethaeo rore madentem*, 5.854).

18. See chap. 11.

hic hasta Aeneae stabat, huc impetus illam
detulerat fixam et lenta radice tenebat.
incubuit voluitque manu convellere ferrum
Dardanides, teloque sequi quem prendere cursu
non poterat. tum vero amens formidine Turnus
"Faune, precor, miserere" inquit "tuque optima ferrum
Terra tene, colui vestros si semper honores,
quos contra Aeneadae bello fecere profanos."
dixit, opemque dei non cassa in vota vocavit.
namque diu luctans lentoque in stirpe moratus
viribus haud ullis valuit discludere morsus
roboris Aeneas. dum nititur acer et instat,
rursus in aurigae faciem mutata Metisci
procurrit fratrique ensem dea Daunia reddit.
quod Venus audaci nymphae indignata licere
accessit telumque *alta ab radice revellit*.
olli sublimes armis animisque refecti,
hic gladio fidens, hic acer et arduus hasta,
adsistunt contra certamine Martis anheli. (12.766–90)

By chance a wild olive with bitter leaves, *sacred to Faunus,* had stood here, wood once venerable to sailors, where those saved from the waves used to fasten their gifts and hang up votive clothing for the Laurentian god. But the Teucrians had destroyed the sacred trunk indiscriminately, that they might do battle on a clear field. Here the spear of Aeneas stood, hither its impetus had brought it and was holding it fixed in the tough root. The son of Dardanus fell upon it and wanted to pluck out the iron with his hand, and to pursue with a missile him whom he could not catch with running. Then, however, mad with fear, Turnus said, "Faunus, I pray, have mercy, and you, oh most excellent Earth, hold fast the iron, if I always cultivated your honors, which by contrast the sons of Aeneas have profaned in war." He spoke, and summoned the god's aid to prayers not unfulfilled. For Aeneas, strug-

> gling long and lingering over the tough stump, was *not* able *with any strength* to open up the bite of the wood. While he strains fiercely and presses on, the Daunian goddess, changed again into the form of the charioteer Metiscus, runs out and returns the sword to her brother. Venus, indignant that this was permitted to the bold nymph, approached and *plucked out* [Aeneas'] weapon *from the deep root*. Lofty in arms and refreshed in spirit, this one trusting in his sword, that one fierce and tall with his spear, the men stand facing each other in the contest of panting Mars.

Like the Golden Bough (6.147), Aeneas' spear is said to be impossible to remove "with any strength," *viribus . . . ullis* (Virgil uses the phrase only in these two places). Venus "plucks it up," *revellit*, not effortlessly, but in language reminiscent of the Polydorus episode (*vellitur* 3.28, *convellere* 3.24, 31), in which Aeneas tries to pluck up a tree with a human voice from a forest of spears. The spear that Venus returns to Aeneas, and with which he will soon bring down his opponent, is later called "tree-like," *arboreum* (12.888). The epithet associates Aeneas with those Giant figures (such as Polyphemus and Mezentius) who wield entire trees, and it also strengthens the connection between the "tree" that is Polydorus and the "tree" that is the spear. The introductory phrase *forte sacer Fauno* echoes the introduction of Chloreus, *forte sacer Cybelo*: this echo reinforces and is enriched by the identification of Chloreus with Attis and Attis with a pine tree.

As suggested in chapter 5, Faunus' tree, strangely hung with votive offerings from sailors "saved from the waves," alludes to Aeneas' eventual manner of death. The species of Faunus' tree, a "wild olive" (*oleaster*), also provides a reminder of the death of Hippolytus. Most interpretations emphasize the nature of the *oleaster*—that is, its barrenness and bitterness—and take it as a comment on the nature of the Italian civilization against which Aeneas is fighting. But the wild olive also played an important role in the myth and cult of Diana's most famous votary. In describing the sacred precinct of Hippolytus at Troezen, Pausanias tells us that this kind of tree was responsible for the hero's death:

> ἐπὶ θάλασσαν δὲ τὴν Ψιφαίαν πορευομένοις κότινος πέφυκεν ὀνομαζόμενος ῥᾶχος στρεπτός. ῥάχους μὲν δὴ καλοῦσι Τροιζήνιοι πᾶν ὅσον ἄκαρπον ἐλαίας, κότινον καὶ φυλίαν καὶ ἔλαιον· στρεπτὸν δὲ ἐπονομάζουσι τοῦτον, ὅτι ἐνσχεθεισῶν αὐτῷ τῶν ἡνιῶν ἀνετράπη τοῦ Ἱππολύτου τὸ ἅρμα. τούτου δὲ οὐ πολὺ τῆς Σαρωνίας Ἀρτέμιδος ἀφέστηκε τὸ ἱερόν, καὶ τὰ ἐς αὐτὸ ἐμήνυσεν ὁ λόγος ἤδη μοι. (2.32.10)

> As you go to the Psiphaean Sea you see a wild olive growing called the "Bent *Rhakhos*." For the Troezenians call *rhakhos* every barren olive, *kotinos* and *phylia* and *elaios*; and they call this one "bent" because the chariot of Hippolytus was overturned when his reins were caught by it. Not far from this stands the temple of Saronian Artemis, and my account has already told about it.

The story that Pausanias tells of Saronian Artemis is as follows:

> μετὰ δὲ Ἄλθηπον Σάρων ἐβασίλευσεν. ἔλεγον δὲ ὅτι οὗτος τῇ Σαρωνίδι τὸ ἱερὸν Ἀρτέμιδι ᾠκοδόμησεν ἐπὶ θαλάσσῃ τελματώδει καὶ ἐπιπολῆς μᾶλλον, ὥστε καὶ Φοιβαία λίμνη διὰ τοῦτο ἐκαλεῖτο. Σάρωνα δὲ—θηρεύειν γὰρ δὴ μάλιστα ἥρητο—κατέλαβεν ἔλαφον διώκοντα ἐς θάλασσαν συνεσπεσεῖν φευγούσῃ· καὶ ἥ τε ἔλαφος ἐνήχετο ἀπωτέρω τῆς γῆς καὶ ὁ Σάρων εἴχετο τῆς ἄγρας, ἐς ὃ ὑπὸ προθυμίας ἀφίκετο ἐς τὸ πέλαγος· ἤδη δὲ κάμνοντα αὐτὸν καὶ ὑπὸ τῶν κυμάτων κατακλυζόμενον ἐπέλαβε τὸ χρεών. ἐκπεσόντα δὲ τὸν νεκρὸν κατὰ τὴν Φοιβαίαν λίμνην ἐς τὸ ἄλσος τῆς Ἀρτέμιδος ἐντὸς τοῦ ἱεροῦ περιβόλου θάπτουσι, καὶ λίμνην ἀπὸ τούτου Σαρωνίδα τὴν ταύτῃ θάλασσαν καλοῦσιν ἀντὶ Φοιβαίας. (2.30.7)

> After Althepus, Saron became king. They said that this man built a temple to Saronian Artemis right on the marshy sea, so that because of this it was called the Phoebaean Lake. It

> happened that as Saron was chasing a deer—for he was quite taken with hunting—he leapt into the sea with her as she was fleeing; and the deer kept swimming farther from land and Saron kept after his quarry, until, in his eagerness, he reached the ocean. Fate overtook him, already exhausted and pummeled by the waves. They buried his body within the sacred enclosure when it emerged at the grove of Artemis by the Phoebaean Lake, and they call the sea in this part the "Saronic Lake" instead of the Phoebaean.

Like the sanctuary that Pausanias describes, Virgil's narrative combines references to deer-hunting (749–55), the danger of drowning (*servati ex undis*, 768), and a wild olive tree (766)—none of which have any inherent connection to one another. If Virgil had access to these myths of Saron and Hippolytus, then it seems likely that he is alluding to them in his combination of these three disparate elements.

One possible literary source for the Troezenian myths is not far to seek. In commenting on the end of Virgil's description of Virbius (7.778), Servius tells us that Callimachus wrote an *aetion* about the reason that horses are barred from Diana's temple:[19]

> VNDE ETIAM TRIVIAE TEMPLO exponit τὸ αἴτιον: nam Callimachus scripsit αἴτια, in quibus etiam hoc commemorat.

> WHEREFORE ALSO FROM THE TEMPLE OF TRIVIA he explains the *aetion*: for Callimachus wrote *aetia*, in which he relates this too.

19. Both of the following quotations are from Pfeiffer (1949–53) ad Call. fr. 190. Callimachus (third century B.C.) wrote a poem called the *Aitia*, "Causes," that explained the mythical and historical origins of various Greek cults, cities, etc. Though only fragments of this poem remain, it was an exemplar of Alexandrian poetics and was much admired by Virgil. See Hollis (1992). Many discussions of Callimachean influence on Virgil, unfortunately, must involve a good deal of speculation about what Callimachus' poem is likely to have contained. Virgil of course knew the myth of Hippolytus, and probably the myth of Saron, from other sources as well. It would be satisfying to have unearthed a literary model in the lost Callimachean poem, but it is not necessary to this book's argument.

A scholiast on Ovid's *Ibis* (line 279, *viscera diversis scissa feruntur equis,* "let [your] guts be torn and carried by horses separate ways") similarly refers to a Callimachean poem now lost to us:

> tangit fabulam de Hippolyto: unde Callimachus: "noluit Hippol. etc.—qui vitae bis reparatur."
>
> He alludes to the story of Hippolytus: about which Callimachus [writes]: "Hippol. did not wish etc.—who was a second time restored to life."

Both of these comments are maddeningly elliptical. As Pfeiffer observes, however, there is little reason to doubt that Callimachus did in fact write a poem that mentioned the Arician cult of Hippolytus/Virbius.[20] Whether Callimachus also treated the legend of Saron we can only guess. Yet it is reasonable to speculate that the poet of the *Aitia,* in writing of Hippolytus' death near the Saronic Lake, at least would have glanced at the remarkable means by which that body of water received its name.[21]

The Troezenians, Pausanias tells us, say that their hero was taken up to the sky and became the constellation called the "Charioteer."[22] They refuse to show visitors his grave, even though they know where it is (2.32.1). As we have seen, another strain of the tradition brings Hippolytus to Italy to found the priesthood of the Arician grove. Still another shows him, like his father Theseus, remaining forever in the Underworld. His ultimate fate remains a mystery. It is fitting that a reminder of his death should precede the final sacrifice performed by Aeneas.

♦ ♦ ♦

> ille, oculis postquam saevi monimenta doloris
> exuviasque hausit, furiis accensus et ira

---

20. Pfeiffer (1949–53) ad Call. fr. 190.

21. See Barrett (1964) ad Eur. *Hipp.* 148–50.

22. As Caviglia (1990) 555–56 points out,Virgil alludes to this tradition while not following it. The resurrection of Hippolytus is described as a return "to the aetherial stars" (*ad sidera rursus / aetheria,* 7.767–68).

> terribilis: "tune hinc spoliis indute meorum
> eripiare mihi? Pallas te hoc vulnere, Pallas
> immolat et poenam scelerato ex sanguine sumit."
> hoc dicens ferrum adverso sub pectore condit
> fervidus; ast illi solvuntur frigore membra
> vitaque cum gemitu fugit indignata sub umbras.
> (12.945–52)

> Aeneas, after he drank in with his eyes the reminder of savage pain and the booty, enflamed with fury and terrible in his wrath—"Are you to be stolen hence from me, clothed in the spoils of my own people? Pallas, Pallas with this wound sacrifices you and exacts the penalty from your accursed blood." While saying this he buries his sword in the chest facing him, seething; but the other's limbs are loosed in cold, and with a groan his life flees, resentfully, to the shades below.

Nowhere is the moral complexity of the *Aeneid* more apparent and more troubling than at its close. The second part of this book has attempted to demonstrate how Virgil's sustained allusion to the rites of the Rex Nemorensis, with its attendant theme of tree violation, contributes to this complexity. In turning himself into a living *tropaeum,* Turnus incurs righteous retribution; yet his assimilation to a violated tree also invites compassion. The doubling that many have seen in that final scene, the uncanny sameness of killer and killed, finds a grim parallel both in the fratricide of civil war and in the reciprocal sacrifice of the Arician cult. The "priest" who slays Turnus is marked as a future victim. Like the slave-kings of Diana's grove, Aeneas, *fato profugus* (1.2), is fated ever to remain a fugitive.

Conclusion

E se furon dinanzi al cristianesmo,
non adorar debitamente a Dio:
e di questi cotai son io medesmo.
Per tai difetti, non per altro rio,
semo perduti, e sol di tanto offesi,
che sanza speme vivemo in disio.

(Dante, *Inferno* 4.37–42)

And if they were before Christianity, they did not worship God as they ought: and I myself am of this sort. For such defects, not for other sin, we are lost, and only so far afflicted that without hope we live in desire.[1]

In analyzing the end of the *Aeneid*, many readers ancient and modern have focused on the morality of Aeneas' sacrifice of Turnus.[2] The assumption underlying most such assessments, baldly stated, is that the rightness or wrongness of Aeneas' final action determines whether Virgil's intention was to praise or to blame Augustus. The present study has a different aim. It has sought to show that Turnus'

1. Virgil speaks these words to Dante, whom he guides through the Inferno and Purgatorio. Virgil vanishes when Dante is on the verge of entering Paradiso.

2. See Horsfall (1995) 192–216, especially 197, quoting Virgil's ancient commentators.

death is inevitable, a *telos* demanded by the religious framework of the poem, and that this sacrifice is the key to understanding Virgil's prophecy of the hero's fate and of the course of Roman history.

The last chapter of a mystery novel should be the best, the "pay-off," with lingering questions answered and clues all slotted into place. The detective should re-read the story to show how he reached his conclusion. The genre is enjoyable partly because it offers the satisfaction of intellectual closure, an assurance that a text initially baffling is in reality both coherent and determinate. In the case of the *Aeneid*, an interpretation that insisted upon such determinacy would ring false: indeterminacy, ambiguity, and ambivalence are the catchwords of Virgilian studies in the modern era, and with good reason. Readings that do not recognize their own partiality—with "partial" meaning both "incomplete" and "biased"—can well be accused of reductionism. On the other hand, fear of overstating their case can sometimes prevent the conscientious from making a case at all.

The thesis of this work is that Virgil casts Aeneas as a priest-king whose sacrifice of Turnus will result in his own sacrificial death, a paradigm of the endless reciprocal human sacrifices demanded by Rome's gods. Crucial to this argument are three extra-textual phenomena familiar to Virgil's ancient Roman readers but unknown to or overlooked by most moderns: the tradition of Aeneas' death by drowning in the Numicus River; the necessity for expiation, through repetition, of a failed sacrifice, especially one whose victim proved unwilling; and the cult of the Rex Nemorensis, in which tree violation led to single combat and the sacrificial death of the priest-king. The investigation has been based in part upon a principle expressed by Mr. Sherlock Holmes: "The more outré and grotesque an incident is the more carefully it deserves to be examined, and the very point which appears to complicate a case is, when duly considered and scientifically handled, the one which is most likely to elucidate it."[3] In allegiance to this principle, the next

3. "The Hound of the Baskervilles," Doyle (1960) 764.

few pages will highlight some of the peculiar twists that led to the conclusions presented in this book.

Like Poe's purloined letter, the most important clue to the whole puzzle is hiding in plain sight: the Golden Bough. Its hesitation—which we should now recognize as deliberate, ritual hesitation—was not in the script laid out by the Sibyl, who had said that it would be either easy or impossible to remove. The discrepancy between her words and the Bough's reluctance shines the spotlight on that critical moment at which Aeneas "greedily" *breaks it off*, thereby determining his own destiny and that of Rome. Servius tells us that, according to the cult of the Rex Nemorensis to which Virgil here alludes, this action must be the cause "of one untimely death." What Servius and others do not care to admit is that, logically, this ultimately must be the *sacrificial death of the one who broke off the bough.*

That Diana's cult was very much on Virgil's mind is not difficult to establish. For instance, there is the strange cameo by the Rex Nemorensis himself—or at least by a mysterious, lonely denizen of the Arician Grove whom legend makes a founder of that priesthood (Virbius, the resurrected Hippolytus). Though Virbius (Junior) receives the last and longest entry in the catalogue of minor Italian warriors, not only is he absent from the rest of the poem, but as Servius recognized, *he should not even exist*: his father is the mythological male most infamous for militant celibacy. Yet as the Arician cult was mirrored on the Aventine, so Virbius is mirrored in the first minor warrior in the list (Aventinus), who also fails to appear again the poem. If we dismiss this anomolous intrusion of Diana's cult apparatus into the catalogue of warriors ("local color"), or close our ears to the bugle call that stirs the lake in her Grove ("romantic circumlocution"), still the goddess will make herself heard. She takes center stage in our first glimpse of Dido and Aeneas' meeting with Venus. She reappears in wounded deer and wounded trees, in shadows of Hippolytus, in the tragic career of her votary Camilla. It could be said that Diana's presence in the *Aeneid* quietly rivals that of obstreperous Juno. As an allusion to the rituals of her Grove, the breaking off of the Bough is hardly alone.

Nor is the Bough an isolated arboreal victim. Attacks on trees, former trees, and humans equated with trees occur repeatedly, even obsessively, throughout the *Aeneid*. Troy's king, slaughtered at the altar before his sacred laurel, becomes a *truncus* moments before the city herself crashes down like a mountain ash. Laocoön attacks the maple, fir, and pine of the enemy's Horse; Turnus attacks the maple, (pitchy) fir, and pine of the enemy's ships. Aeneas' journey begins with the violation of a tree—or more specifically, a man (Polydorus) who has become a tree. And the assimilation of human to tree amid a gruesome display of *pietas* is overt in the trophy that "is" Mezentius. This transformation of the vanquished king stands behind the poem's climactic moment, that instant of recognition and rage when Aeneas sees Turnus "clothed in the spoils" stripped from Pallas, completing the strange parallel between the arming of Turnus and the "arming" of the *tropaeum*. Mezentius himself had wished to make his son a living trophy, "clothed in the spoils" of Aeneas; Evander had wished that Turnus might become a *truncus* like Mezentius. Such wishes have consequences in classical literature. Turnus does not die because he killed Pallas: he dies because he hung Pallas' armor upon his own body *like a tree*.

The final combat, with its chilling denouement, brings this cultic intertext to fruition. After arming himself, Turnus is compared to a bull butting against a tree; when the warriors finally engage in a swordfight, they are compared to bulls butting against one another, fighting to see who will "rule the grove." Aeneas, himself a *rex profugus*, has now become the pursuer. Turnus' sword shatters like ice, and he flees like a deer scared by a crimson feather, summoning unmistakably the recollection of Scythian Diana. The struggle with Faunus' sacred stump recalls the fatal moment when Aeneas first broke the Bough, symbolically marking himself as the Challenger. To become king, he must sacrifice his opponent. And so he does.

As the sacrifice of Turnus is foreordained, so it is destined that Aeneas, like Achilles, will pay with his own life. Images of death by water are especially rife with those anomalies that signal Virgil's ulterior designs, as when Aeneas leaves Tarquitus to the birds and *fishes* with (ostensibly) no river around. The abundant inconsistencies surrounding Palinurus' death bring to mind Aeneas' other drowned comrades. And there is the persistent reappearance of the little Numicus River, cerulean Tiber's sleeping partner and the missing member of the equation in the Sibyl's prophecy of a new Simois and Xanthus in Italy. Aeneas indeed will encounter a formidable opponent in Turnus boiling like the Xanthus, Turnus in full armor saved by the Tiber, Turnus sending bodies rolling like the Simois in Aeneas' opening death-wish. If Aeneas is destined to be lifted up to heaven, as Jupiter says, he also is destined to lie unburied in the sand, as Dido desires. Like so many real and symbolic priests in the *Aeneid*—Laocoön, Panthus, Pyrrhus, Haemonides—he is marked as a victim.

Small wonder, then, if Juno leaves heaven happy. Her wrath is the force that motivates the poem's action; what is most important to her, she tells us, is to receive sufficient *honores*. Yet whenever Aeneas tries to placate her, reassured by prophets that the proper sacrifices will do so, he fails—until Jupiter's promise at the very end. This riddle admits of only two solutions: either the prophets are lying (and prophets do not, as a rule, lie) or *Aeneas has failed to make the proper sacrifices*. Only at the end is Juno made happy, through Jupiter's promise that the Romans will surpass all nations in celebrating her *honores*. The final act in the poem is a human sacrifice. It is not a great step further to surmise that the offerings she craves must be *human* sacrifices, of which Turnus is the first.

And yet there is something wrong even with that offering. Time and again, the poet shows us humans offered in a sacrificial manner: Sinon the escaped victim, Laocoön like the screaming bull, Palinurus the "one head given for many"—the list goes on. The quality that these all share is their resistance. If sacrifices, even symbolic ones, are made *to* someone, then it matters a great deal how the recipient reacts. How could such offerings be seen as pleasing to the gods, when it was common (Roman) knowledge that a victim's unwillingness indicated the gods' rejection of the gift? Unless—and here is the heart of the darkness that Virgil saw in human existence—unless the gods are such that the very fact of repetition, the unending necessity for further acts of expiation, *is what pleases them most*.

♦ ♦ ♦

To our modern sensibilities, there is nothing shocking, or even remarkable, about "the theme of sacrifice in the *Aeneid*." The widespread figurative use of the term "sacrifice" has sapped the word of its ancient power and sense. Although the idea of actual ritual slaughter may still lurk in the background for some, the word largely has come to mean simply "to forfeit (something of value) for something considered to have a higher claim."[4] It seems natural, then, that Aeneas must perform (symbolic) sacrifices in the service of the community. In his suffering for the sake of a higher good that he will never see—except, perhaps, after his deification—*pius Aeneas* fits readily into a modern Judeo-Christian model of morality. Viewed in this light, the *Aeneid* is edifying. Sacrifices, however painful, are ultimately for the best.

This model causes us to miss Virgil's point. For the Romans, sacrifice was part of daily life, and it was loud, smelly, and bloody. It had no genteel figurative meaning. We should try to imagine the probable effect when a recalcitrant animal, like the bull in the simile for Laocoön, ran screaming from the scene. Could there be any doubt that the gods were angry and would not accept the offering? Even if an animal might be tricked into the appearance of willingness, the evils of life did not go away. Could any amount of repetition cause the gods' anger to cease? It is against this backdrop that "the theme of sacrifice in the *Aeneid*" must be considered—that is, a world in which sacrifice could be seen to be not only futile but dangerous to those who performed it. The sacrificial death of Palinurus is indeed paradigmatic, but not because he is a successful scapegoat. His unwillingness suggests that the offering will be ineffectual in appeasing the gods and will necessitate further offerings

4. *American Heritage Dictionary* (Boston, 1976), s.v. "sacrifice" (verb) 2.

in expiation. The *Aeneid* offers no evidence that the sacrifice of Turnus will be any different. The final adjective in the poem, *indignata,* echoes like a curse throughout Roman history.

In the strange rituals of the Rex Nemorensis, Virgil found a cultic paradigm for this endless cycle of sacrifice. He also found a potent symbol of man's uneasy relationship with what we would call "Nature." Readers have long recognized the analogy that Virgil develops between humans and trees, and scholars have recently begun to appreciate the religious implications of tree violation in the ancient world. But what is remarkable is the frequency with which humans shift from being violators of trees to being violated trees themselves—just as Laocoön is a priest one moment and a victim the next. Turnus enters as "Erysichthon," he attacks Cybele's pines in various manifestations, yet he ends as a living *tropaeum.* This reversal of roles is demanded by the cult of Diana Nemorensis. The identification between the priest-king and the sacred tree meant that the violator of the tree (the Challenger), if successful in the ensuing combat, would eventually be subject to a similar attack at the hands of the next Challenger. By assimilating his characters alternately to trees and to violators of trees, Virgil illustrates the moral complexity of men's relationships with one another and with the natural world. By presenting these reversals in a context of religious necessity, he shows both human responsibility and human helplessness in the face of *religio,* the caprice and cruelty of the gods.

What then is implied in Aeneas' final sacrifice of Turnus? The answer has less to do with morality than with Roman religious practice. For the Romans, the two were quite separate. Whether or not a sacrifice was efficacious had nothing to do with whether the practitioner was a good man. Aeneas may try to conciliate Juno with heartfelt prayers, but these will be to no avail if he fails to follow the proper procedures. The "one head given for many" accomplishes nothing—or worse than nothing—if the victim is unwilling. The rites of Diana Nemorensis, with their cycle of priest-become-victim, reflect the cycle of bloodshed that characterized Roman history from its beginnings. The first part of this book ends with the *honores* of Juno and the second part with the *honores* of Diana; despite bitter squabbles within the Olympian pantheon, at day's end, both amount to the same thing. The sacrifice of Turnus does not "work." According to the logic of the poem, that sacrifice is necessary, but its consequence will be the sacrifice of Aeneas and many after him.

Roman history would confirm the truth of the *Aeneid*'s prophecy. What Virgil could not have foreseen is the role that he himself would play in linking classical antiquity with a religion yet to be born, one that would hold up a single sacrifice as efficacious and final. "Without hope we live in desire": innocent of ancient cult and modern critical theory, Dante in his Christian reading of the *Aeneid* recognized his master's longing for a consummation eternally deferred.[5] "It is not thanks to the Fourth Eclogue alone," writes C. S. Lewis, "that [Virgil] has become almost a great Christian poet."[6] Almost. The pagan prophet, sensing that sacrifice was at the core of human history, did not envision the possibility of redemption. He could guide his pupil only through the realm of shadows.

---

5. On Dante's Christian reading of the *Aeneid*, see Martindale (1993) 43–48, especially 47–48: "Dante's implication seems to be that Virgil's inability to reconcile *amor* and *fatum* springs, ultimately, from his paganism, which he partly—but only partly—transcended."

6. Lewis (1942) 19. Virgil's poem about a child whose birth would herald a new Golden Age was seen until modern times as a prophecy of Christ; on "Virgil's Fourth Eclogue in Christian Interpretation," see Benko (1980). Among the most persuasive interpretations of the Eclogue is that of Petrini (1997) 111–21.

Bibliography

Ahl, Frederick. 1984. "The Art of Safe Criticism in Greece and Rome." *AJP* 105: 174–208.

Alföldi, Andrew. 1960. "Diana Nemorensis." *AJA* 64: 137–44.

Ambrose, Z. P. 1980. "The Etymology and Genealogy of Palinurus." *AJP* 101: 449–57.

Ampolo, Carmine. 1993. "Boschi sacri e culti federali: l'esempio del Lazio." In de Cazanove and Scheid (1993), 159–67.

Anderson, William S. 1969. *The Art of the "Aeneid."* Englewood Cliffs, New Jersey.

———. 1999. "*Aeneid* 11: The Saddest Book." In Perkell (1999), 195-209.

Austin, R. G. 1955. *P. Vergili Maronis Aeneidos Liber Quartus*. Oxford.

———. 1964. *P. Vergili Maronis Aeneidos Liber Secundus*. Oxford.

———. 1971. *P. Vergili Maronis Aeneidos Liber Primus*. Oxford.

———. 1977. *P. Vergili Maronis Aeneidos Liber Sextus*. Oxford.

Baldwin, Barry. 1993. "Half-Lines in Virgil: Old and New Ideas." *SO* 68: 144–51.

Bandera, Cesáreo. 1981. "Sacrificial Levels in Virgil's *Aeneid*." *Arethusa* 14: 217–39.

Barchiesi, Alessandro. 1978. "Il lamento di Giuturna." *MD* 1: 99–121.

———. 1984. *La traccia del modello: Effetti omerici nella narrazione virgiliana*. Pisa.

———. 1994. "Rappresentazioni del dolore e interpretazione nell' *Eneide*." *A&A* 40: 109–24.

———. 1997. *The Poet and the Prince: Ovid and Augustan Discourse*. Berkeley and Los Angeles.

Barrett, W. S. 1964. *Euripides: Hippolytus*. Oxford.

Basanoff, V. 1943. *Regifugium: La Fuite du Roi, Histoire et Mythe*. Paris.

Beard, Mary. 1992. "Frazer, Leach, and Virgil: The Popularity (and Unpopularity) of *The Golden Bough*." *CSSH* 34: 203–24.

———. 1993. "Frazer et ses bois sacrés." In de Cazanove and Scheid (1993), 171–80.

Beard, Mary, and John North, eds. 1990. *Pagan Priests*. Ithaca, New York.

Beard, Mary, John North, and Simon Price. 1998a. *Religions of Rome. Volume 1: A History*. Cambridge.

———. 1998b. *Religions of Rome. Volume 2: A Sourcebook*. Cambridge.

Benko, Stephen. 1980. "Virgil's Fourth Eclogue in Christian Interpretation." *ANRW* 2.31.1: 646–705.

Bing, Peter. 1988. *The Well-Read Muse: Present and Past in Callimachus and the Hellenistic Poets*. Göttingen.

Blagg, Thomas F. C. 1993. "Le mobilier archéologique du sanctuaire de Diane *Nemorensis*." In de Cazanove and Scheid (1993), 103–109.

Bleisch, Pamela R. 1998. "Altars Altered: The Alexandrian Tradition of Etymological Wordplay in *Aeneid* 1.108-12." *AJP* 119: 599–606.

Bloch, Raymond. 1963. *Les Prodiges dans l'antiquité classique*. Paris.

Boyle, Anthony J. 1993. *Roman Epic*. London.

———. 1999. "*Aeneid* 8: Images of Rome." In Perkell (1999), 148–61.

Bremmer, J. N., and N. M. Horsfall. 1987. *Roman Myth and Mythography*. London.

Brenk, F. E. 1984. "*Unum pro multis caput*: Myth, History, and Symbolic Imagery in Vergil's Palinurus Incident." *Latomus* 43: 776–801.

———. 1988. "Wind and Waves, Sacrifice and Treachery: Diodorus, Appian and the Death of Palinurus in Vergil." *Aevum* 62: 69–80.

Briggs, Ward W. 1980. *Narrative and Simile from the "Georgics" in the "Aeneid." Mnemosyne* Suppl. 58. Leiden.

———. 1981. "Virgil and the Hellenistic Epic." *ANRW* 2.32.2: 948–84.

Bronzini, Giovanni Battista. 1990. "Tradizioni popolari." *EV* 5*: 230–44.

Brotherton, Blanche. 1931. "Vergil's Catalogue of the Latin Forces." *TAPA* 62: 192–202.

Burke, Paul F., Jr. 1974. "Mezentius and the First-Fruits." *Vergilius* 20: 28–29.

Cairns, Francis. 1989. *Virgil's Augustan Epic*. Cambridge.

Capdeville, M. Gérard. 1976. "*Taurus et bos mas*." In *Mélanges offerts a Jacques Heurgon: L'Italie preromaine et la Rome republicaine*, 115–23. Rome.

Casali, Sergio. 1995. "Aeneas and the Doors of the Temple of Apollo." *CJ* 91: 1–10.

Caviglia, Franco. 1990. "Virbio (*Virbius*)." *EV* 5*: 553–58.

Christmann, Eckhard. 1976. "Der Tod des Aeneas und die Pforten des Schlafes." In *Studien zum Antiken Epos Franz Dirlmeier und Viktor Pöschl gewidmet*, eds. H. Görgemanns and E. Schmidt, 251–79. *Beiträge zur klassischen Philologie* 62. Meisenheim.

Clark, Raymond J. 1979. *Catabasis: Vergil and the Wisdom-Tradition*. Amsterdam.

———. 1992. "Vergil, *Aeneid* 6: The Bough by Hades' Gate." In Wilhelm and Jones (1992), 167–78.

Clausen, Wendell. 1964. "An Interpretation of the *Aeneid*." In Commager (1966), 75–88.

———. 1987. *Virgil's "Aeneid" and the Tradition of Hellenistic Poetry*. Berkeley, Los Angeles, and London.

Clay, Diskin. 1988. "The Archaeology of the Temple to Juno in Carthage (*Aen*. 1.446-93)." *CP* 83: 195–205.

Coarelli, Filippo. 1987. *I santuari del Lazio in età repubblicana*. Rome.

Commager, Steele, ed. 1966. *Virgil: A Collection of Critical Essays*. Englewood Cliffs, New Jersey.

Conington, John. 1883. *P. Vergili Maronis Opera*. 3rd ed. Rev. by Henry Nettleship. London.

Connors, Catherine. 1991. "Simultaneous Hunting and Herding at *Ciris* 297–300." *CQ* 41: 556–59.

———. 1992. "Seeing Cypresses in Virgil." *CJ* 88: 1–17.

Conte, Gian Biagio. 1986. *The Rhetoric of Imitation: Genre and Poetic Memory in Virgil and Other Latin Poets*. Trans. Charles Segal. Ithaca, New York and London.

Cook, Arthur Bernard. 1902. "The Golden Bough and the Rex Nemorensis." *CR* 16: 365–80.

Cruttwell, Robert W. 1947. *Virgil's Mind at Work: An Analysis of the Symbolism of the "Aeneid."* Oxford.

D'Arms, John H. 1964. "Vergil's *Cunctantem (Ramum): Aeneid* 6.211." *CJ* 59: 265–68.

Davidson, J. F. 1992. "Tragic Daughter of Atlas?" *Maia* 45: 367–71.

de Cazanove, Olivier, and John Scheid, eds. 1993. *Les Bois Sacrés*. Naples.

Dee, James H. 1981. "*Iliad* 1.4 f. and Catullus 64.152 f.: Further Considerations." *TAPA* 111: 39–42.

Doyle, Arthur Conan. 1960. "The Hound of the Baskervilles." In *The Complete Sherlock Holmes*, 669–766. Garden City, New York.

Duclos, Gloria S. 1969. "Dido as 'Triformis' Diana." *Vergilius* 15: 33–41.

———. 1971. "Nemora Inter Cresia." *CJ* 66: 193–95.

Dumézil, Georges. 1961. "Joui tauro uerre ariete immolari non licet." *REL* 39: 242–50.

———. 1970. *Archaic Roman Religion*. 2 vols. Trans. Philip Krapp. Baltimore and London.

———. 1979. "Jupiter et les victimes mâles." In *Mariages Indo-Européens, suivi de quinze Questions Romaines*. Paris.

Dunn, Francis M., Don Fowler, and Deborah H. Roberts, eds. 1997. *Classical Closure: Reading the End in Greek and Latin Literature*. Princeton.

Dyson, Julia T. 1996a. "*Caesi Iuvenci* and *Pietas Impia* in Virgil." *CJ* 91: 277–86.

———. 1996b. "*Septima Aestas*: The Puzzle of *Aen*. 1.755–56 and 5.625." *CW* 90: 41–43.

———. 1997a. "*Fluctus Irarum, Fluctus Curarum*: Lucretian *Religio* in the *Aeneid*." *AJP* 118: 449–57.

———. 1997b. "Birds, Grandfathers, and Neoteric Sorcery in *Aeneid* 4.254 and 7.412." *CQ* 47: 314–15.

Edgeworth, Robert J. 1986. "The Ivory Gate and the Threshold of Apollo." *C&M* 37: 145–60.

———. 1992. *The Colors of the "Aeneid."* New York and Frankfurt am Main.

Edlund, Ingrid E. M. 1987. *The Gods and the Place: Location and Function of Sanctuaries in the Countryside of Etruria and Magna Graecia (700–400 B.C.)*. Stockholm.

Eitrem, S. 1915. *Opferritus und Voropfer der Griechen und Römer*. Kristiana.

Ernout, A., and A. Meillet. 1931. *Dictionnaire étymologique de la langue latine: histoire des mots*. Paris.

Fantham, Elaine. 1990. "*Nymphas . . . E Navibus Esse*: Decorum and Poetic Fiction in *Aeneid* 9.77–122 and 10.215–59." *CP* 85: 102–19.

———. 1998. *Ovid: Fasti IV*. Cambridge.

———. 1999. "Fighting Words: Turnus at Bay in the Latin Council (*Aeneid* 11.234–446)." *AJP* 120: 259–80.

Farrell, Joseph. 1991. *Vergil's "Georgics" and the Traditions of Ancient Epic: The Art of Allusion in Literary History*. Oxford.

———. 1997. "The Virgilian Intertext." In Martindale (1997), 222–38.

Feeney, Denis C. 1984. "The Reconciliations of Juno." In Harrison (1990), 339–62.

———. 1991. *The Gods in Epic: Poets and Critics of the Classical Tradition*. Oxford.

———. 1998. *Literature and Religion at Rome: Cultures, Contexts, and Beliefs*. Cambridge.

Fontenrose, J. 1978. *The Delphic Oracle: Its Responses and Operations*. Berkeley, Los Angeles, and London.

Fordyce, C. J. 1977. *P. Vergili Maronis "Aeneidos" Libri VII–VIII with a Commentary*. Ed. John D. Christie. Oxford.

Foss, Clive, and Peter Knox, eds. 1998. *Style and Tradition: Studies in Honor of Wendell Clausen*. Stuttgart and Leipzig.

Fowler, Don P. 1990. "Deviant Focalisation in Virgil's *Aeneid*." *PCPhS* 36: 42–63.

———. 1991. "Narrate and Describe: The Problem of Ekphrasis." *JRS* 81: 25–35.

———. 1997. "The Virgil Commentary of Servius." In Martindale (1997), 73–78.

Fraenkel, Eduard. 1957. *Horace*. Oxford.

Frazer, James G. 1890. *The Golden Bough: A Study in Comparative Religion*. London.

———. 1922. *The Golden Bough: A Study in Magic and Religion*. Abridged edition. London.

Gale, Monica R. 1994. *Myth and Poetry in Lucretius*. Cambridge.

Galinsky, G. Karl. 1969. *Aeneas, Sicily, and Rome*. Princeton.

———. 1988. "The Anger of Aeneas." *AJP* 109: 321–48.

———, ed. 1974. *Perspectives of Roman Poetry: A Classics Symposium*. Austin, Texas.

Girard, René. 1977. *Violence and the Sacred*. Trans. Patrick Gregory. Baltimore.

Glenn, Justin. 1971. "Mezentius and Polyphemus." *AJP* 92: 129–55.

Goold, G. P. 1970. "Servius and the Helen Episode." In Harrison (1990b), 60–126.

Gordon, A. E. 1934. *The Cults of Aricia*. University of California Publications in Classical Archaeology 2.1. Berkeley.

Gotoff, H. C. 1984. "The Transformation of Mezentius." *TAPA* 114: 191–218.

Gottlieb, Gunther. 1998. "Religion in the Politics of Augustus." In Stahl (1998), 21–36.

Graf, Fritz. 1979. "Das Götterbild aus dem Taurerland." *AW* 10: 33–41.

Gransden, K. W. 1976. *Virgil, "Aeneid," Book VIII*. Cambridge.

———. 1984. *Virgil's "Iliad."* Cambridge.

———. 1985. "The Fall of Troy." In McAuslan and Walcot (1990), 121–33.

———. 1991. *Virgil, "Aeneid," Book XI*. Cambridge.

Green, C. M. C. 1994. "'The Necessary Murder': Myth, Ritual, and Civil War in Lucan, Book 3." *CA* 13: 203–34.

———. 2000. "The Slayer and the King: *Rex Nemorensis* and the Sanctuary of Diana." *Arion* 7.3: 24–63.

Griffin, Jasper. 1998. "Chopping Off the Golden Bough." Review of Fritz Graf, *Magic in the Ancient World*, and John Boardman, *The Great God Pan: The Survival of an Image*. *New York Review of Books* (8 October 1998), 44–47.

Gurval, Robert Alan. 1995. *Actium and Augustus: The Politics and Emotions of Civil War*. Ann Arbor.

Hardie, Philip R. 1984. "The Sacrifice of Iphigeneia: An Example of 'Distribution' of a Lucretian Theme in Virgil." *CQ* 34: 406–12.

———. 1986. *Virgil's "Aeneid": Cosmos and Imperium*. Oxford.

———. 1991. "The *Aeneid* and the *Oresteia*." *PVS* 20: 29–45.

———. 1993. *The Epic Successors of Virgil*. Cambridge.

———. 1994. *Virgil, "Aeneid." Book IX*. Cambridge.

———. 1997a. "Virgil and Tragedy." In Martindale (1997), 312–26.

———. 1997b. "Closure in Latin Epic." In Dunn, Fowler, and Roberts (1997), 139–62.

Harrison, Edward L. 1970. "Cleverness in Virgilian Imitation." In Harrison (1990b), 445–48.

———. 1972–73. "Why did Venus wear boots?" *PVS* 12: 10–25.

———. 1980. "The Structure of the *Aeneid*: Observations on the Links between the Books." *ANRW* 2.31.1: 359–93.

———. 1984. "The *Aeneid* and Carthage." In Woodman and West (1984), 95–115.

———. 1989. "The Tragedy of Dido." *EMC* 33: 1–21.

———. 1995. "The Metamorphosis of the Ships (*Aeneid* 9.77–122)." *PLLS* 8: 143–64.

Harrison, Stephen J. 1990a. "Dictamnum and Moly: Vergil *Aeneid* 12.411–19." *PLLS* 6: 45–47.

———. 1991. *Vergil, "Aeneid" 10*. Oxford.

———. 1998. "The Sword-belt of Pallas: Moral Symbolism and Political Ideology." In Stahl (1998), 223–42.

———, ed. 1990b. *Oxford Readings in Vergil's "Aeneid."* Oxford.

Heinze, Richard. 1993. *Virgil's Epic Technique*. Trans. Hazel and David Harvey and Fred Robertson. Berkeley and Los Angeles.

Hershkowitz, Debra. 1991. "The *Aeneid* in *Aeneid* 3." *Vergilius* 37: 69–76.

Hexter, Ralph. 1989–90. "What Was the Trojan Horse Made Of? Interpreting Vergil's *Aeneid*." *YJC* 3: 109–31.

Hickson, Frances V. 1993. *Roman Prayer Language: Livy and the "Aneid"* [sic] *of Vergil*. Stuttgart.

Highet, Gilbert. 1972. *The Speeches in Vergil's "Aeneid."* Princeton.

Hinds, Stephen. 1987a. "Generalising About Ovid." *Ramus* 16: 4–31.

———. 1987b. *The Metamorphosis of Persephone: Ovid and the Self-Conscious Muse*. Cambridge.

———. 1998. *Allusion and Intertext: Dynamics of Appropriation in Roman Poetry*. Cambridge.

Holland, Louise Adams. 1961. *Janus and the Bridge*. Rome.

Hollis, A. S. 1992. "Hellenistic Colouring in Virgil's *Aeneid*." *HSCP* 94: 269–85.

Hopkinson, Neil. 1988. *A Hellenistic Anthology*. Cambridge.

Hornsby, Roger. 1966. "The Armor of the Slain." *PhQ* 45: 347–59.

Horsfall, Nicholas M. 1986. "The Aeneas-Legend and the *Aeneid*." *Vergilius* 9: 8–17.

———. 1991. *Virgilio: l'epopea in alambicco*. Naples.

———. 1999. *Virgil, "Aeneid" 7: A Commentary*. Leiden, Boston, and Köln.

———, ed. 1995. *A Companion to the Study of Virgil*. Leiden.

Hunter, Richard. 1989. "Bulls and Boxers in Apollonius and Vergil." *CQ* 39: 557–61.

Huskey, S. J. 1999. "Turnus and Terminus in *Aeneid* 12." *Mnemosyne* 52: 77–80.

Hutchinson, G. O. 1988. *Hellenistic Poetry*. Oxford.

Jocelyn, H. D. 1966. "The Roman Nobility and the Religion of the Republican State." *JRH* 4: 89–104.

Johnson, W. R. 1976. *Darkness Visible: A Study of Vergil's "Aeneid."* Berkeley and Los Angeles.

Kaster, Robert A. 1988. *Guardians of Language: The Grammarian and Society in Late Antiquity*. Berkeley, Los Angeles, and London.

Kennedy, Duncan F. 1992. "'Augustan' and 'Anti-Augustan': Reflections on Terms of Reference." In Powell (1992b), 26–58.

Kenney, E. J. 1979. "*Iudicium Transferendi*: Virgil, *Aeneid* 2.469–505 and Its Antecedents." In West and Woodman (1979), 103–20.

Kepple, Laurence R. 1976. "Arruns and the Death of Aeneas." *AJP* 97: 344–60.

Ketterer, R. C. 1991. "The Rainbow at the End of *Aeneid* 4." *Syll. Class.* 3: 21–23.

Kinsey, T. E. 1979. "Virgil, *Aeneid* VI 88–90." *Maia* 31: 267.

Kleinknecht, Hermann. 1944. "Laokoon." *Hermes* 79: 66–111.

Klingner, Friedrich. 1967. *Virgil: Bucolica, Georgica, Aeneis*. Zurich.

Knauer, Georg Nicolaus. 1964. *Die Aeneis und Homer: Studien zur poetischen Technik Vergils mit Listen der Homerzitate in der Aeneis*. Hypomnemata 7. Göttingen.

Knox, Bernard M. W. 1950. "The Serpent and the Flame." In Commager (1966), 124–42.

Knox, Peter E. 1997. "Savagery in the *Aeneid*." *CJ* 92: 225–33.

Kraggerud, Egil. 1987. "Perusia and the *Aeneid*." *SO* 62: 77–87.

Krause, C. 1894. *De Romanorum Hostiis Quaestiones Selectae*. Ph.D. diss., Marburg.

———. 1931. "Hostia." *RE* Suppl. V: 236–82.

Kyle, Donald G. 1998. *Spectacles of Death in Ancient Rome*. London and New York.

La Penna, Antonio. 1980. "Mezentio: Una Tragedia della Tirannia e del Titanismo Antico." *Maia* 32: 3–30.

Latte, Kurt. 1960. *Römische Religionsgeschichte*. Munich.

Le Gall, J. 1953. *Recherches sur le culte du Tibre*. Paris.

Leach, Edmund. 1985. "Reflections on a visit to Nemi: Did Frazer get it wrong?" *Anthropology Today* 1: 2–3.

Lee, M. Owen. 1981. "The Sons of Iasus and the End of the *Aeneid*." In Quinn (2000), 207–10.

———. 1988. "*Per Nubila Lunam*: The Moon in Virgil's *Aeneid*." *Vergilius* 34: 9–14.

———. 1992. "Seven Suffering Heroines and Seven Surrogate Sons." In Wilhelm and Jones (1992), 82–92.

Lehr, Heinrich. 1934. *Religion und Kult in Vergils Aeneis*. Ph.D. diss., Jena.

Leigh, Matthew. 1993. "Hopelessly Devoted to You: Traces of the Decii in Virgil's *Aeneid*." *PVS* 21: 89–110.

Lewis, C. S. 1942. *A Preface to "Paradise Lost."* Oxford.

Liebeschuetz, J. H. W. G. 1979. *Continuity and Change in Roman Religion*. Oxford.

Linderski, Jerzy. 1984. Review of *Le délit religieux dans la cité antique (Table ronde, Rome, 6–7 avril 1978)*. In Linderski (1995), 592–95.

———. 1986. "The Augural Law." *ANRW* 2.16.3: 2146–312.

———. 1993. "Roman Religion in Livy." In Linderski (1995), 608–19.

———. 1995. *Roman Questions: Selected Papers 1958–1993*. Stuttgart.

Lloyd, Robert B. 1954. "On *Aeneid*, III, 270–80." *AJP* 75: 288–99.

Losada, Luis A. 1983. "Maple, Fir, and Pine: Vergil's Wooden Horse." *TAPA* 113: 301–10.

Lyne, R. O. A. M. 1983. "Vergil and the Politics of War." In Harrison (1990b), 316–38.

———. 1987. *Further Voices in Vergil's "Aeneid."* Oxford.

———. 1989. *Words and the Poet: Characteristic Techniques of Style in Vergil's "Aeneid."* Oxford.

———. 1994. "Vergil's *Aeneid*: Subversion by Intertextuality. Catullus 66.39–40 and Other Examples." *G&R* 41: 187–204.

MacBain, Bruce. 1982. *Prodigy and Expiation: A Study in Religion and Politics in Republican Rome*. Brussels.

MacCormick, A. G. 1983. *Mysteries of Diana: The Antiquities from Nemi in Nottingham Museums*. Nottingham.

Mack, Sara. 1978. *Patterns of Time in Vergil*. Hamden, Connecticut.

———. 1999. "The Birth of War: A Reading of *Aeneid* 7." In Perkell (1999), 128–47.

Mackie, C. J. 1988. *The Characterisation of Aeneas*. Edinburgh.

———. 1992. "Vergil's Dirae, South Italy, and Etruria." *Phoenix* 46: 352–61.

Makowski, John F. 1996. "Bisexual Orpheus: Pederasty and Parody in Ovid." *CJ* 92: 25–38.

Malavolta, Mariano. 1990. "Tropaeum." *EV* 5*: 296–97.

Mancini, Marco. 1990. "Tumeo." *EV* 5*: 312–13.

Mannhardt, Wilhelm. 1905. *Wald- und Feldkulte*. Vol. 2. Berlin.

Martindale, Charles. 1993. *Redeeming the Text: Latin Poetry and the Hermeneutics of Reception*. Cambridge.

———, ed. 1997. *The Cambridge Companion to Virgil*. Cambridge.

McAuslan, Ian, and Peter Walcot, eds. 1990. *Virgil*. Oxford.

McLeod, W. 1970. "The Wooden Horse and Charon's Barque: Inconsistency in Virgil's 'Vivid Particularization.'" *Phoenix* 24: 144–49.

Merkelbach, Reinhold. 1961. "Aeneas in Cumae." *MH* 18: 83–99.

Michels, Agnes Kirsopp. 1945. "The Golden Bough of Plato." *AJP* 66: 59–63.

Mitchell, Robin N. 1991. "The Violence of Virginity in the *Aeneid*." *Arethusa* 24: 219–38.

Mitchell-Boyask, Robin. 1996. "*Sine Fine*: Vergil's Masterplot." *AJP* 117: 289–307.

Moles, John. 1988. "The Tragedy and Guilt of Dido." In Whitby, Hardie, and Whitby (1988), 153–61.

Montanari, Enrico. 1990. "Victima." *EV* 5*: 531–33.

Montepaone, Claudia. 1993. "L'*alsos* / *lucus*, forma idealtipica artemidea: il caso di Ippolito." In de Cazanove and Scheid (1993), 69–75.

Morgan, Gareth. 1994. "Dido the Wounded Deer." *Vergilius* 40: 67–68.

Moskalew, Walter. 1982. *Formular Language and Poetic Design in the Aeneid*. Leiden.

Murgia, Charles E. 1987. "Dido's Puns." *CP* 82: 50–59.

Musgrove, Margaret Worsham. 1997. "Change of Perspective in Ovid, *Metamorphoses* 12.11–23." *AJP* 118: 267–83.

Mynors, R. A. B. 1969. *P. Vergili Maronis Opera*. Oxford.

Nagy, Gregory. 1979. *The Best of the Achaeans*. Baltimore and London.

Narducci, Emanuele. 1990. "Truncus." *EV* 5*: 305–306.

Nethercut, William R. 1974. "Snakes in the *Aeneid*: Two Comments." *Vergilius* 20: 20–23.

Nicoll, William S. M. 1988. "The Sacrifice of Palinurus." *CQ* 38: 459–72.

Nielson, Kristina P. 1983. "The *Tropaion* in the *Aeneid*." *Vergilius* 29: 27–33.

Nisbet, R. G. M., and M. Hubbard. 1970. *A Commentary on Horace: Odes, Book I*. Oxford.

Noonan, J. D. 1993. "Daunus/Faunus in *Aeneid* 12." *CA* 12: 111–25.

Norden, Eduard. 1957. *P. Vergilius Maro Aeneis Buch VI*. 4th ed. Stuttgart.

North, John A. 1976. "Conservatism and Change in Roman Religion." *PBSR* 44: 1–12.

O'Hara, James J. 1989. "Messapus, Cycnus, and the Alphabetical Order of Vergil's Catalogue of Italian Heroes." *Phoenix* 43: 35–38.

———. 1990. *Death and the Optimistic Prophecy in Vergil's "Aeneid."* Princeton.

———. 1993. "A Neglected Conjecture at *Aeneid* 12.882." *RhM* 136: 371–74.

———. 1994. "They Might Be Giants: Inconsistency and Indeterminacy in Vergil's War in Italy." *Colby Quarterly* 30: 206–26.

———. 1996. *True Names: Vergil and the Alexandrian Tradition of Eymological Wordplay*. Ann Arbor.

Ogilvie, R. M. 1970. *A Commentary on Livy Books 1–5*. Oxford.

Otis, Brooks. 1964. *Virgil: A Study in Civilized Poetry*. Oxford.

Page, T. E. 1929. *The "Aeneid" of Vergil: Books VII–XII*. London.

Pairault, Françoise-Hélène. 1969. "Diana Nemorensis: Déesse Latine, Déesse Hellénisée." *MEFRA* 81: 425–71.

Panoussi, Vassiliki. 1998. *Epic Transfigured: Tragic Allusiveness in Vergil's "Aeneid."* Ph.D. diss., Brown University.

Pascal, C. Bennet. 1990. "The Dubious Devotion of Turnus." *TAPA* 120: 251–68.

Pease, Arthur S. 1935. *P. Vergili Maronis Aeneidos Liber Quartus*. Cambridge, Massachusetts.

Perkell, Christine. 1997. "The Lament of Juturna: Pathos and Interpretation in the *Aeneid*." *TAPA* 127: 257–86.

———. 1999. *Reading Vergil's "Aeneid": An Interpretive Guide*. Norman, Oklahoma.

Perotti, Pier Angelo. 1991. "Dorica Castra, Alius Achilles (Aen. VI 88–90)." *Maia* 43: 195–98.

Petrini, Mark. 1997. *The Child and the Hero: Coming of Age in Catullus and Vergil*. Ann Arbor.

Pfeiffer, Rudolph. 1949–53. *Callimachus*. 2 vols. Oxford.

Pigoñ, Jakub. 1991. "Dido, Diana, and Penthesilea: Observations on the Queen's First Appearance in the 'Aeneid.'" *Eos* 79: 45–53.

Porte, Danielle. 1985. *L'etiologie religieuse dans les Fastes d'Ovide*. Paris.

Pöschl, Viktor. 1962. *The Art of Vergil: Image and Symbol in the "Aeneid."* Trans. Gerda Seligson. Ann Arbor.

Powell, Anton. 1992a. "The *Aeneid* and the Embarrassments of Augustus." In Powell (1992b), 141–74.

———, ed. 1992b. *Roman Poetry and Propaganda in the Age of Augustus*. Bristol.

Putnam, Michael C. J. 1965. *The Poetry of the "Aeneid": Four Studies in Imaginative Unity and Design*. Cambridge, Massachusetts.

———. 1995. *Virgil's "Aeneid": Interpretation and Influence*. Chapel Hill and London.

Quinn, Kenneth. 1968. *Virgil's "Aeneid": A Critical Description*. London.

Quinn, Stephanie, ed. 2000. *Why Vergil? A Collection of Interpretations*. Wauconda, Illinois.

Quint, David. 1993. *Epic and Empire: Politics and Generic Form from Virgil to Milton*. Princeton.

Raaflaub, Kurt A., and Mark Toher, eds. 1990. *Between Republic and Empire: Interpretations of Augustus and His Principate*. Berkeley, Los Angeles, and London.

Rauk, John. 1991. "Androgeos in Book Two of the *Aeneid*." *TAPA* 121: 287–95.

———. 1995. "Macrobius, Cornutus, and the Cutting of Dido's Lock." *CP* 90: 345–54.

Reckford, Kenneth J. 1974. "Some Trees in Virgil and Tolkien." In Galinsky (1974), 57–91.

Renehan, R. 1979. "New Evidence for the Variant in *Iliad* 1.5." *AJP* 100: 473–74.

Rosenstein, Nathan. 1990. *Imperatores Victi: Military Defeat and Aristocratic Competition in the Middle and Late Republic*. Berkeley.

Ross, David O., Jr. 1987. *Virgil's Elements: Physics and Poetry in the "Georgics."* Princeton.

Rowland, Robert J., Jr. 1992. "*Ductor Rhoeteius*: Vergil, *Aeneid* 12.456." In Wilhelm and Jones (1992), 237–43.

Ryberg, Inez Scott. 1955. *Rites of the State Religion in Roman Art*. Rome.

Scheid, John. 1981. "Le délit religieux dans la Rome tardo-républicaine." In *Le délit religieux dans la cité antique*, 117–71. Rome.

———. 1985. *Religion et piété à Rome*. Paris.

Scullard, H. H. 1981. *Festivals and Ceremonies of the Roman Republic*. Ithaca, New York.

Segal, Charles P. 1968. "The Hesitation of the Golden Bough: A Reexamination." *Hermes* 96: 74–79.

Simon, Erika. 1984. "Diana" (Introduction). *LIMC* 2.1: 792–95.

Skutsch, Otto. 1985. *The Annals of Quintus Ennius*. Oxford.

Smith, Jonathan Z. 1978. *Map Is Not Territory: Studies in the History of Religions*. Leiden.

Smith, Rebekah M. 1999. "Deception and Sacrifice in *Aeneid* 2.1–249." *AJP* 120: 503–23.

Spence, Sarah. 1991. "Cinching the Text: The Danaids and the End of the *Aeneid*." *Vergilius* 37: 11–19.

———. 1999. "*Varium et Mutabile*: Voices of Authority in *Aeneid* 4." In Perkell (1999), 80–95.

Stahl, Hans-Peter. 1990. "The Death of Turnus: Augustan Vergil and the Political Rival." In Raaflaub and Toher (1990), 174–211.

———, ed. 1998. *Vergil's "Aeneid": Augustan Epic and Political Context*. Wales.

Starr, Raymond J. 1997. "Aeneas as the *Flamen Dialis*? Vergil's *Aeneid* and the Servian Exegetical Tradition." *Vergilius* 43: 63–70.

Tarrant, Richard J. 1997. "Aspects of Virgil's Reception in Antiquity." In Martindale (1997), 56–72.

———. 1998. "Parenthetically Speaking (in Virgil and Other Poets)." In Foss and Knox (1998), 141–57.

Thomas, Richard F. 1979. "On a Homeric Reference in Catullus." *AJP* 100: 475–76.

———. 1982. "Gadflies (Virg. *Geo.* 3.146–148)." *HSCP* 86: 81–85.

———. 1986. "Virgil's *Georgics* and the Art of Reference." *HSCP* 90: 171–98.

———. 1988a. *Virgil, "Georgics."* 2 Vols. Cambridge.

———. 1988b. "Tree Violation and Ambivalence in Virgil." *TAPA* 118: 261–73.

———. 1993. Review of N. M. Horsfall, *Virgilio: l'epopea in alambicco* (Naples, 1991). *Vergilius* 39: 76–80.

———. 1998. "The Isolation of Turnus: *Aeneid* Book 12." in Stahl (1998), 271–302.

Traina, Alfonso. 1992. "Ancora *Alius Achilles* (Verg. *Aen.* 6,88–90)." *Maia* 44: 159.

———. 1994. "Il Libro XII dell' *Eneide*." *AVM* 62: 19–36.

Treggiari, Susan. 1991. *Roman Marriage: Iusti Coniuges From the Time of Cicero to the Time of Ulpian*. Oxford.

Tromp, S. P. C. 1921. *De Romanorum Piaculis*. Lugduni Batavorum.

Tupet, A.-M. 1970. "Didon Magicienne." *REL* 48: 229–58.

Turcan, Robert. 1988. *Religion Romaine. 2: Le Culte*. Leiden.

Vermaseren, Maarten J. 1977. *Cybele and Attis: The Myth and the Cult*. London.

Versnel, H. S. 1970. *Triumphus: An Inquiry into the Origin, Development, and Meaning of the Roman Triumph*. Leiden.

———. 1981. "Self-Sacrifice, Compensation and the Anonymous Gods." In *Le Sacrifice dans l'antiquité. Entretiens sur l'antiquité classique* 27: 135–94.

Warmington, E. H. 1956. *Remains of Old Latin: Vol. I.* Cambridge, Massachusetts.

Watson, Patricia A. 1993. "Stepmothers and *Hippomanes: Georgics* 3.282f." *Latomus* 52: 842–47.

Weber, Clifford. 1990. "Some Double Entendres in Ovid and Vergil." *CP* 85: 209–14.

———. 1995. "The Allegory of the Golden Bough." *Vergilius* 41: 3–35.

———. 1999. "Dido and Circe Dorées." *CJ* 94: 317–27.

West, David. 1987. "The Bough and the Gate." In Harrison (1990), 224–38.

West, David, and Tony Woodman, eds. 1979. *Creative Imitation and Latin Literature*. Cambridge.

West, Grace Starry. 1985. "Chloreus and Camilla." *Vergilius* 31: 22–29.

Whitby, M., P. Hardie, and M. Whitby, eds. 1988. *Homo Viator: Essays in Honor of John Bramble*. Bristol.

White, Peter. 1993. *Promised Verse: Poets in the Society of Augustan Rome*. Cambridge, Massachusetts.

Wigodsky, Michael. 1972. *Vergil and Early Latin Poetry. Hermes* Einzelschriften 24. Wiesbaden.

Wilhelm, Robert M. 1989. "Cybele: The Great Mother of Augustan Order." *Vergilius* 34: 77–101.

Wilhelm, Robert M., and Howard Jones, eds. 1992. *The Two Worlds of the Poet: New Perspectives on Vergil*. Detroit.

Williams, Gordon. 1983. *Technique and Ideas in the "Aeneid."* New Haven and London.

Williams, R. D. 1960. *P. Vergili Maronis Aeneidos Liber Quintus*. Oxford.

———. 1962. *P. Vergili Maronis Aeneidos Liber Tertius*. Oxford.

———. 1973. *The Aeneid of Virgil: Books 7–12*. London.

Wills, Jeffrey. 1996. *Repetition in Latin Poetry*. Oxford.

Wiltshire, Susan Ford. 1989. *Public and Private in Vergil's "Aeneid."* Amherst.

———. 1999. "The Man Who Was Not There: Aeneas and Absence in *Aeneid* 9." In Perkell (1999), 162–77.

Winkler, John J. 1985. *Auctor & Actor: A Narratological Reading of Apuleius's "The Golden Ass."* Berkeley, Los Angeles, and London.

Wiseman, T. P. 1984. "Cybele, Virgil, and Augustus." In Woodman and West (1984), 117–28.

———. 1995. *Remus: A Roman Myth*. Cambridge.

Wissowa, Georg. 1912. *Religion und Kultus der Römer*. 2nd ed. Munich.

Woodman, Tony, and David West, eds. 1984. *Poetry and Politics in the Age of Augustus*. Cambridge.

Zanker, G. 1987. *Realism in Alexandrian Poetry: A Literature and Its Audience.* London, Sidney, and Wolfeboro, New Hampshire.

Zarker, J. W. 1966–67. "Aeneas and Theseus in *Aeneid* VI." *CJ* 62: 220–26.

Zetzel, James E. G. 1978. "A Homeric Reminiscence in Catullus." *AJP* 99: 332–33.

———. 1989. "*Romane Memento*: Justice and Judgment in *Aeneid* 6." *TAPA* 119: 263–84.

———. 1997. "Rome and Its Traditions." In Martindale (1997), 188–203.

Index of Passages Cited

ACCIUS
Tragicorum Romanorum Fragmenta
156: 122
AELIAN
Varia Historia
13.14: 101n. 13
AESCHYLUS
Agamemnon
1066–67: 102n. 16
APOLLODORUS
Bibliotheca
1.4.3–5: 181
APOLLONIUS
Argonautica
2.1–97: 107–10
2.88–97: 108
3.876–85: 148
4.125f: 64n. 27
AULUS GELLIUS
Noctes Atticae
1.12.15: 103n. 19
2.26: 60n. 18
10.15: 10n. 20
10.16.11–13: 152

CALLIMACHUS
Hymn to Demeter
6.31–119: 197
Fragmenta Incerti Libri Aetiorum
190 Pfeiffer: 225–26
Fragmenta Incertae Sedis
587 Pf: 101n. 13
CATULLUS
Carmina
64.105–11: 212–13
64.152–53: 90
101.1: 216n. 6
CICERO
De Natura Deorum
3.5: 34
Pro Sestio
129: 37n. 15

DIODORUS
Anthologia Palatina
6.245.3–5: 118n. 10
DIONYSIUS OF HALICARNASSUS
Roman Antiquities
1.64.4–5: 52–53
1.70: 156, 159

ENNIUS
Annales
54 Vahlen, 26 Skutsch: 115n. 7
65V, 54S: 75n. 5
384–85V, 377–78S: 60n. 18
EURIPIDES
Hecuba
28–30: 62
Hippolytus
509–10, 514: 150

FESTUS, SEXTUS POMPEIUS
abridgement of Verrius Flaccus
p. 343 Müller: 217–18

HERODOTUS
Histories
1.34–45: 204n. 25
HOMER
Iliad
1.3–4: 99
1.4–5: 90
1.352: 92
2.308–13: 64n. 28
6.476–81: 122n. 16
8.555, 558–59: 163
12.22–23: 57n. 21
12.132–34: 201
14.292: 196n. 5
15.612: 92
16.20, 584, 693, 744, 754, 787, 812, 843: 87n. 27
16.41: 97
16.300: 163n. 42
16.852–54, 855–57: 97
18.39–40: 86
21.27: 106n. 26
21.84–85, 108–13: 92
21.122–27, 136–38: 91
21.218–20: 57n. 21, 74n. 3
21.234–39: 57n. 12
21.281: 74
21.300–27, 362–65: 116
22.209–13: 119–20
22.358–60, 361–63: 97
23.70–76: 87n. 27
23.175: 106n. 26
Odyssey
5.312: 74
6.102–109: 148
9.275–78: 179
10.302–305: 220n. 15
11.72: 62n. 22
24.473–88: 128
HORACE
Carmen Saeculare
1–2: 163
Odes
1.5.13–16: 118n. 10
3.29.33–41: 72n. 51
4.7.25–26: 153
4.7.14–16: 153n. 16

LIVY
Ab Urbe Condita
1.2.6: 52
1.3: 67
2.10.11: 115n. 7
2.14.5–9: 209n. 33
21.63.13–14: 105n. 22
8.9, 10.28: 119
LUCAN
Bellum Civile
1.135–43: 170n. 6
1.140–41: 171n. 7
1.151–57: 170n. 6
LUCIAN
Amores
53: 101n. 13
LUCRETIUS
De Rerum Natura
1.86, 92: 167
1.200–201: 181n. 27
1.280–87: 72n. 51
2.1031–32: 163
4.1068: 175n. 13
6.256–59: 202

MACROBIUS
Saturnalia
1.24.16, 3.2.1: 10n. 19
3.5.8: 84n. 23
3.5.10: 189–90n. 9
3.10: 31
3.11.1: 35
MARTIAL
Epigrams
13.25.1: 196n. 2

OVID
Ars Amatoria
1.257–60: 140
1.259–60: 215
Fasti
1.178: 30
1.579, 588: 33
2.485–88: 76n. 5
3.271: 215
3.545–656: 53n. 7

4.223–44: 205
6.755: 219
Ibis
279: 226
Metamorphoses
10.103–105: 195–96
10.110–11: 160–61
12.13: 64n. 28
14.328, 426: 67n. 38
14.603: 53
14.615–16: 67n. 38
14.593–608: 53
15.535: 220n. 15

PAUSANIAS
Description of Greece
2.27.4: 144–45
2.30.7: 224–25
2.32.1: 226
2.32.10: 224–25
PLINY THE ELDER
Natural History
28.17: 37n. 15
29.72: 65n. 30
PLUTARCH
Coriolanus
25: 49n. 34
POLYBIUS
Histories
1.37.4: 79
PROPERTIUS
Carmina
2.32.9–10: 140
2.34.66: 9n. 17

SENECA
Troades
140–41: 89n. 30
SERVIUS
ad Aeneidem
1.259: 51n. 4
1.706: 12
2.31: 196n. 2
2.116: 142, 198n. 10, 208, 219
2.341: 101n. 13
2.557: 170–71n. 7
3.21: 31
3.46: 198n. 11
3.64: 61
3.279: 31, 38–39
3.681: 179
4.29, 103, 137, 262, 263, 339, 374, 518: 10n. 20
4.620: 51–52, 73
4.646: 10n. 20, 11
5.814–15: 81–82
6.88: 58
6.136: 136–39
6.153: 40n. 20
6.176: 74n. 1
6.617–18: 152–53
7.31: 60
7.84: 50n. 1
7.150: 51n. 4, 58–59
7.198: 61
7.415–16: 162
7.487: 159
7.761: 196n. 3
7.776: 153–54
7.778: 225–26
7.797: 10, 51n. 4, 59
8.95: 66
8.813: 113–14
8.552: 11
10.198: 177
11.84: 187
12.175: 215
12.727: 120–21
12.768: 118–19
12.794: 51n. 4, 52
12.940: 192
SOPHOCLES
Ajax
550–51
STATIUS
Silvae
3.1.55: 215
3.1.56: 198n. 10
STRABO
Geography
5.3.12: 213–17
SUETONIUS
De Grammaticis
11: 219n. 13
Vita Augusti
13: 89n. 31
Vita Neronis
54: 7n. 10

Vita Vergilii
23–24, 35–42: 6
32: 80n. 15
SUIDAS (lexicon)
s.v. Koroibos

VALERIUS FLACCUS
Argonautica
2.300–305: 179–80
VARRO
De Re Rustica
2.5.6: 110
VIRGIL
Aeneid
1.2: 216, 227
1.2–3: 54
1.4: 125
1.7: 157
1.8–11: 38, 129
1.11: 129
1.29, 32: 216
1.44: 170
1.46–49: 129
1.48–49: 42–43
1.55: 72n. 51
1.87: 173
1.94–101: 72n. 49, 74
1.100–101: 57, 117
1.108: 79
1.108–17: 77
1.113–15: 81–82
1.148–53: 80n. 14
1.190: 160–61
1.259–60: 54, 93
1.273: 158–59
1.314–401, 329, 334: 162
1.337: 148
1.376: 216n. 6
1.389: 102
1.390–400: 81
1.401: 102
1.452–93: 66n. 33
1.498–504: 149
1.535, 560: 7n. 10
1.582–85: 82
1.743: 41n. 21
2.16, 112: 199
2.130–31, 140: 85
2.176: 216n. 6
2.201–19: 104
2.220–27: 104–105
2.230: 169, 200
2.258: 199
2.319–21: 103
2.367–68: 98
2.381: 61n. 20, 64, 66
2.387–90: 102–103
2.387–98: 98–99
2.402–30: 99
2.424–30: 100–101
2.429–30: 103
2.430: 107
2.471–75: 65n. 31, 66
2.472: 66
2.479–82: 169
2.496–99: 66
2.512–17: 171
2.550: 88, 105, 171
2.552: 110
2.553: 170
2.557–58: 88–89, 170–71
2.623: 7n. 10
2.626–31: 168
2.627: 169
2.631: 170
2.637: 169
2.639, 649: 170
2.663: 105, 171
2.767: 7n. 10
2.782: 56
3.5–6: 199
3.19–21: 29–35
3.22–46: 35–38
3.22–48: 147n. 24
3.22–68: 199
3.24: 182, 223
3.25: 185
3.28, 31: 223
3.33: 203
3.35: 186
3.42: 185
3.45: 181
3.46: 182
3.63–64: 61
3.64: 181
3.111: 206n. 30
3.120: 41n. 21
3.194–95: 62

3.208: 63n. 24
3.209: 119
3.325: 216n. 6
3.332: 105, 138n. 6, 171
3.405: 44
3.426–27: 62–63
3.432: 62
3.433–40: 43–46
3.439–40: 88
3.497–501: 57
3.500: 50, 56
3.543–47: 44–46
3.639: 181
3.642: 41n. 21
3.659: 178, 181
3.677–81: 178–80
4.31–55: 150
4.60–66: 96n. 3
4.68–73: 218–19
4.232: 127n. 7
4.235: 126–27
4.242–43: 174
4.271: 126–27
4.272: 127n. 7
4.300–303: 150n. 7
4.396: 113
4.441–49: 210–11
4.443: 173
4.469–70: 150n. 7
4.495–97: 150
4.506–507: 149
4.507–508: 150
4.511: 149
4.515–16: 150–51
4.583: 63n. 24
4.620: 51, 71
4.624, 638–39: 96n. 3
4.645–46: 11
4.701: 65
5.10–11: 62
5.82–83: 50, 56
5.82–89: 64–66
5.92: 66n. 33
5.95–96: 65
5.100: 66n. 33
5.123: 63
5.219: 216n. 6
5.240: 86
5.263: 203n. 24
5.362–484: 32, 107–11, 122
5.366: 109, 110
5.368–74: 107n. 31
5.372: 62n. 23
5.382: 109, 110
5.394–400: 110
5.399: 109
5.432, 455, 458–60: 111
5.470: 110
5.472, 473: 109
5.475: 111
5.477: 109
5.481: 109, 124n. 19
5.483–84: 109
5.502–504: 166
5.545–603: 204
5.563–69: 204–205
5.597: 204
5.698–99: 81n. 17
5.766: 69–70, 70n. 46
5.777: 68, 75
5.779–871: 68, 75
5.797: 50, 56, 75n. 3
5.800–15: 75
5.800–21: 85
5.804–10: 75n. 3
5.806–808: 57
5.813: 75n. 3
5.814: 82
5.814–15: 75
5.814–21: 75n. 3
5.820–21: 68
5.821: 68–69
5.822–26: 85–86
5.840: 87n. 27
5.843: 221n. 17
5.848–51: 69–70
5.852: 85
5.854: 77, 221n. 17
5.856: 221n. 17
5.870–71: 71
6.18–22: 100
6.21–22, 38–39: 81n. 17
6.86–89: 58
6.86–94: 101
6.87: 56
6.88–89: 56n. 11
6.89: 102
6.95–97: 102–103

6.100: 103n. 17
6.101–102: 101n. 16
6.119–23: 152
6.138: 42
6.145–55: 39–42
6.146–48: 220–21
6.147: 223
6.149: 82
6.153: 40n. 20, 41n. 21
6.171–74: 63, 82
6.176–77, 183: 40
6.210–11: 41, 147n. 24, 175
6.211: 221n. 17
6.212, 236: 40
6.247: 162
6.294: 166n. 48
6.303: 63
6.333–39: 78
6.333–83: 75
6.334–36: 80
6.338: 79, 80
6.343–46: 87
6.355–56: 79
6.359–62: 87
6.362: 62
6.364–71: 87n. 27
6.384: 63n. 26
6.405–407: 175
6.409: 174
6.410: 63
6.445–49: 81n. 17
6.451–54: 149
6.556: 70
6.558: 173
6.617–18: 152
6.760–66: 156–57
6.763–69: 157
6.765: 157n. 21
6.773–818: 157n. 23
6.778: 157
6.779: 157n. 21
6.899: 113
7.30–36: 54
7.58–70: 172–73
7.108, 140: 162
7.149–51: 55, 56n. 11
7.171–72: 173
7.173: 174
7.178: 173
7.190: 173–74
7.198: 63n. 24
7.240–242: 55–56, 56n. 11
7.286: 124n. 19
7.302–303: 50
7.302–304: 63
7.323–40: 128
7.346: 64
7.372: 124n. 19
7.413–74: 197–98
7.454–55: 198
7.462–66: 115–16
7.485–87: 159
7.505–10: 161–62
7.514–16: 162, 215
7.659–61: 158–59
7.728: 216n. 6
7.733: 158n. 25
7.738: 216n. 6
7.761–64: 207n. 31
7.761–82: 143–44
7.764: 156–57
7.767–68: 226n. 22
7.769: 153, 220
7.770–73: 154
7.778–80: 155–56
7.783: 124n. 20
7.789–92: 123
7.790: 110n. 36, 124n. 19
7.797–798: 56
8.31–96: 50
8.40–41: 73
8.59–62: 46–48
8.61–62: 73, 88, 109
8.61–64: 60
8.68–73: 46–48
8.69–70: 113
8.72: 115n. 7
8.79–80: 69
8.79–83: 47–48
8.84–85: 48–49, 69
8.86: 66
8.86–89: 68–70
8.90: 63n. 26
8.94: 69, 70n. 46
8.330: 62, 67
8.330–32: 67
8.538–40: 57, 117
8.539: 117
8.585–86: 11
8.619–23: 63

8.645: 186
8.650: 114
8.658–61: 206n. 29
8.672: 71
8.711–13: 117n. 9
8.713: 71
8.714–15: 72
8.726–28: 72–73
8.728: 113
8.731: 112
8.813–15: 176
9.3–4: 162–63
9.18, 20–21: 163
9.22–24: 113
9.30–32: 117n. 9
9.47–76: 205
9.49: 205
9.74–76: 202n. 23
9.75: 202
9.80–106: 196, 207
9.86–89: 198–200
9.105: 202
9.116: 199
9.226: 167
9.327: 216
9.329–34: 166–67
9.341: 167
9.368: 216
9.384, 386–91: 164
9.402–15: 164–66
9.405: 163, 208–209
9.415: 167
9.457: 202
9.485–86: 90–91
9.488: 70
9.527: 99n. 9
9.551–52: 178
9.575: 205
9.581–85: 206–207n. 31
9.617–20: 195
9.669–71: 111
9.673–74: 200
9.679–82, 84: 200–201
9.706: 201–202
9.728: 216
9.743: 201
9.762–65: 205n. 27
9.765: 203n. 24
9.785: 99n. 9
9.812–816: 201–202
9.815–18: 113
9.816: 72n. 50
10.47: 90
10.206–208: 177
10.209–12: 63
10.267: 216
10.421–23: 191
10.501–505: 190–91
10.518–20: 106
10.519: 186
10.521–60: 155
10.524–25: 89
10.529: 106
10.535: 110
10.537–42: 89, 106–107
10.541: 106
10.541–42: 186
10.545–49, 550–60: 89
10.551, 555: 176
10.557–60: 89–93
10.565–70: 115n. 6
10.570–74: 155–56
10.763–68: 180–81
10.773–76: 189–90
10.775: 186n. 5, 191
10.783–86: 185n. 3
10.803–10: 111
10.835–36: 182
10.856–58: 185n. 3
10.886–89: 182
10.893–94, 904–906: 185n. 3
11.4: 185
11.5–16: 184–85, 187–91
11.7: 186n. 5
11.16: 178
11.81–84: 186–87
11.172: 186n. 5
11.172–79: 192–93
11.173–75: 193n. 16
11.199: 41n. 21
11.224: 186n. 5, 194
11.385: 186n. 5
11.440–42: 119n. 12
11.486–89: 188
11.532–94: 196, 207
11.541, 545: 208
11.552–60: 208–209
11.591–92: 209
11.675: 205n. 27
11.768–77: 206–207

11.782: 206
11.790: 186n. 5
11.831: 72n. 51, 95n. 1
11.863: 173
12.51: 203
12.87–95: 188–90
12.104–106: 108n. 31, 212–13
12.134–35: 196
12.171: 41n. 21
12.175: 215
12.175–94: 71n. 48
12.203–11: 174–75
12.221: 111
12.266: 202–203
12.289, 294: 177
12.296: 109, 176
12.302: 110
12.311–15, 318–25: 203
12.328–29: 117
12.363: 203n. 24
12.371–83: 203
12.392: 221n. 17
12.400–406: 219
12.401: 220
12.411–15, 423–24: 219–21
12.430–32: 188
12.435–36: 122
12.453–54: 161n. 38
12.456: 122
12.457: 161n. 38
12.503–504: 190n. 10
12.512: 185
12.590: 173
12.668: 111
12.710–952: 211–27
12.715: 212
12.715–24: 123–24, 211–13
12.716: 124
12.721: 212
12.725–27: 120–21
12.739–45: 214–17
12.742: 216n. 6
12.749–51: 216–17
12.749–55, 766: 225
12.766–71: 117–19
12.766–90: 176, 221–26
12.768: 225
12.770–71: 147n. 24
12.794–95: 54, 93
12.796: 126–27
12.808–28: 128
12.811–12: 124
12.830–33: 128–29
12.838–40: 42–43, 129
12.841–42: 127–28
12.843–68: 202n. 23
12.845–54: 128
12.869: 173
12.876–86: 93–94
12.882: 93n. 43
12.888: 223
12.896–907: 192n. 13
12.905: 111
12.928–29: 214–15
12.930: 193
12.938–52: 3–4
12.944: 177
12.945–49: 191–92
12.945–52: 226–27
12.948: 193
12.949: 106, 187
12.952: 72n51, 95n. 1
Eclogues
6.49: 41n. 21
Georgics
1.244: 66
2.84: 219
2.161–62: 72n. 51
2.395: 84n. 23
3.24: 66
3.201: 216n. 6
3.219: 110
3.219–41, 232–34: 108n. 31
3.233: 212
3.280–83: 150–51
3.341: 70
3.363–65: 216
3.368: 41n. 21
3.372: 217
3.454: 175n. 13
3.471, 480: 41n. 21
4.338: 86n. 25
4.538, 550: 124n. 20
[VIRGIL]
Ciris
300: 219n. 13

General Index

Achilles: Aeneas as, 16, 83, 102, 102–103n. 17, 106, 211; altar to, 105; and Hector, 17, 92, 95, 97, 99, 119–20; and Lycaon, 90–93; and Patroclus, 85–87, 89, 95, 97, 99, 102; and Priam, 4n. 2; as tree, 147; Turnus as, 99n. 9, 102–103n. 17, 106n. 24. *See also* Apollo; death (watery); sacrifice (human)
Actium, battle of. *See* Augustus
Aegaeon. *See* Jupiter
Aeneid: as mystery, 4–5, 229; audience for, 7–8; half-lines in, 7n. 10; incompletion of, 4n. 2, 6; intentionality in, 7–8; religion in, 10–13. *See also* Augustus; prophecy; Trojan Horse; Virgil, "errors" of
Aeneas: passim. *See especially* Achilles; death (watery); Dido; *flamen*; Golden Bough; Juno; Numicus (river); *pietas*; prophecy; Pyrrhus; Rex Nemorensis; sacrifice (animal); sacrifice (human); Tiber (river); tree violation; Turnus; Venus
Ajax (son of Oileus), 170
Ajax (son of Telamon), 17, 122
Albula (river), 67
Alexandrianism, 5, 205n. 27
Allecto: and Dira, 128; and Turnus, 22, 115, 197–98, 202, 203; bugle-call of, 20, 162, 215, 230; snakes of, 64, 198
Amata, 64, 198
Ambiguity, 187n. 6, 203
Amycus, 107–10
Anchises, 64, 66n. 33, 156, 162. *See also* sacrifice (human); tree violation
Androgeos, 64, 100
Anna, 53
Antony, 71–72, 117n. 9
Anxur, 89, 155
Aphodite, 149. *See also* Venus
Apollo: and Achilles, 97; and Panthus, 103, 107; temple of, 100, 105, 152. *See also* prophecy
Araxes (river), 72–73, 113
Arcens, son of: as hybrid of Chloreus/Attis and Virbius, 206–207n. 31
Aristeia, 92, 106, 115n. 6, 188
Armor: of enemy, 16, 98–99, 101, 103, 111, 190–92; of Turnus and *tropaeum*, 21, 187–89, 231
Arruns, 51n. 2, 95n. 1, 209n. 33
Artemis. *See* Diana
Ascanius: and Aeneas, 122; and Lavinia, 156, 159; and Troy Game, 204–205; and Venus, 90. *See also* Silvia; Silvius
Athena, 128. *See also* Minerva
Attis, 22, 195–96, 203n. 24, 204–207, 223. *See also* Arcens, son of; Chloreus; Virbius

Atys, 204–205
Augustus: *Aeneid* as temple to, 4, 139; and "Augustan poetry," 8; and battle of Actium, 71–73; and Perusia, 130, 177; and recitation of *Aeneid*, 80–81n. 15; criticism of, 24; cruelty of, 85n. 24, 89n. 31; *imperium* of, 69n. 44; mother of, 139, 204; priesthood of, 103n. 18
Aulestes. *See* sacrifice (human); tree violation
Auspicium, 34–35, 37n. 15
Aventine Hill, 19, 141, 159, 217, 230
Aventinus: and Virbius, 158–59, 230

Bitias. *See* Pandarus and Bitias
Boxing match, 17, 107–111, 122–23
Bullfight: and Juno, 17, 122–24; and Rex Nemorensis, 23, 211–13, 231
Butes, 62n. 23, 107–108n. 31

Caeruleus, 15, 60–67, 73, 75–76n. 5, 113, 117n. 9, 232
Caesar. *See* Augustus; Julius Caesar
Caieta, 83
Camilla: death of, 51n. 2, 72n. 51, 81n. 17, 95n. 1; and Chloreus, 22, 206–207; and Diana, 22–23, 181, 207–209, 230; in catalogue, 143, 158; victims of, 205n. 27
Capito, C. Ateius, 30–31
Cassandra, 99, 101–102
Charon, 15, 63, 175
Chloreus, 203n. 24, 205–207, 223; and Gauls, 206n. 29. *See also* Arcens, son of; Camilla
Circe, 67n. 38, 173–74
Civil war, 130, 157, 159, 227
Cleopatra, 71–72, 117n. 9
Coroebus. *See* sacrifice (human)
Crassus, 50n. 1
Creusa. *See* sacrifice (human)
Croesus, 45n. 28, 204n. 25
Cybele, 22, 195–209, 234. *See also* Diana; Jupiter; pines
Cyclopes. *See* Polyphemus
Cypresses, 20, 61, 148, 149, 160–61, 178–79, 181, 219

Dante, 228, 235
Dares, 62n. 23, 107–111
Death (watery), 24; and Achilles, 74, 75n. 3, 115–16; and Odysseus, 74; of Misenus, 16, 63, 81n. 17, 82–84, 96; of Orontes, 16, 77–83, 94, 96; of Palinurus, 15, 51n. 2, 62, 67–71, 73, 74–88, 94, 96, 109, 232; of Polydorus, 61–62, 83, 96; of Priam, 16, 88–89, 94, 96; of Tarquitus, 16, 89–93, 96, 106, 155, 232. *See also* Numicus (river); Tiber (river)
Deer: and Diana, 160; and Saron, 23, 224–25; Dido as, 23, 160, 218–21; killed by Aeneas, 160, 218; of Silvia, 20, 160–62, 167, 218; Turnus as, 23, 216–18, 225
Demeter, 22, 197–98
Devotio, 197; of Dido, 96n. 3; of Mezentius, 185n. 3; of Turnus, 96n. 3, 119n. 12
Diana, 19, 148–49; and Cybele, 22, 196, 207; and Nisus and Euryalus, 20, 149, 163–67, 208–209; lake of, 163, 215; torch of, 198n. 10; transportation of, 179–80. *See also* Allecto, bugle-call of; Camilla; cypresses; deer; Dido; Hippolytus; Iris; Juno; Rex Nemorensis; Venus
Dictynna, 23, 219
Dido: affair with, 126; and hunting, 148; and Medea, 59n. 16; as Diana, 19, 148–49, 167, 197, 230; as *flaminica*, 10–11; as Phaedra, 19, 149–51, 167; curse of, 51–52, 93, 152, 232; death of, 63n. 24, 85n. 24, 122n. 16. *See also* deer; *devotio*; Iris; sacrifice (human)
Dira. *See* Allecto
Dittany, 23, 218–21
Donatus, 9n. 16
Drowning. *See* death (watery)
Dryope, 176

Elpenor, 62n. 22, 83–84
Entellus, 107–111
Erysichthon. *See* Turnus
Euphrates (river), 50n. 1, 72–73

Euryalus, 81n. 17, 90. *See also* Diana; Nisus; sacrifice (human)
Evander, 21, 63n. 24, 67, 176, 192–93, 231

Faunus, 176, 182. *See also* Tiber (river); tree violation; Turnus
Flamen, 33; Aeneas as, 10–11
Flaminica. *See* Dido

Golden Ass: as mystery novel, 5n. 3
Golden Bough: and Aeneas' arrow-wound, 23, 220–21; and Aeneas' catabasis, 198n. 11; and Aeneas' soul, 147n. 26; and Aeneas' spear, 223; and Circe's wand, 174; and Latinus' scepter, 20, 174–75, 182–83; and *moly*, 220n. 16; and Palinurus, 85, 221n. 17; and Rex Nemorensis, 19, 135–39, 147, 175; breaking off of, 49, 139n. 7, 147n. 24, 199, 223, 230, 231. *See also* Sibyl

Haemonides. *See* sacrifice (human)
Hecate. *See* Diana
Hector: Aeneas as, 122n. 16; burial of, 4n. 2. *See also* Achilles
Helenus. *See* prophecy
Hercules, 33
Herodotus, 45n. 28
Hippolytus, 19, 149–57; Niphaeus as, 155–56; death of, 23, 209, 223–26. *See also* Rex Nemorensis; Virbius
Hippomanes, 150–51
Hitchcock, Alfred, 45n. 28
Horatius Cocles, 115n. 7. *See also* Turnus
Hyrtacides. *See* tree violation

Iapyx, 219–21; as brother of Palinurus, 221n. 17
Ilia, 115n. 7. *See also* Rhea Silvia
Indignatus. *See* Turnus
Io, 17, 110n. 36, 123–24n. 19
Iphigeneia. *See* sacrifice (human)
Iris: and Dido, 65–66, 198n. 11; as Diana, 20, 162–63
Iulus. *See* Ascanius

Julius Caesar, 141–42, 170n. 6. *See also* Rex Nemorensis; sacrifice (human)
Juno: and Diana, 230, 235; pursuit of Aeneas, 216; spectating of, 196; temple of, 66n. 33; wrath of, 33–34, 38–39, 42–49, 63, 73, 113, 123–24, 125–29, 232. *See also* Jupiter; sacrifice (animal); sacrifice (human)
Jupiter: and Aegaeon, 115n. 6; and Cybele, 202; and Juno, 93, 125–29; and Juturna, 94; and Mercury, 126–27; and Romulus/Remus, 75–76n. 5; and *spolia opima*, 99n. 7; and Venus, 93; scales of, 120–22; forest of, 21, 178–80, 200; thunderbolt of, 170, 202; thunderstorm of, 81n. 17; Turnus as, 201–202. *See also* prophecy; sacrifice (animal)
Juturna, 16, 93–94

Laocoön. *See* sacrifice (animal); sacrifice (human); tree violation
Latin League, 19, 140
Latinus, 117, 203. *See also* Golden Bough; laurels; tree violation
Laurels, 20, 171–73, 176n. 16, 182, 198, 200
Lausus, 81n. 17, 158, 181, 189, 231
Lavinia. *See* Ascanius
Lavinium, 54–55
Luna. *See* Diana

Macrobius, 10
Mad Hatter, 45n. 28
Magus, 89, 155
Marcellus, 81n. 17
Mars, 11, 37, 76n. 5, 186
Medea, of Apollonius, 59n. 16, 148, 149n. 4
Mercury, 18, 174. *See also* Jupiter
Mezentius: and Orion, 180–81; and Polyphemus, 21, 178–81, 197, 223; in catalogue, 158. *See also devotio*; Polydorus; Tiber (river); tree violation
Mincius (river), 66, 177
Minerva, 16, 44–46, 99, 100

Misenus: burial of, 39–41. *See also* death (watery)

Neptune: altars of, 81n. 17; calming of waters, 68–69, 80n. 14, 85. *See also* prophecy
Nile (river), 71–73, 117n. 9
Niphaeus. *See* Hippolytus
Nisus, 81n. 17. *See also* Diana; sacrifice (human); tree violation
Numa, 35
Numanus Remulus: 195
Numicus (river): and Aeneas' death, 9–10, 15, 16, 50n. 1, 51–60, 73, 94, 116, 196n. 4, 229, 232

Odysseus, 4n. 2, 13, 64n. 28, 83, 147. *See also* death (watery)
Oebalus, 158n. 25
Oleaster, 223–225
Optimists and pessimists, 8–9, 125, 130, 192
Orestes: and Pyrrhus, 105, 171. *See also* Rex Nemorensis
Orion. *See* Mezentius
Orontes. *See* death (watery); sacrifice (human)
Orpheus, 153, 160, 195

Palinurus. *See* death (watery); Golden Bough; sacrifice (human)
Pallas (Athena). *See* Athena; Minerva
Pallas (son of Evander), 81n. 17; and Turnus' death, 192–93; funeral of, 186–87; swordbelt of, 21–22, 190–91, 231
Pandarus and Bitias: 22, 200–201, 203
Panthus. *See* Apollo; sacrifice (human)
Patroclus. *See* Achilles
Pax deorum, 11–12, 38–39, 130
Penthesilea, 149n. 4
Pentheus, 150n. 7
Perusia. *See* Augustus
Pessimists. *See* optimists and pessimists
Phaedra. *See* Dido
Phegeus. *See truncus*
Picus, 20, 67n. 38. *See also* tree violation
Pietas, 29, 38, 77n. 9, 89, 100, 103, 129–30, 185, 192–93, 231, 233
Pines, 22, 196, 199–200, 202, 203, 223, 234
Polites, 105, 204
Polydeuces, 107–10
Polydorus: as prodigy, 14, 30–31, 35–38, 49, 198n. 11; and Polyphemus, 181; and Mezentius, 21, 181–82. *See also* death (watery); tree violation
Polyphemus. *See* Mezentius; Polydorus
Pompey, 88n. 30, 141–42, 170n. 6, 170–71n. 7, 197. *See also* Rex Nemorensis
Priam (grandson of king), 204
Priam (king). *See* Achilles; sacrifice (human); tree violation
Prodigy. *See* Polydorus
Prophecy: *Aeneid* as, 5–6, 234–35; by Apollo, 56, 87–88; by Helenus, 14, 43–46, 87–88; by Jupiter, 15, 18, 42–43, 54, 93, 158–59, 232; by Neptune, 75, 82–84, 87; by Sibyl, 14, 57–58, 97, 101–103, 232; by Tiber, 14, 15, 46–49, 73, 88, 94, 109; by Venus, 81–82
Proserpina, 42
Pyrrhus (king of Epirus): 45n. 28; Pyrrhic victory, 12n. 24
Pyrrhus (son of Achilles): Aeneas as, 106, 172–73; and snakes, 65n. 31, 66; and river, 66. *See also* Orestes; sacrifice (human); tree violation

Regifugium, 215n. 4
Remus. *See* Romulus; *truncus*
Rex Nemorensis, 14, 18–19, 24, 134–41, 169n. 3, 173n. 9, 180, 234–35; and Aeneas/Turnus, 23, 196–97, 200, 211–27, 229–231; and Hippolytus/Virbius, 18, 19, 142–46, 149, 151–52; and Orestes, 18, 19, 142–43, 171, 208, 216; in Lucan, 19, 141–42, 170n. 6, 197. *See also* Golden Bough; tree violation
Rhea Silvia, 157–60
Romulus, 35; and Remus, 69n. 44, 75–76n. 5, 157–59, 166–67

Sacrifice (animal): 12–14, 75, 84, 94, 105n. 22, 130; after boxing match, 17, 107–111; before catabasis, 39–41, 81n. 17, 82–83n. 18; in *Georgics*, 84n. 23, 124n. 20; in Laocoön episode, 16–17, 104–105, 233; to Juno, 14, 46–49, 69, 73; to Jupiter, 14, 29–35, 45, 110
Sacrifice (human): 12–13, 24, 94, 130, 233–35; and role-reversal, 96–111; of Anchises, 96; of Aulestes, 17, 20, 109, 177, 183; of Coroebus, 16, 98–103; of Creusa, 81n. 17, 96; of Dido, 81n. 17; of eight youths (by Aeneas), 106, 186–87; of Euryalus, 167; of Haemonides, 16, 89, 106–107, 111, 155, 177, 186–87, 232; of Iphigeneia, 84n. 22, 142, 167; of Laocoön, 13n. 25, 16–17, 65, 104–105, 107n. 28, 111, 232, 234; of Misenus, 81n. 17; of Nisus, 167; of Orontes, 16, 77–83, 94; of Palinurus, 15–16, 74–88, 94, 232, 233; of Panthus, 16, 100, 103–104, 107, 232; of Priam, 16, 17, 88–89, 94, 105, 107n. 28, 111; of Pyrrhus, 17, 105–106, 111, 138n. 6, 232; of Sinon, 85, 130n. 17; of Turnus, 3–5, 17–18, 23–24, 51n. 2, 96, 106, 112–24, 129–30, 177, 185–87, 226–35; of twelve youths (by Achilles), 106n. 26; to Divus Julius, 130, 177; to Juno, 17–18, 129, 232–33. *See also devotio*; Rex Nemorensis
Sagaris, Sagaritis, Sangarius, 203n. 24, 205
Saron. *See* deer
Scamander (river). *See* Xanthus
Scylla, 62–63
Scythians, 23, 216–18, 231
Selene. *See* Diana
Servius Tullius, 141, 157n. 23, 159, 217
Servius (*grammaticus*), 9–11
Sibyl: and Cassandra, 101–102n. 16; and Golden Bough, 39–42, 45, 175, 220–21, 230; and Theseus, 152–53. *See also* prophecy
Silvia: and Silvius, 159–60. *See also* deer
Silvius: and Virbius, 19–20, 156–57; legend of, 159–60
Simois (river), 56–59, 72n. 49, 91, 196n. 4, 232. *See also* Turnus
Sinon, 13n. 25, 104. *See also* sacrifice (human)
Snakes, 15, 63–67, 73, 169, 198
Styx (river), 63, 74n. 1, 78, 87n. 27, 202

Tarquitus. *See* death (watery); *truncus*
Theseus: and Minotaur, 212–13; in Underworld, 19, 152–54, 226
Tiber (river): and Aeneas' death, 50–73, 75n. 3, 77, 196n. 4, 232; and Faunus, 119, 223; and Mezentius, 181–82; and Pallas, 191; and Simois, 117, 232; and Trojan camp, 164; and Turnus, 17, 72n. 50, 112–17, 201, 232; king Tiberinus/Thybris, 67, 73. *See also* prophecy
Tree violation: 18, 146–47, 196, 231, 234; and Aeneas, 210–11; and Anchises, 169–70; and Aulestes, 20, 176–77, 183; and Faunus, 20, 23, 147n. 24, 176, 221–23, 231; and Hyrtacides, 165–66; and Italians, 160–62, 167; and kings, 167–69, 182; and Laocoön, 169, 200, 231; and Latinus, 20, 173–75, 182, 198; and Mezentius, 21–22, 147, 178–83, 184–92, 209, 223, 231; and Nisus, 165–66; and Picus, 173–74, 182; and Polydorus, 21, 22, 35–38, 147n. 24, 185, 186, 199, 203, 223; and Pyrrhus/Priam, 20, 169–73, 182, 185, 198, 199–200, 231; and Trojan Horse, 22, 169, 199–200, 231; and Troy, 20, 147, 168–72, 182, 199–200, 231; and Turnus, 21–22, 197–205, 221, 231. *See also* armor; Golden Bough; Rex Nemorensis; *truncus*
Triton, 16, 63
Trivia. *See* Diana
Trojan Horse: as *Aeneid*, 199n. 16; as ship, 200n. 18. *See also* tree violation

Truncus, 146; Phegeus as, 22, 203, 221; Priam as, 20, 170–71, 182, 185, 200, 231; Remus as, 166–67; Tarquitus as, 176; Turnus as, 21–22, 193, 231

Tucca. *See* Varius and Tucca

Turnus: and Hippolytus, 154; and Horatius Cocles, 17, 114–15, 201; and Xanthus, 115–16, 232; and Simois, 116–17, 232; and Faunus' tree, 17, 117–19; and Iris, 162–63; as Erysichthon, 22, 197–98, 234; as *indignatus*, 72n. 51, 154, 234; as *tropaeum*, 21, 185–93, 203; cruelty of, 185; flight of, 69n. 43, 216; impiety of, 192n. 13; in catalogue, 143, 158. *See also* Allecto; deer; *devotio*; Jupiter; Pallas (son of Evander); Rex Nemorensis; sacrifice (human); Tiber (river); tree violation; *truncus*

Tyrrhus, 159

Varius and Tucca, 6

Venus: advice of, 102–103; and Aeneas' death, 53, 90; and Aeneas' spear, 223; and Lemnian women, 179n. 24; and Neptune, 68n. 40; and *venenum*, 151n. 12; as Diana, 20, 162, 230; boots of, 148; born from foam, 118n. 10. *See also* Aphrodite; Jupiter; prophecy

Virbius, 230; and Attis, 196; healed, 220; placed in Grove, 219. *See also* Arcens, son of; Aventinus; Hippolytus; Rex Nemorensis; Silvius

Virgil, "errors" of, 6–7, 68–70; Conington, 163n. 42; Edgeworth, 88; Fordyce, 69–70, 116, 173n. 10; Hardie et al., 198n. 11; Highet, 67, 69, 90; Horsfall, 54–55, 76n. 6; Mackie, 77n. 9; Page, 163n. 42, 67; Quint, 77n. 9; G. Williams, 76n. 7; R. Williams, 68n. 41, 76–80

Xanthus (river), 17, 56–59, 90, 91, 196n. 4, 232. *See also* death (watery); Turnus

Zeus, 119–20. *See also* Jupiter